MW00584254

NAVAL OFFICER'S GUIDE
to the
PENTAGON

Titles in the Series

The Bluejacket's Manual
Career Compass
The Chief Petty Officer's Guide
Command at Sea
Dictionary of Modern Strategy and Tactics
Dictionary of Naval Abbreviations
Dictionary of Naval Terms
Division Officer's Guide
Dutton's Nautical Navigation
Farwell's Rules of the Nautical Road
Fleet Tactics and Naval Operations
International Law for Seagoing Officers
Naval Ceremonies, Customs, and Traditions
The Naval Institute Guide to Naval Writing
The Naval Officer's Guide
Naval Shiphandler's Guide
Newly Commissioned Naval Officer's Guide
Operations Officer's Guide
Principles of Naval Engineering
Principles of Naval Weapon Systems
The Professional Naval Officer: A Course to Steer By
Reef Points
A Sailor's History of the U.S. Navy
Saltwater Leadership
Shiphandling Fundamentals for Littoral Combat Ships and the New Frigates
Watch Officer's Guide

NAVAL OFFICER'S GUIDE
to the
PENTAGON

RDML Fred W. Kacher, USN

LCDR Douglas A. Robb, USN

Foreword by ADM James G. Stavridis, USN (Ret.)

NAVAL INSTITUTE PRESS

ANNAPOLIS, MARYLAND

Naval Institute Press
291 Wood Road
Annapolis, MD 21402

Names: Kacher, Fred W., author. | Robb, Douglas A., date, author.
Title: Naval officer's guide to the Pentagon / RDML Fred W. Kacher, USN, and
    LCDR Douglas A. Robb, USN.
Description: Annapolis, MD : Naval Institute Press, [2019] | Series: The U.S.
    Naval Institute blue & gold professional library | Includes
    bibliographical references and index.
Identifiers: LCCN 2019010849 | ISBN 9781682474662 (hardcover : alk. paper)
Subjects: LCSH: United States. Navy—Officers' handbooks. | Pentagon (Va.) |
    United States. Navy—Military life—Handbooks, manuals, etc.
Classification: LCC V133 .K326 2019 | DDC 355.709755/295—dc23 LC record available at
https://lccn.loc.gov/2019010849

♾ Print editions meet the requirements of ANSI/NISO z39.48-1992 (Permanence of Paper).
Printed in the United States of America.

27 26 25 24 23 22 21 20 19   9 8 7 6 5 4 3 2 1
First printing

CONTENTS

List of Illustrations ix

Foreword

ADM James G. Stavridis, USN (Ret.) xiii

Acknowledgments xv

List of Acronyms, Initialisms, and Abbreviations xix

Introduction 1

PART I. THE BUILDING

1. The Pentagon: A Brief History
   LCDR Rachael A. Gosnell, USN 7
2. Navigating the Pentagon
   LCDR Jonathan "Shank" Lushenko, USN 19

PART II. KEY ORGANIZATIONS

3. The Navy (OPNAV) Staff
   LCDR Doug Robb, USN 38
4. The Navy Secretariat
   Sarandis Papadopoulos, PhD 59
5. The Joint Staff
   Col Doug Douds, USMC (Ret.) 77
6. The Office of the Secretary of Defense
   CAPT Thane Clare, USN 97

PART III. THE PENTAGON AT WORK

7. The Budget Process
   CDR Rob Niemeyer, USN 118
8. Action Officers: The Lifeblood of Pentagon Staffs
   CAPT Grady Musser, USN 134
9. Front Office and Personal Staff
   CAPT Matthew Duffy, USN 146
10. Speechwriter: The Principal's Voice
    CDR Guy Snodgrass, USN (Ret.) 159

11. Pentagon Safety Tips
     RDML Fred W. Kacher, USN   169

12. Reflections on Service at the Pentagon
     VADM Doug Crowder, USN (Ret.)   175

PART IV. "ACROSS THE RIVER"

13. The White House
     CAPT Joseph A. Gagliano, USN   186

14. Working with Congress
     LCDR James Hagerty, USN   204

15. Interagency Coordination
     CDR Michael Wisecup, USN   220

16. Think Tanks and Fellowships
     CDR Micah Murphy, USN   232

17. Research and Development Organizations
     CDR Kyle Gantt, USN   242

PART V. LIFE IN WASHINGTON, DC

18. Finding the Right Place to Live
     LCDR Doug Robb, USN   254

19. Pursuing Graduate Education in DC
     LT Kaitlin Smith, USN   264

20. Enrichment Opportunities
     LCDR Doug Robb, USN   276

Index   283

ILLUSTRATIONS

PHOTOGRAPHS

Main Navy and munitions buildings ("Main Navy")   9
One of the Pentagon's 131 stairways   29
The Chief of Naval Operations is the uniformed
  leader of the U.S. Navy   40
Secretary of the Navy Dan Kimball's Pentagon office, 1953   64
Secretary of the Navy Spencer at a Pentagon briefing   71
The Joint Chiefs meet over lunch, 1943   78
Secretary of Defense Robert McNamara with
  assistant secretaries and the JCS   99
The Office of the Secretary of Defense has evolved
  markedly since its creation   103
Serving as a flag aide is a unique, rewarding, and
  challenging opportunity   148
Speechwriters must understand their principal's
  persona and speaking preferences   162
VADM Doug Crowder addressing sailors in
  Yokosuka, Japan   176
The White House complex   187
The National Security Council advises and assists the President   193
Members of the Joint Chiefs of Staff appearing
  before the U.S. Senate   207
Annual posture hearings provide congressional
  oversight of the DOD   211
The interagency process brings together executive branch leaders   222
Think tanks provide venues for leaders to discuss
  important policy issues   235
Numerous graduate degree opportunities exist
  in Washington, DC   266
Several Civil War battlefields are close to the DC area   281

FIGURES

2-1	Pentagon Reservation Parking Map	25
2-2	Map of the Pentagon	28
3-1	OPNAV Principal Officers	43
4-1	Navy Secretariat Organization	73
5-1	Joint Staff Organization	83
6-1	OSD Structure	104
7-1	Requirements–Budgeting–Acquisitions System Interdependencies	125

TABLES

3-1	Military and Civilian Pay Grades	57
6-1	Comparison between Senior OSD and Military Staff Leadership	113
14-1	Budget and Appropriations Timeline	213
17-1	Federally Funded Research and Development Centers (FFRDC)	248
17-2	University Affiliated Research Centers (UARCs)	251
18-1	Military Bases and Services in the Greater Washington Area	260
19-1	Post–9/11 GI Bill	271

TEXT BOXES

3-1	OPNAV Reorganizations	44
5-1	CCDR vs. CCMD vs. COCOM	81
6-1	The Defense Agencies and the Defense Field Activities	101
6-2	Deputy Undersecretaries of Defense	106
7-1	PBIS	120
7-2	The Importance of Budget Exhibits	122
7-3	Continuing Resolutions	124
8-1	Working with Civilian Teammates	136
8-2	Unanticipated Funding Requests	139
8-3	Internal, Pre-decisional, or Sensitive Information	141
15-1	Importance of Cooperation	223
15-2	Achieving Interagency and Civil Interoperability	224
16-1	Law vs. Regulation vs. Policy	233
20-1	Ethics Determination for Attendance	279

FOREWORD

Buried deep on page 272 of the *Division Officer's Guide* (11th edition) I wrote, "Into most successful careers, a little Washington must fall." More than fifteen years later, that declaration has never been more true. Navy officers in command and staff today often navigate complex issues that are influenced by the interagency, joint world, public–private developments, and coalition ramifications. Simply put, officers and leaders today confront challenges that are no less daunting than those of their predecessors, but are composed of more layers of complexity.

The Naval Institute Press was founded in 1898 and has published thousands of guides, manuals, and maritime books. This *Naval Officer's Guide to the Pentagon* is a masterful work offering precisely what any Navy officer considering or ordered to a tour in Washington needs. It serves as a comprehensive reference that covers pertinent topics from detailed descriptions of the different Pentagon staffs, to tangible front office mechanics, insights, and vignettes on the various think tanks, nongovernmental organizations (NGOs), and federal agencies in the national capital region. This text is one that will also serve families who are seeking a better understanding of Navy life and opportunities in Washington.

Washington service affords officers exposure to the "corporate Navy" at our principal headquarters. Washington is also the ideal location for rising leaders to witness senior officer and civilian decision-making firsthand. It provides an excellent position to observe policy development, and in many cases the opportunity to help craft the various strategies that guide our collective national defense. In short, and as you will discover herein, service in the Pentagon offers a glimpse of the strategic process—with the President and Secretary of Defense determining the ends, the Joint Staff and combatant commands formulating the ways, and the individual services furnishing the means.

Any career-minded Navy officer would be well served by executing at least one tour in Washington. You will gain critical insights and develop new skills to be a more effective leader and operator in the fleet. You will learn how our organization functions and witness some of the best examples of leadership and leaders in our Navy. Washington service is typically demanding and will test your abilities. However, it will expand both your knowledge base and valuable relationships. Most importantly, almost all officers who have served in Washington will claim that the experience was extremely rewarding.

Having served many tours in Washington, I can attest that the purpose of this book is arguably overdue, and that this text is certain to be the go-to reference for Washington service. Consuming the rich chapters contained herein will best prepare any officer embarking on their first Washington tour. This inaugural edition of the *Naval Officer's Guide to the Pentagon* rightfully takes its place alongside other iconic Naval Institute Press works. Enjoy this text and welcome to Washington!

ADM James G. Stavridis is a distinguished 1976 graduate of the U.S. Naval Academy. He served thirty-seven years in uniform, including seven years as a four-star admiral. Formerly Dean of the Fletcher School of Law and Diplomacy at Tufts University, he currently serves as Chairman of the Board for the U.S. Naval Institute. He is the author or co-author of eight books, including *Sea Power: The History and Geopolitics of the World's Oceans*, *Command at Sea*, and *Destroyer Captain: Lessons of a First Command*.

ACKNOWLEDGMENTS

Life and work in the Pentagon is the ultimate "team sport." Nothing gets done—from the most seemingly menial task to the most consequential decision—alone. It takes groups, shifts, teams, and organizations operating in harmony—and, occasionally, in tension—to plan, orchestrate, direct, execute, and evaluate everything large and small. So, too, is the case with this book, which is a proud product of collaboration and teamwork.

The Pentagon is a world unto itself and this project was borne out of a desire to help our fellow cadre of officers (and civilians) reporting for duty at the Pentagon—some for the first time and others, perhaps, returning after tours in the fleet. Our hope is that this group will find the information compiled here useful and that it will help make them more effective in their new roles.

This book is a testament to modern communications as our writing team worked "after hours" while serving in sea and shore assignments all over the world—every single one of them juggling the demands of an important day job (and family life at home). We are grateful for their time and contributions, as well as those of LT Hans Lauzen, who shared his experiences as a White House social aide; Tara Slye, who offered insights on life in the DC metro area; and LT Kaitlin Smith, who helped compile photographs and illustrations to make this work more complete.

In addition to these contributors, many others supported us in this endeavor.

Fred is grateful to have worked for some senior leaders in the Pentagon and the fleet who have shared their insights and mentorship over the years—ADM Mike Mullen, USN (Ret.); ADM Phil Davidson, USN; VADM John Morgan, USN (Ret.); VADM Doug Crowder, USN (Ret.); VADM Tom Rowden, USN (Ret.); RADM Charlie Williams, USN (Ret.); and CDR Bryan McGrath, USN (Ret.).

Most of all, Fred would like to thank his family for their support. His wife, Pam, has always been willing to read and reflect on his writing despite being an incredibly busy and dedicated wife and mother of Jen and Katie, who have perhaps had to sacrifice the most during their childhood while their dad worked in a profession that he has loved. Fred also thanks his parents, Fred and Nancy Kacher, for serving as the original examples of leadership and patriotism in his life.

This is Doug's first book and he owes a debt of gratitude to many people—too many to list here, but a few deserve special recognition. To ADM Harry B. Harris Jr., USN (Ret.), for taking a chance on him as a high school student and keeping him under his wing throughout their shared time in uniform. To RDML Paul Schlise, his former captain, who recruited him for Pentagon duty. To Mike Shane, Don Blottenberger, and RADM Ron Boxall for coaching him through the machinations of the budget process and Pentagon staff work. To CDR Guy Snodgrass, USN (Ret.), RDML George Wikoff, and ADM John Richardson for the opportunity to observe, learn from, and contribute to the Navy's business at the highest levels.

Finally, Doug is deeply thankful to his parents, Stephen and Margret Robb, for giving him the gift of reading, thinking, and writing critically. His dad has never once been too busy to offer editing help. His wife, Kate, has provided immeasurable encouragement and patience and has acquiesced whenever she was presented with a request to work late on this project. And finally, to his children, Lincoln and Genevieve, for offering unconditional love to their dad—despite no understanding of what the Navy is or what he does in it—and for taking an occasional weekend nap during which he could chip away at this book.

Just as leadership is essential in the Pentagon and in the fleet, it is also a critical ingredient in the making of a book. Together, Fred and Doug are grateful to the Naval Institute Press for its teamwork; specifically, two extraordinary mentors, ADM James Stavridis, USN (Ret.), for penning the foreword, and USNI CEO and publisher, VADM Pete Daly, USN (Ret.), for supporting this title. Finally, we also thank the legendary LCDR Tom Cutler, USN (Ret.), as well as Jim Dolbow, copyeditor Aden Nichols, and production editor Rachel Crawford for their stewardship and care throughout the process.

An additional note: While we have loved working on this book with so many talented professionals, any opinions expressed here are solely those of the authors and should not be construed as those of the United States government, the Department of Defense, or the Department of the Navy. Additionally, any omissions, errors, or oversights fall on our shoulders alone.

Getting things done in the Pentagon is both an art and a science. We hope the knowledge in this book, and that which will be learned on the job starting one's very first day, will arm civilian and Navy professionals—from junior officers to senior leaders—to not only survive but to thrive in their roles as leaders in the world's greatest Navy. This book is dedicated to the members of this team—past, present, and future—who by their service make a difference in our Navy, our nation, and the world.

Fred W. Kacher
Douglas A. Robb

ACRONYMS, INITIALISMS, AND ABBREVIATIONS

If, as it is often said, military members "speak their own language"—one filled with acronyms and colloquialisms—then those stationed within the Beltway share a distinct dialect. Below are some of the organizational and programmatic acronyms and abbreviations one may encounter during a tour in the Pentagon or Washington, DC. In addition to this list, the Defense Acquisition University's online glossary provides an extensive list of acronyms, abbreviations, and terms commonly used in defense acquisition processes (https://www.dau.mil/glossary).

ACAT	acquisition category
ACJCS	Assistant to the Chairman of the Joint Chiefs of Staff
ACMC	Assistant Commandant of the Marine Corps
ADCOM	Administrative Command
ADCON	Administrative Control
AFCEA	Armed Forces Communications and Electronics Association
AFRICOM	U.S. Africa Command
AGC	assistant general counsel
A_o	operational availability ("A-sub-oh")
AO	action officer
AOA	analysis of alternatives
AOR	area of responsibility
APEX	adaptive planning and execution
APL	Applied Physics Laboratory
APN	Aircraft Procurement, Navy (appropriations)
APNSA	Assistant to the President for National Security Affairs
APPN	appropriation
APSA	Asia-Pacific security affairs
APUC	average procurement unit cost
ARL	Applied Research Laboratory
ARP	advance research program
ART	Arlington Transit
AS	Acquisition Strategy
ASD	Assistant Secretary of Defense
ASN	Assistant Secretary of the Navy
ASNE	American Society of Naval Engineers

AT&L	acquisition, technology, and logistics
AT/FP	antiterrorism force protection
ATSD(PA)	Assistant to the Secretary of Defense for Public Affairs
AVF	All-Volunteer Force
BAM	baseline assessment memorandum
BD	business development
BES	budget estimate submission
BISOG	blue in support of green
BLUF	bottom line up front
BRAC	Base Realignment and Closure
BSO	Budget Submitting Office
BUMED	Bureau of Medicine and Surgery
BUPERS	Bureau of Naval Personnel
C	comptroller
C2	command and control
C4	command, control, communications, and computers
C4ISR	command, control, communications, computers, intelligence, surveillance, and reconnaissance
CAC	common access card
CAE	component acquisition executive
CAG	commander's/chairman's action group
CAPE	cost assessment and program evaluation
CBA	capabilities-based assessment
CBRN	chemical, biological, radiological, and nuclear
CCDR	combatant commander (functional and geographic)
CCMD	combatant command
CDC	child development center
CDD	capability development document
CEC	Civil Engineer Corps
CENTCOM	U.S. Central Command
CFR	Council on Foreign Relations
CGA	capabilities gap assessment
CHINFO	Chief of Information
CIA	Central Intelligence Agency
CIC	commander in chief
CIMS	Congressional Information Management System
CIO	Chief Information Officer
CJCS	Chairman of the Joint Chiefs of Staff

CLA	Chief of Legislative Affairs
CLF	Combat Logistics Force
CMC	Commandant of the U.S Marine Corps
CMO	Chief Management Officer
CMSI	China Maritime Studies Institute
CNA	Center for Naval Analyses
CNAS	Center for a New American Security
CNGB	Chief of the National Guard Bureau
CNIC	Commander, Naval Installations Command
CNO	Chief of Naval Operations
CNOG	Chief of Naval Operations guidance
CNP	Chief of Naval Personnel
CNR	Chief of Naval Reserve; or Chief of Naval Research
CNWS	Center for Naval Warfare Studies (NWC)
COCOM	combatant command (authority)
CODEL	congressional delegation
COG	continuity of government
CONEMP	concept of employment
CONOP	concept of operation
COOP	continuity of operations
COR	contracting officer's representative
CP	critical path
CPA	chairman's program assessment
CPD	capability production document
CPR	component parking representative; or chairman's program recommendation
CR	continuing resolution
CRA	continuing resolution authority; or chairman's risk assessment
CRS	Congressional Research Service; or Chairman's Readiness System
CSA	Chief of Staff of the U.S. Army; or combat support agencies
CSAF	Chief of Staff of the U.S. Air Force
CSBA	Center for Strategic and Budgetary Assessments
CSIS	Center for Strategic and International Studies
CSM	command sergeant major
CY	calendar year

DAB	defense acquisition board
DAE	defense acquisition executive
DANTES	Defense Activity for Nontraditional Education Support
DAPNSA	Deputy Assistant to the President for National Security Affairs
DARPA	Defense Advanced Research Projects Agency
DAS	defense acquisition system
DASD	Deputy Assistant Secretary of Defense
DASH	Driving Alexandria Safely Home
DASN	Deputy Assistant Secretary of the Navy
DAU	Defense Acquisition University
DBB	Defense Business Board
DC	Deputies Committee (NSC)
DCMA	Defense Contract Management Agency
DCMO	Deputy Chief Management Officer
DCNO	Deputy Chief of Naval Operations
DD	deputy director
DDO	deputy director of operations
DEA	deputy executive assistant
DEF	Defense Enterprise Forum
DEPOPSDEPs	Deputy Operations Deputies (of the Joint Chiefs of Staff)
DEPORD	deployment order
DEPSECDEF	Deputy Secretary of Defense
DHS	Department of Homeland Security
DIA	Defense Intelligence Agency
DIMEFIL	diplomatic, information, military, economic, financial, intelligence, and legal
DJAG	Deputy Judge Advocate General
DLA	Defense Logistics Agency
DMAG	Deputy's Management Action Group
DNI	Director of National Intelligence; or Director of Naval Intelligence
DNS	Director, Navy Staff
DOD	Department of Defense
DODAF	Department of Defense Architecture Framework
DOE	Department of Energy
DOJ	Department of Justice
DOM	Director of Management
DON	Department of the Navy
DON/AA	Department of the Navy administrative assistant

DOS	Department of State
DOT&E	Director of Operational Test and Evaluation
DOTMLPF	doctrine, organization, training, matériel, leadership, and education, personnel, and facilities
DPB	Defense Policy Board
DPG	defense planning guidance
DSB	Defense Science Board
DSG	defense strategic guidance
DTRA	Defense Threat Reduction Agency
DUSN	Deputy Undersecretary of the Navy
EA	executive assistant
ECP	engineering change proposal
EEOB	Eisenhower Executive Office Building
EI&E	energy, installations, and environment
EIS	environmental impact statement
EMD	engineering and manufacturing development
EOC	early operational capability
EOD	explosive ordnance disposal
EOP	Executive Office of the President
EUCOM	U.S. European Command
EW	electronic warfare
EXORD	execution order
FADM	fleet admiral
FAFSA	free application for federal student aid
FAO	foreign area officer
FAR	federal acquisition regulation
FCB	functional capabilities board
FDD	Foundation for the Defense of Democracies
FEA	front-end assessment
FEF	federal executive fellowship
FFRDC	Federally Funded Research and Development Center
FLAGSEC	flag secretary
FMA	Fiscal Administrative Division
FM&C	financial management and comptroller
FMB	financial management and budget
FMBE	Office of Appropriations Matters
FMO	Office of Financial Operations
FMP	Office of Financial Policies and Systems

FMS	foreign military sale
FOC	full operational capability
FOS	family of systems
FRP	full-rate production
FSEP	Fleet Scholar Education Program
FY	fiscal year
FYDP	Future Years Defense Program
GAI	Government Affairs Institute
GAO	Government Accountability Office
GC	general counsel
GCC	global combatant commander
GEF	global employment of the force
GEV	graduate education voucher
GFE	government-furnished equipment
GFM	global force management
GO/FO	general officer/flag officer
GS	general schedule; or government service
HAC	House Appropriations Committee
HASC	House Armed Services Committee
HD	homeland defense
HON	Head of Navy (foreign)
HQMC	Headquarters Marine Corps
HSC	Homeland Security Council
I	intelligence
IA	information assurance
IAA	integrated analytic agenda
IB	industrial base
IC	intelligence community
ICD	Initial Capability Document
IDC	Information Dominance Corps
IFWS	Institute for Future Warfare Studies
IG	inspector general
INDOPACOM	U.S. Indo-Pacific Command
INSURV	Board of Inspection and Survey
IO	information operations
IOC	initial operational capability
IOT&E	initial operational test and evaluation

IPL	Integrated Priority List
IPR	in-process review; or interim program review
IPT	integrated product team
IRAD	independent (or internal) research and development
ISA	international security affairs
ISIC	immediate superior in command
ISR-T	intelligence, surveillance, and reconnaissance and targeting
IT	information technology
IW	information warfare
J-1	Manpower and Personnel Directorate (JCS)
J-2	Intelligence Directorate (JCS)
J-3	Operations Directorate (JCS)
J-4	Logistics Directorate (JCS)
J-5	Strategic Plans and Policy Directorate (JCS)
J-6	Command, Control, Communications, and Computers/Cyber Directorate (JCS)
J-7	Joint Force Development Directorate (JCS)
J-8	Force Structure, Resources, and Assessment Directorate (JCS)
JAG	judge advocate general
JBA	Joint Base Andrews
JBAB	Joint Base Anacostia-Bolling
JBMHH	Joint Base Myer-Henderson Hall
JCB	Joint Capabilities Board
JCIDS	Joint Capabilities Integration and Development System
JCS	Joint Chiefs of Staff
JCTD	Joint Capability Technology Demonstration
JDAL	joint duty assignment list
J-DIR	Joint-Code Director (Joint Staff)
J-Dirs	Joint Staff Directorates
JEON	joint emergent operational need
JF	joint force
JFC	joint force commander
JHU APL	Johns Hopkins University Applied Physics Laboratory
JIAMDO	Joint Integrated Air and Missile Defense Organization
JLOC	Joint Logistics Operations Center
JPME	Joint Professional Military Education
JQO	joint qualified officer

JQS	Joint Qualification System
JROC	Joint Requirements Oversight Council
JS	Joint Staff
JSAP	Joint Staff Action Process
JSCP	Joint Strategic Capabilities Plan
JSO	joint specialty officer
JSPS	Joint Staff Planning System
JUON	Joint Urgent Operational Need
KM/DS	knowledge management/decision support
KPP	key performance parameter
KSA	key system attribute
LA	legislative affairs
LC	legal counsel
LCC	life cycle cost
LDO	limited duty officer
LL	legislative liaison
LRIP	low-rate initial production
MA	military assistant
M&RA	Manpower and Reserve Affairs
MCPON	Master Chief Petty Officer of the Navy
MDA	Missile Defense Agency; or Milestone Decision Authority
MDAP	Major Defense Acquisition Program
MEF	Marine Expeditionary Force
METOC	meteorology and oceanography
MILCON	military construction
MILPERS	military personnel
MISO	military information support operations
MLA	military legislative assistant
MOA	memorandum of agreement
MOE	measure of effectiveness
MOP	measure of performance
MOS	measure of suitability
MOU	memorandum of understanding
MPN	Military Personnel Navy (appropriations)
MPTE	manpower, personnel, training, and education
MS	milestone

MSA	matériel solution analysis
MSC	Military Sealift Command
MTBP	Mass Transportation Benefit Program
MWR	morale, welfare, and recreation
MYP	multiyear procurement
N00	Office of the Chief of Naval Operations (personal staff)
N09	Office of the Vice Chief of Naval Operations
N1	Manpower, Personnel, Training, and Education (OPNAV)
N2/N6	Information Dominance (OPNAV)
N3/N5	Operations, Plans, and Strategy (OPNAV)
N4	Fleet Readiness and Logistics (OPNAV)
N7	Warfighting Development (OPNAV; announced December 2018)
N8	Integration of Capabilities and Resources (OPNAV)
N9	Warfare Systems (OPNAV)
NAO	Navy Analytic Office
NATO	North Atlantic Treaty Organization
NAVAIR	Naval Air Systems Command
NAVFAC	Naval Facilities Engineering Command
NAVSAFCEN	Naval Safety Center
NAVSEA	Naval Sea Systems Command
NAVSUP	Naval Supply Systems Command
NAWC	Naval Aviation Warfare Center
NCA	National Command Authority
NCB	Navy Capabilities Board
NCCA	Naval Center for Cost Analysis
NCIS	Naval Criminal Investigative Service
NCO	noncommissioned officer
NCR	National Capital Region
NDAA	National Defense Authorization Act
NDS	National Defense Strategy
NEOB	New Executive Office Building
NETC	Naval Education Training Command
NGA	National Geospatial-Intelligence Agency
NGO	non-governmental organization
NHHC	Naval History and Heritage Command
NJOIC	National Joint Operations and Intelligence Center
NMCC	National Military Command Center

NMCS	National Military Command System
NMRP	Navy Munitions Requirements Program
NMS	National Military Strategy
NOC	Navy Operations Center
NORTHCOM	U.S. Northern Command
NPC	Naval Personnel Command
NPS	Naval Postgraduate School
NR	Naval Reactors
NRL	Naval Research Laboratory
NRO	National Reconnaissance Office
NRP	Naval Research Program
NSA	National Security Agency
NSB	Naval Studies Board
NSC	National Security Council
NSFP	National Security Fellows Program
NSS	National Security Strategy
NSTC	Naval Service Training Command
NSW	Naval Special Warfare
NSWC	Naval Surface Warfare Center
NUWC	Naval Undersea Warfare Center
NWC	Naval War College
O&M	Operations and Maintenance
O&S	Operating and Support
OGC	Office of the General Counsel
OIPT	Overarching Integrated Product Team
OJAG	Office of the Judge Advocate General
OLA	Office of Legislative Affairs
OMB	Office of Management and Budget
OMN	Operations and Maintenance [Appropriation], Navy
ONR	Office of Naval Research
OOOM	OPNAV Operations and Organization Manual
OPM	Office of Personnel Management
OPNAV	Office of the Chief of Naval Operations, or Navy Staff
OPO	OPNAV Principal Office
OPSDEPs	Operations Deputies (of the Joint Chiefs of Staff)
OSD	Office of the Secretary of Defense
OT	Operations Team
OWLS	Officer Women Leadership Symposium

PAC	Pentagon Athletic Center
PACB	Pentagon Access Control Branch
P&D	Production and Deployment
P&R	Personnel and Readiness; or Programs and Resources
PAO	public affairs officer
PB	President's budget
PBAD	Program and Budget Analysis Division
PBCG	Program Budget Coordinating Group
PBIS	Program Budget Information System
PBR	Program and Budget Review
PC	Principals Committee (NSC)
PCD	principal civilian deputy
PDM	Program Decision Memorandum
PDUSD	Principal Deputy Undersecretary of Defense
PE	program element
PEO	Program Executive Office
PESTONI	Personnel, Equipment, Supply, Training, Networks, Ordnance, and Infrastructure
PFPA	Pentagon Force Protection Agency
PLANORD	planning order
PM	Program Manager
PMB	Parking Management Branch
PMD	Principal Military Deputy
PME	professional military education
PNT	positioning, navigation, and timing
POAM	Plan of Action and Milestones
POC	point of contact
POLAD	political advisor
POLMIL	politico-military
POM	Program Objective Memorandum
POR	Program of Record
POTUS	President of the United States
PPBE	planning, programming, budgeting, and execution
PPBS	Planning, Programming, and Budgeting System
PRR	Program Requirements (or Readiness) Review
PRTC	Potomac and Rappahannock Transportation Commission
PSA	Principal Staff Assistant
PSB	Presidential Service Badge
PSD	protective service detail
PSM	professional staff member

RAH	read-ahead
R&D	research and development
R&E	research and engineering
RD&A	research, development, and acquisition
RDT&E	research, development, test, and evaluation
RFI	request for information
RM	requirements manager
RMD	Resource Management Decision
RMSI	Russia Maritime Studies Institute
RO	requirements officer
ROM	rough order of magnitude
RPED	rapid prototyping, experimentation, and demonstration
SAC	Senate Appropriations Committee
SAE	Service Acquisition Executive
S&T	science and technology
SAP	Special Access Program
SAPCO	Special Access Program Coordinator
SAS	United States Navy League Sea-Air-Space Exposition
SASC	Senate Armed Services Committee
SCN	Shipbuilding and Conversion, Navy
SCO	Strategic Capabilities Office
SCRA	Servicemembers Civil Relief Act
SEAC	Senior Enlisted Advisor to the Chairman (of the Joint Chiefs of Staff)
SEAL	Sea, Air, and Land (NSW)
SECAF	Secretary of the Air Force
SECDEF	Secretary of Defense
SECNAV	Secretary of the Navy
SECSTATE	Secretary of State
SES	Senior Executive Service
SHAPE	Supreme Headquarters Allied Powers Europe
S-JDAL	standard joint duty assignment
SLEP	Service Life Extension Program
SME	subject matter expert
SNA	Surface Navy Association
SOCOM	U.S. Special Operations Command
SO/LIC	special operations and low-intensity conflict
SORD	Strategic and Operational Research Department (NWC)
SOS	System of Systems

SOUTHCOM	U.S. Southern Command
SOW	statement/scope of work
SPA	systems planning and analysis
SPAWAR	Space and Naval Warfare Systems Command
SROC	Senior Readiness Oversight Council
STAFFDEL	staff delegation
STO	Special Technical Operations
STRATCOM	U.S. Strategic Command
SVTC	secure video teleconference
SYSCOM	Systems Command
T&E	test and evaluation
TD	technology development
TEMP	Test and Evaluation Master Plan
TOA	Total Obligation Authority
TRANSCOM	U.S. Transportation Command
TRL	technology readiness level
UARC	University Affiliated Research Center
UAS	unmanned aerial systems
UAV	unmanned aerial vehicles
UNSECNAV	Undersecretary of the Navy
UON	urgent operational need
URL	unrestricted line
USA	U.S. Army
USAF	U.S. Air Force
USAID	U.S. Agency for International Development
USCG	U.S. Coast Guard
USD	Undersecretary of Defense
USG	U.S. government
USMC	U.S. Marine Corps
USN	U.S. Navy
USNA	U.S. Naval Academy
USNI	U.S. Naval Institute
UUV	unmanned underwater vehicles
VA	Veterans Affairs
VCJCS	Vice Chairman of the Joint Chiefs of Staff
VCNO	Vice Chief of Naval Operations
VD	Vice Director

VDJS	Vice Director of the Joint Staff
VPOTUS	Vice President of the United States
VRE	Virginia Railway Express
VTC	video teleconference
WAG	widely attended gathering
WARNORD	warning order
WH	White House
WHLO	White House Liaison Office
WHMO	White House Military Office
WHS	Washington Headquarters Services
WHSR	White House Situation Room
WIPT	working-level integrated product team
WMATA	Washington Metropolitan Area Transit Authority
WMD	weapons of mass destruction
WNY	Washington Navy Yard
WPN	Weapons Procurement, Navy (appropriations)
WRNMMC	Walter Reed National Military Medical Center
WSCA	warfighting and support capability assessment
WSERB	Weapon System Explosives Safety Review Board

INTRODUCTION

Your next assignment is taking you to the Pentagon—congratulations! Although relocating to Washington, coupled with the prospect of beginning a new job, can seem daunting, the authors of this book hope to ease the transition by offering useful information to make your adjustment smooth and pleasurable.

No guidebook—no matter how thorough and well conceived—can substitute for knowledge and insights experienced directly. That is how it should be. Your experiences will be somewhat unique, reflecting your personal and professional needs. Rather, this volume seeks to provide some basic, but helpful, information as you embark on what for many is a life-altering and career-enhancing journey.

At the Pentagon, you will join approximately 3,400 uniformed Navy officers serving in the National Capital Region and will follow in the footsteps of the many thousands who preceded you to this unique place. Working in our nation's capital is equal parts demanding, challenging, insightful, and rewarding. Observing firsthand how and why decisions are made that can affect the Navy and the nation provides an often-humbling perspective that will remain with you after you leave the Pentagon and return to leadership positions on the waterfront or flight line that comprise the true core of the naval profession.

The organization and purpose of this book will be familiar to those who have consulted previous Naval Institute Press *Guides* titles, which for decades have served as repositories of information related to the naval profession. These works include guidance for newly commissioned officers and captains at sea; essentials of division officer leadership and fundamentals of watchstanding; administrative management; naval writing; customs and ceremonies; etiquette, and more. This book should not be construed as an exhaustive treatment of everything you might encounter during your time at the Pentagon; rather, it is a stimulus to encourage your own search to becoming more acquainted with aspects of the profession you may not have encountered before this assignment.

Collectively, the chapters in this book offer a wide range of information about the Pentagon and its workings—from the building's inception and construction during World War II to its many functions today. This book highlights what life is like inside its imposing limestone walls; it discusses some of the major staff tenants housed within what is colloquially termed "the Building" with whom you may work; describes some of the common staff roles and functions for which you may be responsible; explores some of the actors and organizations in Washington with whom you can expect to interact; and gives you some things to think about as you prepare for your tour. While other books have been written on one or more of these topics—for example, the excellent *Assignment Pentagon*, by Maj Gen Perry Smith, USAF (Ret.), and COL Daniel Gerstein, USA (Ret.)—none have been tailored exclusively for naval officers living and working in Washington.

This reference seeks to fill that literary void. It brings together insights from professionals who have excelled in jobs in Washington and around the globe. Contributors and their topics were paired to match subjects to expertise, bringing a variety of academic backgrounds, experiences, perspectives, warfighting designators, and ashore subspecialties to the task. If you have heard negative things about working in Washington, we encourage you to open your mind and let this book expand your horizons.

A quick review of active and retired flag officer biographies reveals that nearly every single one of them served at least one tour in Washington. While this is not to say that Pentagon duty is a promotion-earning prerequisite, it does demonstrate that working in DC is almost universally appreciated for providing naval leaders with a broader sense of our institution and the forces that shape its funding, organization, and future. It also means you can take comfort in knowing that your boss—and your boss' boss—understand the challenges and opportunities you face because they, too, likely faced them in their careers.

Moreover, you may be surprised to meet a number of retired officers who chose to permanently settle with their families in and around DC, or the cadre of "repeat offenders" who voluntarily return to the city for successive tours—an indicator of the area's impact on those who have served here. This is because not only is the work meaningful and important but also because the region can be a rewarding place to live and raise a family. Perhaps most importantly, serving in Washington will affirm your appreciation for how the Navy fits into the larger national defense picture, from the creation of the service budget to the formulation of operational plans to the enactment of grand security strategies. Here, the daily interactions of our constitutionally created co-equal branches of government can be observed up close. This is also a prime opportunity to meet fleet, government, academic, and industry experts who plan, test, acquire, and field the concepts and systems critical for preserving our war-fighting advantage. And you will work alongside some of the finest military and civilian professionals in the nation.

When deliberating about where to move his wartime headquarters, FADM Ernest J. King observed, "Where the power is that is where the headquarters have to be." So join us as we explore what it is like to live and work in one of the world's largest office buildings; one of the most consequential architectural landmarks of the twentieth century; and a monumental structure whose name is synonymous with the size, power, and the security of the United States. Welcome aboard!

PART I
THE BUILDING

1

THE PENTAGON: A BRIEF HISTORY

LCDR RACHAEL A. GOSNELL, USN

Receiving orders to the Pentagon for the first time can be daunting, particularly when one realizes they will be joining more than 30,000 others who trek to "the Building" every day for work. Thousands of naval officers have reported for duty in the Pentagon—just as you soon will. Yet this is no standard workplace, despite being recognized as one of the world's largest office buildings. This behemoth complex that hosts the Department of Defense (DOD) has a history as peculiar and impressive as the structure itself. Understanding this background will offer a greater appreciation of both its creators and the important work that happens daily in the building—it may even impress your guests when they ask for the requisite Pentagon tours!

THE IDEA

Washington, DC, was a solemn place in the spring of 1941. Adolf Hitler's Third Reich already controlled much of Europe and was preparing to launch Operation Barbarossa, a massive invasion of the Soviet Union. On May 27, President Franklin D. Roosevelt addressed the nation via radio, painting a dire picture of Nazi domination across the European continent. He proceeded to declare a state of unlimited national emergency in response to the alarming events that were developing "into a world war for world domination." Though President Roosevelt was hesitant to commit troops, he clearly detailed a policy to protect shipping in the Atlantic by increasing U.S. shipbuilding, providing additional aid to Britain, and establishing a civilian defense—all while placing the armed forces in a strategic military position. President Roosevelt reaffirmed that the nation would not hesitate to use the armed forces to repel any attack.

In response, the War Department began to swell massively. Personnel flooded the city as the war machine spooled up, though policy mandated civilian attire in an attempt to conceal the growing numbers. The department desperately needed a new headquarters for the 24,000 workers who were literally bursting out of the nearly two dozen disparate offices scattered across the city in temporary structures, apartment buildings, rented garages, and even private homes. A July 1941 congressional hearing noted the pressing need to find a suitable alternative to the inefficient office structures in place. With authorization from Army Chief of Staff GEN George C. Marshall, BG Brehon Burke Somervell, head of the Army's Construction Division, seized upon the opportunity to design and construct a suitable new headquarters. Described by a 1943 *Life* article as "dynamite in a Tiffany box," General Somervell was a shrewd operator who would deftly guide the massive project through immense budgetary, programmatic, and political obstacles that would be formidable even to today's program managers.

LOCATION, LOCATION, LOCATION

President Roosevelt had previously approved the construction of an $18 million new headquarters for the War Department at Foggy Bottom. However, when it opened in June 1941, the small facility was already inadequate. Secretary of War Henry L. Stimson grappled to determine the political feasibility of requesting a new headquarters so quickly after the completion of the Foggy Bottom complex. Knowing full well that the Foggy Bottom offices could not meet the expanding needs of a department churning toward war, Somervell focused on finding an appropriate solution to the challenge of housing the department's employees. Foggy Bottom would later become the home of the State Department instead.

Somervell faced a daunting task as he envisioned a headquarters with a capacity of 40,000 workers and parking for 10,000 cars. Upon a preliminary survey of available land, engineers soon realized that the location would have to be moved across the Potomac River to Virginia. The first Virginia location selected—the old Washington-Hoover Airport that had been vacated when the modern National Airport was constructed—was quickly ruled out due to flooding concerns. The search for a suitable location moved northward along the Potomac.

Somervell's brilliant Chief of Design, LTC "Pat" Casey, selected a large tract of land just east of Arlington National Cemetery, an area known as Arlington Farms. Part of Robert E. Lee's estate that had been

Foreground: main Navy and munitions buildings ("Main Navy"). *Background:* Reflecting Pool, Lincoln Memorial, Memorial Bridge, and Potomac River. *Official U.S. Navy photo, now in the collections of the National Archives*

confiscated in 1861, Arlington Farms had recently been returned to the War Department by presidential decree for use by infantry and cavalry troops stationed at the neighboring Fort Myer. Upon surveying the land and discounting other options nearby, Somervell approved of the Arlington Farms site as the location of the new Department of War headquarters. Notable architect George Edwin Bergstrom was hired to design what would become the largest project of his distinguished career.

THE DESIGN

On July 18, 1941, Bergstrom gathered his assistants. The challenge before them was immense: Somervell demanded "500,000 square feet ready in six months, the whole thing [4 million square feet] ready in a year." There were many obstacles to overcome—the physical restrictions of the oddly shaped plot, height limitations (to prevent obstructing the views of Washington and due to matériel shortages), and a tight project timeline. Even the building materials would pose a challenge—the preferred choice, steel, was simply not an option. War in Europe had decimated steel sup-plies, and the construction of new warships took priority for the scarce steel reserves. The building could not rely on steel-supported height for the requisite office space, but instead would have to find an innovative solution to meet Somervell's requirements.

The asymmetrical shape of the Arlington Farms location—bounded by roads or obstacles on each of its five sides—inspired a junior architect to propose an asymmetrical pentagonal structure for the new headquar-ters. Other more standard designs, such as a traditional rectangle, were quickly discarded due to inefficiencies and space limitations. Architects worked feverishly to refine the innovative five-sided design. Conceived and sketched in a mere three days, Somervell presented the building plan to Secretary Stimson, who was immediately attracted to the simplicity and practicality of the building. Somervell promised that construction would be completed within a year and assured the secretary that it would result in a 25 to 40 percent improved efficiency of the department. Stimson was convinced and permitted Somervell to seek funding from the House Appropriations Committee.

President Roosevelt was briefed on the plan on July 24 and, spurred by his growing fear that the United States could not avoid war with Germany, quickly approved it. In just one week—in what has to be a record for military construction projects—Somervell proposed a plan, drafted an initial design, gained the support of the cabinet secretary, and received funding from the Appropriations Committee.

THE CONTROVERSY

Yet, every project faces unforeseen challenges. In the case of the Pentagon, the ghost of Washington's founding architect Pierre L'Enfant foiled the plans for the new headquarters. The Chairman of the U.S. Commission of Fine Arts, Gilmore D. Clarke, was concerned that such a building would obstruct L'Enfant's view of the city from his tomb and embarked on a crusade to prevent construction. Clarke found an ally in the National Capital Park and Planning Commission Chairman, Frederic A. Delano (the brother of President Roosevelt's mother, whom the President [POTUS] called "Uncle Fred"). Delano noted that the site would also pose further transportation problems and asked for a meeting with his nephew to dissuade the President of its construction. Harold D. Smith, director of the

United States Bureau of the Budget, joined the meeting, asserting that the massive structure was unnecessary given the only temporary enlargement of the War Department in response to the Nazi threat. Surely, he reasoned, the building would be underutilized after the threat has passed and would be viewed by taxpayers as a wasteful misuse of funds.

Swayed by these arguments, the President rationalized that a building capacity of 20,000 employees would be a more practical solution. While the House of Representatives had already approved the project, he urged the Senate to reconsider and instead approve a smaller building. Opponents launched a robust campaign to derail the project and nearly succeeded. However, the size that was originally requested passed in the Senate by a thin margin. Despite Congress' unity, Washington was now in an uproar over the project and the building's proposed location proved the main source of contention. Secretary of the Interior Harold L. Ickes wrote a furious letter to the President, begging him not to permit "this rape of Washington."

As a result of the discord, Clarke proposed an alternae site just south of Arlington Farms, where the Army had recently commenced construction of a quartermaster depot. Yet Somervell refused to consider the new location known as Hell's Bottom—a low-lying plot located among brickyards and shanties—because he felt it inappropriate to situate the new headquarters in such a sordid neighborhood. Clarke, however, had the support of the Senate—and now of the POTUS. Roosevelt's lingering sense of guilt over persuading President Wilson to authorize the temporary construction of the Navy building (called "Main Navy") and the munitions building along the National Mall in 1917—and their continued presence decades later—made him hesitant to further upset the aesthetics of the city. Roosevelt had decided that a better solution would be to move the headquarters to the alternate site, with a small portion extending slightly onto the Arlington Farms plot so as to satisfy the congressional funding requirement that approved construction of the new headquarters at that location.

Though the unique pentagonal shape was no longer needed on the new site, Bergstrom did not have time to change the plans. Indeed, the unusual blueprint offered efficiencies in walking distances within the building, as well as improved office space and utilities distribution throughout the headquarters. The sides were updated to make them symmetrical, which

improved the aesthetics over the asymmetrical design that was neces-
sitated by the Arlington Farms site limitations. However, challenges to
the unique design were mounted; the President was unconvinced that the
unusual shape was ideal and Clarke wielded the power of his commission
to reexamine the plans.

A special congressional hearing was arranged in early September, where
famous architects gathered to ridicule the design. Notable architect and
commission member Paul Phillipe Cret aptly predicted that if a visitor
wandered into the wrong corridor, "he is lost." The commission vocally
opposed the design but Congress was not swayed by their testimony. Plans
were adjusted slightly, and Somervell and Bergstrom received approval
from the POTUS—much to the chagrin of the Fine Arts Commission.
Upon the commission's final appeal to the President, Roosevelt is known
to have exclaimed support for the building because "nothing like it has
ever been done that way before."

CONSTRUCTION

On September 11, 1941, the War Department initiated construction on the
Pentagon. The project was a monumental one and the timeline exceed-
ingly short. By early December, 3,000 workers had converged onto the
site, led by building contractor John McShain and Corps of Engineers
MAJ Leslie R. Groves (who would later be chosen to head the Manhattan
Project). Despite falling behind schedule, construction was spurred on
with a greater urgency after the Japanese attack on Pearl Harbor and
subsequent declaration of war. Thousands of workers were added—their
numbers reached nearly 15,000 at the height of construction. Work was
divided into three shifts that would permit progress twenty-four hours a
day, aided by floodlights to illuminate the site at night. Construction moved
at such a breathtaking clip that work often began before the blueprints
were finished—despite the employment of nearly 1,000 architects.

The scope of construction itself was massive. First, 5.5 million cubic
yards of earth were brought in to stabilize the swampland on which the
new headquarters was to rest. Another 689,000 tons of sand and gravel
were repurposed from the Potomac River as ingredients to mix into the
building's concrete—a wartime alternative to the scarce steel typically used
for large-scale construction projects. More than 41,000 concrete pilings
were placed on the site to provide a stable foundation. Indiana limestone
was selected for the façade, with more than 460,000 cubic feet covering

the outermost ring and the interior wall surrounding the courtyard. No marble was utilized since the primary source of marble—Italy—had signed the Tripartite Pact establishing the Axis powers the year before. Under the demanding guidance of Somervell, Bergstrom, and Groves, the project would take a mere sixteen months to transform into the functioning military headquarters we recognize today.

Originally known as the New War Department Building in Arlington, workers quickly bestowed the nickname "pentagonal building." War Department employees moved into their new offices as soon as sections were completed; the first office workers began work in the building in late April 1942. Those early days saw office workers and construction workers laboring alongside one another, both focused on their respective tasks. In May 1942 the War Department changed the name to the Pentagon Building and a year later it was simplified to the Pentagon. As with many military projects, cost overruns for the Pentagon were rampant; Somervell's proposed $35 million project became a $75 million investment (approximately $1.1 billion in today's dollars), with the entire Pentagon Reservation complex costing $83 million in total. The completed structure, which contained 6.24 million square feet of office space, officially opened on January 14, 1943. Upon completion, the Pentagon housed nearly 30,000 defense workers focused on winning World War II.

THE WORLD'S LARGEST OFFICE BUILDING

With the official opening, the Pentagon was bestowed with the title of "the world's largest office building." In the decades since, taller buildings have emerged that call the precise definition of "largest" into question. For example, the Burj Khalifa in Dubai, the world's tallest building, contains office space within it. However, the Pentagon's 6.7 million square feet of floor area—nearly three times that of the Empire State Building—is still among the largest in the world. For those eager to maintain a level of fitness while assigned to a staff job, the corridors total nearly 17.5 miles across five concentric rings with five stories above ground and two below. Each outer wall is 921 feet long. The outer ring—the E-ring—is approximately one mile in length, with each ring inside progressively smaller. The central courtyard comprises five acres and is one of the largest "no hat, no salute" zones in the United States. Yet despite the sheer size of the building, as you will learn in the next chapter, it takes only seven minutes to walk between any two points—if you know where you are going. Even then the Army Chief of Staff, GEN Dwight D. Eisenhower, famously got lost trying to return to his new office, remarking that no enemy would ever be able to successfully infiltrate the building.

To facilitate movement between floors, there are 131 stairways and 19 escalators (which tend to be turned off in the evenings, much to the chagrin of the dedicated action officer). The lack of steel available during the war precluded elevators—indeed, there were only 13 freight elevators in the original design—and gave rise to the innovative ramps that connect floors throughout the building (elevators were installed, however, during subsequent renovations). While early messengers took to the Pentagon corridors on roller skates and bikes, today's Pentagon relies more heavily on telephones at every desk and email to pass messages. Electric vehicles were popular during the 1960s for expeditious transport, but they were limited after Secretary of the Air Force Eugene M. Zuckert was struck by one while attempting to cross the busy hallway intersection near his office.

The building includes 691 water fountains (one is purple—see if you can find it!) and 284 restrooms—far more than a typical building of its size because the initial design had segregated restrooms to comply with Virginia state law. However, when President Roosevelt visited the construction site on May 2, 1942, he was confounded by the "prodigality of lavatory space." The justification of compliance with Virginia segregation laws was in violation of his June 1941 Executive Order 8802 that outlawed discrimination in the national defense establishment. After Roosevelt's visit, signs marking "colored" or "white" were never painted on the restrooms. As a result, the Pentagon earned the distinction of being the first non-segregated government building in Virginia. As the next chapter will detail, the concourse (main) entrance hosts a bus terminal, metro station, and a mini shopping mall that offers necessities ranging from various food and coffee options, dry cleaning, a post office, a Virginia Department of Motor Vehicles office, and a rotating assortment of merchandise shops. Thoughtful planners included a flower shop, jewelry store, and chocolate shop for those requiring last-minute gifts—or those hoping to offer an apology for too many late nights in the office.

The outside of the building is equally impressive, comprising 583 acres with 67 acres devoted to 8,700 parking spaces (still vastly insufficient to meet demand). The 30 miles of access highways surrounding the building include 21 overpasses and bridges. Though the region—and the Department of Defense—has evolved immensely since the doors of the Pentagon first opened, the Pentagon remains a massive architectural marvel that has played a critical role in defense planning from the day its first office workers moved in during the height of World War II.

WORLD WAR II IS OVER—NOW WHAT?

The Allied victory of World War II cast doubt on the future of the Pentagon—most assumed that the War Department would have little reason to remain in such a massive building once the war had ended. Calls in Washington came for conversion of the building into a university or a hospital instead. It was even suggested that the space could be better utilized as warehouse storage. The Army, however, was reluctant to relinquish the building.

Indeed, tensions mounted among the Allied powers that, while unified to eradicate a common enemy, found that they ultimately had irreconcilable differences in terms of political philosophy and national ambitions. The Cold War was quickly forming as the Soviet Union sought to extend its influence and communist ideology while Western democracies rushed to counter the expanding threat. The 1947 National Security Act sought to reorganize the military in advance of the growing Soviet threat. President Truman recognized the value of headquartering the Navy, Army, and newly created Air Force together in the Pentagon, and relied on the first Secretary of Defense (SECDEF), James V. Forrestal, to enact his vision. As a result, the President declared that the Pentagon would serve as the headquarters for the newly created National Military Establishment, known today as the Department of Defense.

PENTAGON DURING THE COLD WAR

The massive military headquarters continued to churn at the Pentagon as the fierce global rivalry between the United States and Soviet Union took off. The Korean War witnessed another increase in department staffing, which reached nearly 33,000 employees. By this point, the Pentagon had become a recognizable symbol of American military strength and determination. In 1962, Secretary of Defense Robert McNamara authorized the National Military Command Center (NMCC) in the building, allowing close coordination among the services for emerging events and urgent crises.

While seen by many as an admirable symbol of military might, the Pentagon was targeted during the Vietnam War by antiwar protesters who viewed the building in a far more negative light. Nearly 35,000 protesters marched on the Pentagon in October 1967 vowing to "levitate" the building to disrupt the war effort. Approximately 2,000 soldiers guarded the Pentagon under orders to "fix bayonets" as the protesters approached. Violence ensued but surprisingly not a single shot was fired and no protesters were killed. Nevertheless, the Pentagon remained a target of antiwar protests. In 1972 a bomb planted by an antiwar group, the Weather Underground, exploded in a women's restroom. Though no one was injured, the damage totaled $75,000 and served as a stark reminder of the primary function of the Pentagon. When its doors first opened to visitors in 1976, the Pentagon also became a popular Washington tourist attraction.

For the duration of the Cold War, the Pentagon maintained the dubious distinction of being "Ground Zero" in the event of a hot war with the Soviet Union. The hotdog stand in the center of the courtyard was affectionately known as the Ground Zero Café. It was rumored to have confounded Soviet planners who watched the vast numbers of military officers entering and exiting that location each day—they were just seeking lunch, not heading to a secret command center for a classified briefing.

The collapse of the Soviet Union in 1991 was celebrated as a victory for democracy, but the Defense Department would soon grapple with how best to adjust to the evolving international security environment. The Pentagon itself was also facing challenges posed by its aging infrastructure. Designated a national historic landmark in 1992, the Pentagon was showing its age and the Defense Department recognized the need to modernize. Massive renovations—authorized by Congress in 1994 with an appropriation totaling more than $1 billion—were critical to ensure the building kept pace with the challenges of a rapidly evolving world. Much like the original project, the renovations went significantly over budget and fell behind schedule.

THE PENTAGON ON SEPTEMBER 11, 2001

The modernization budget and time delays meant that on September 11, 2001, the renovations were in their final stages. That day—exactly sixty years after the initiation of construction on the building—American Airlines Flight 77, hijacked by terrorists, crashed into the northwestern side of the building. The damage was shocking. The aircraft punctured the three outer rings, creating a hole thirty yards wide. Fires raged for nearly three days, and 184 people were killed, 125 of whom were Pentagon employees working in their offices. Heroic actions undoubtedly saved many more lives that day. The sacrifices made cannot be appropriately captured on these pages, but no tour in the Pentagon is complete without visiting the Pentagon's 9/11 Memorial.

The $500 million Phoenix project was quickly authorized to repair the devastation, with the objective to restore the damaged wing so that it would blend seamlessly into the rest of the exterior. Within days of the attack, Pentagon officials approached the Indiana Limestone Company—providers of the original limestone façade—asking for replacement stone. Yet the company had long since scrapped the saws used on the original contract, posing a dilemma. The officials desired the same grooved striations, known as "shot sawn" that the original saws had left in the façade. A nearby company, Bybee Stone, still had these older saws and was awarded the contract. The 2.5 million pounds of limestone was sourced from a quarry barely twenty miles from the original in order to retain the same geological appearance. While the renovation project aimed to complete in one year, the scope of the project had been vastly enlarged to add security upgrades, including moving the Pentagon's command centers to the basement for added protection. The project finished in February 2003 at a cost of $5 billion and with the military's focus on the war in Afghanistan (and then Iraq) the people in the building never stopped working. Much like the early days of construction, laborers repairing the building worked alongside staff officers and Defense Department civilians planning war, each superbly executing their assigned tasks. While the Pentagon had sustained a massive attack, those working within it quickly demonstrated perseverance and toughness—qualities embodied by the U.S. Department of Defense.

THE PENTAGON TODAY

Shaped by its impressive history, the Pentagon remains the physical and spiritual center of the U.S. Department of Defense. In 2011 an enormous renovation was completed to prepare the building for the evolving threat environment; it took nearly twenty years and cost $4.5 billion. The café still stands at the center of the courtyard, harkening back to the Cold War era—even as the world is ominously facing greater nuclear instability. More than 25,000 workers pass through its corridors each day, and the headquarters envisioned by Somervell still directs the nation's military. Forged from innovative plans, dogged perseverance, and expert project management, the Pentagon remains a recognizable symbol of U.S. military might.

FURTHER READING

In writing this brief historical overview of the Pentagon, the author relied on a number of sources that also offer additional information for those readers who wish to explore the Pentagon's history more deeply.

Bland, Larry, Sharon Ritenour Stevens, and Clarence Wunderlin. *The Papers of George Catlett Marshall.* (Lexington, Va.: The George C. Marshall Foundation, 2016).

Brinkley, David. *Washington Goes to War.* (New York: Ballantine Books, 1989).

Fine, Lenore, and Jesse A. Remington. *The Corps of Engineers: Construction in the United States.* (Washington, DC: Office of the Chief of Military History, U.S. Army, 1972).

Goldberg, Alfred. *The Pentagon: The First Fifty Years.* (Washington, DC: Historical Office, Office of the Secretary of Defense, 1992).

Goldberg, Alfred, et al. *Pentagon 9/11.* (Washington, DC: Department of Defense, 2007).

Mullen, William. "Indiana Rock to Restore Pentagon." *Chicago Tribune.* December 20, 2001. http://articles.chicagotribune.com/2001-12-20 /news/0112200259_1_bybee-limestone-pentagon.

Murphy, Charles. "Somervell of the SOS: His Getting the Right Things to the Right Places at the Right Time Means Our Success." *Life*, March 8, 1943, 83–94.

Pentagon Tours (Department of Defense). "Facts." https://pentagontours.osd.mil /Tours/facts.jsp.

Roosevelt, Franklin D. "Radio Address Announcing an Unlimited National Emergency" [May 27, 1941]. In Gerhard Peters and John T. Woolley, *The American Presidency Project.* http://www.presidency.ucsb.edu/ws/?pid=16120.

Vogel, Steve. *The Pentagon: A History: The Untold Story of the Wartime Race to Build the Pentagon and to Restore It Sixty Years Later.* (New York: Random House, 2007).

LCDR Rachael A. Gosnell served in the Pentagon in both OPNAV N513 Strategy and Policy and as the speechwriter for the Chief of Naval Operations. She was previously a surface warfare officer, serving at sea on board USS *Shiloh* (CG 67), USS *Harry S. Truman* (CVN 75), and USS *Stockdale* (DDG 106). She is pursuing a PhD from the University of Maryland and holds master's degrees in international security studies from Georgetown University and in engineering management from Old Dominion University, and a BS in political science from the U.S. Naval Academy.

2

NAVIGATING THE PENTAGON

LCDR JONATHAN "SHANK" LUSHENKO, USN

Whether reporting to the Pentagon for first time or returning for another tour in "the Building," you are embarking on an adventure that is both personally and professionally rewarding. Working in one of the world's largest office complexes is a unique experience—and not simply because of the fast-paced, high-visibility environment in which you will operate. Physically making your way through the Pentagon—traversing the levels and passageways—is a challenge in and of itself. Though it is not uncommon, even for Pentagon veterans, to take an occasional wrong turn or to stop and ask for directions to an obscure space, this chapter will arm you with some basic logistical guideposts to help plan your daily commute to and from the Pentagon, navigate miles of corridors, and familiarize yourself with some of the goods and services offered within this not-so-mini city.

The Pentagon Reservation is a sprawling complex of buildings and roadways in Arlington, Virginia, that sits along the western bank of the Potomac River just north of I-395. In addition to the five-sided centerpiece, the grounds are home to an adjacent library and conference center, immense fitness center, sprawling outdoor memorial park, remote delivery facility, and several large parking lots. Because original construction predated satellite systems and fiber-optic cables, the building underwent a massive renovation project that began in the late 1990s and was completed in 2011. In addition to interior piping, flooring, wiring, and aesthetic upgrades, the project included construction of a new aboveground bus terminal and visitor's entrance. Construction facts drawn from popular sources such as the History Channel, encyclopedias, and even the public affairs guide brochure published by the Department of Defense underscore the enormity of this iconic complex:

Construction commences:	September 11, 1941
Construction finishes:	January 15, 1943
Architectural style:	Stripped Neo-Classical
Primary building material:	Concrete
Total land area:	583 acres
Total floor space:	6,636,360 square feet
Total corridor length:	17.5 miles
Total windows:	7,754
Total light fixtures:	16,250
Total restrooms:	284
Total stairways:	131
Length of each outer wall:	921 feet
Façade material:	Indiana limestone
Total employees:	~30,000
Number of zip codes:	Six
Total parking lots:	16 (~8,770 vehicles)
Total project cost:	$83 million (1943 dollars), ~$1.2 billion (2019 dollars)

GETTING TO THE PENTAGON

There are many ways to commute to the Pentagon—bus, train, automobile, carpool, motorcycle, bicycle, walking, and so on. Through the course of your tour, the realities imposed by a potentially demanding work schedule and other personal and professional commitments will likely cause you to rely on more than one means of getting to and from the Pentagon. Understanding these options can help reduce stress by saving you valuable time.

MASS TRANSIT

Residents of the greater Washington area enjoy access to one of the nation's most robust mass transit systems. The Pentagon is easily accessible by car, rail, and bus, and this section will familiarize you with these popular commuting options.

Washington Metropolitan Area Transit Authority (WMATA). Metro-rail—or, simply, the Metro—is one of the most convenient and cost-efficient means of transportation to and from the Pentagon, and has been a prime choice of traveling in and around the District since beginning operations in 1973. The Metro now comprises 91 stations across 117 miles of track to provide a highly reliable, user-friendly commuting option. Smartphone Metro applications supplement online services—schedules, maps, rider guide, fares, services—to provide real-time updates on service outages and delays. WMATA operates two lines to and from the Pentagon: the Blue Line, which runs between the Franconia/Springfield Station in Virginia and the Largo Town Center in Maryland, and the Yellow Line, which operates between the Huntington Station in Virginia and Fort Totten in Maryland. During peak morning and evening rush hours, the Yellow Line also runs between the Franconia/Springfield Station in Virginia and the Greenbelt Station in Maryland.

Government employees who elect to forgo applying for a parking permit are eligible to receive a commuting stipend that subsidizes nearly the entire cost of your morning and evening commute. Additionally, regular Metro commuters should invest in SmarTrip, a plastic stored-value payment card that provides automated entry and exit of Metrorail station fare gates. SmarTrip is easily linked with the Mass Transportation Benefit Program (MTBP) to renew and receive your stipend automatically each month, and you can use your card for many other area transit providers, including Metrobus and Metro facility parking. More information on SmarTrip and WMATA is available online (www.wmata.com).

Metrobus. Metrobus is an efficient and reliable public transportation option that provides added flexibility when traveling around DC, Maryland, and Northern Virginia. Metrobus conducts more than 400,000 trips daily, serving 11,500 bus stops with a fleet of 1,500 buses operating across 325 routes. Service adjustments, trip eliminations, and bus stop notifications are communicated in advance using the WMATA smartphone application or by checking the website.

Arlington Transit (ART). ART buses operate within Arlington County, Virginia, to supplement Metrobus routes. Most ART buses operate on clean burning natural gas and serve to link riders to other Metrorail and Virginia Railway Express (VRE) options. More information on Arlington Transit is available online (www.arlingtontransit.com).

Driving Alexandria Safely Home (DASH). Similar to its Arlington counterpart, DASH provides bus service within the City of Alexandria and connects with Metrorail, Metrobus, Virginia Railway Express, and all local bus systems. During morning and evening peak commute hours, DASH serves all Alexandria Metrorail Stations and the Pentagon Metrorail Station. More information is available on their website (www.dashbus.com).

Fairfax Connector. The Fairfax Connector provides bus service within Fairfax County and connects with Metrobus, Metrorail, Virginia Railway Express, and all local bus systems. Maps, schedules, and additional information can be found online (www.fairfaxcounty.gov/connector).

COMMUTER AND COACH BUS

Some riders—especially those with longer commutes into the city—may prefer the comfort and ease of a coach bus. These buses pick up riders at designated locations outside the city (for example, at Park & Ride facilities in outlying suburbs) and offer riders a hassle-free commute during which they are free to work, read, or rest. Additionally, these buses—to include Metrobus—travel in designated High Occupancy Vehicle (HOV) lanes on some of the area's busiest highways, thereby expediting your commute.

Loudoun County Transit. This morning and late afternoon rush hour service operates from Park & Ride lots in Loudoun to Metrorail Stations that include West Falls Church and Wiehle-Reston East, with additional stops in Rosslyn, Crystal City, the Pentagon, and Washington, DC. Text messaging alert sign-up and additional information is available online (www.loudoun.gov/).

Martz Commuter Bus. The Martz Group, a coach (bus) company currently under contract with the Maryland Transit Administration, provides fixed-route round-trip commuter bus service between Virginia Park & Ride lots and various locations in southern Maryland and Washington, DC. Routes, schedules, and additional information are provided on their website (www.martzgoldline.com/mta-commuter-service).

OmniRide. This weekday rush hour service is operated by the Potomac and Rappahannock Transportation Commission (PRTC) to provide transportation from Virginia locations throughout Prince William County, Manassas, and Gainesville to various destinations including the Mark Center, Pentagon, Crystal City, Rosslyn, Tysons Corner, downtown Washington, DC, and the Washington Navy Yard. Midday service is also available on most routes. Designated commuter lots are also serviced by OmniRide near major thoroughfares. Hours of operation and schedule information are available online (www.prctransit.org/commuter-bus/index.html).

COMMUTER RAIL

These trains, which share tracks in Maryland and Virginia with Amtrak regional trains, offer commuting options that avoid the vehicular gridlock for which the city is famous. Because trains depart at set times from designated stations that require follow-on connection via Metro or bus, these commuter rail options may only offer a viable alternative for those with more flexible work schedules.

Virginia Railway Express (VRE). VRE is a weekday rail option that services Virginia commuters on two lines, the Fredericksburg Line and the Manassas Line. VRE runs northbound into Washington, DC, in the mornings and southbound in the afternoon and evening. The Fredericksburg Line operates between the Fredericksburg Station in Fredericksburg, VA, and Union Station in Washington, DC. The Manassas Line operates between the Broad Run Station in Bristow, VA, and Union Station. VRE connects with Metrorail and Metrobus at five locations and does not run on federal holidays. Public transportation connections from VRE are available at Alexandria, Crystal City, and L'Enfant Metrorail Stations. Additional information is available on the website (www.vre.org).

MARC Train. Operated by the Maryland Transit Administration, the MARC Train provides service along three routes—Brunswick Line, Camden Line, and Penn Line—to commuters from Maryland (Harford County, Baltimore City, Brunswick, Frederick), West Virginia (Martinsburg), and Washington, DC. The Brunswick Line runs between Martinsburg, WV, and Union Station in Washington, DC (Monday through Friday). The Camden Line runs between the Baltimore/Camden Station in Baltimore, MD, and Union Station in Washington, DC (Monday through Friday). The Penn Line runs between Baltimore/Perryville, MD, and Union Station in Washington, DC (seven days a week).

MARC tickets are only available for purchase at Quik Trak machines, Amtrak Ticket Agents, Commuter Direct Ticket Agents, or online. Connections from MARC to Metrorail are available at several stations along the Red, Yellow, Blue, and Green Lines. Additional information is available online (https://mta.maryland.gov/marc-train).

RIDESHARING

Ridesharing is a cost-effective and environmentally friendly means of transportation that offers added social benefits. The Pentagon has a robust ridesharing culture that is actively supported by several local communities and municipal governments:

Alexandria City—www.alexandriava.gov (search "rideshare")

Arlington County Commuter Services—https://arlingtontransportationpartners.com

Commuter Connections—www.commuterconnections.com

GW Ride Connect—www.gwrideconnect.org

PRTC—www.prtctransit.org

Tri-County Council for Southern Maryland—http://tccsmd.org

WMATA—www.wmata.com

ADDITIONAL COMMUTING OPTIONS

Several other transportation alternatives are available for Washington Metropolitan Area commuters traveling to and from the Pentagon. These options may afford you additional flexibility, which can in turn reduce stress:

- Slugging: A unique form of commuting often referred to as "instant" or "casual" carpooling (www.slug-lines.com).
- Zip Cars: Membership-based car sharing company providing vehicle reservations to members on an hourly or daily rate (www.zipcar.com).
- Guaranteed Ride Home (GRH): A free service provided to Washington Area commuters who regularly (twice a week) carpool, vanpool, bicycle, walk, or take other public transportation in the event of a personal emergency or at the request of a supervisor (www.commuterconnections.com).
- Bicycle: A healthy alternative to avoid rush hour traffic. The Pentagon and all Metrorail stations have plenty of designated rack space near main entrances to lock up bicycles (http://bikewashington.org).

PARKING

In addition to the commuting options described above, many Pentagon employees choose to drive personally owned vehicles (POV) (including motorcycles) to and from the Building each day. Having knowledge of Pentagon parking organization and management is important to ensure you avoid illegally parking since unauthorized vehicles are subject to citations, booting, or towing to an impound lot at the owner's expense. Moreover, permit holders who receive three or more parking violations within a twelve-month period are subject to parking restrictions for a year or more.

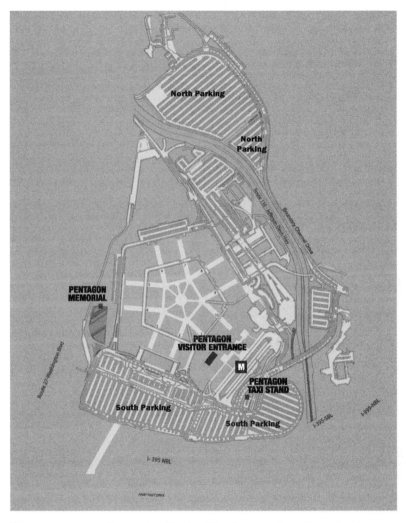

Figure 2-1. Pentagon Reservation Parking Map. *Pentagon Force Protection Agency*

The Pentagon has sixteen parking lots on the north and south sides of the grounds. Parking services at the Pentagon, Mark Center, and Suffolk Building facilities are managed by the Washington Headquarters Services (WHS) Parking Management Branch (PMB). PMB is located on the Pentagon Concourse adjacent to Pentagon Federal Credit Union in room 2D1039 and operates Monday through Friday. All individuals desiring to park on the Pentagon Reservation must register their vehicles (whether for a permanent or temporary pass) to ensure each vehicle on the complex has been identified. Administrative Instruction (AI) 88 establishes parking policies and assigns responsibilities governing all guests, visitors, contractors, and other DOD personnel approved to use Pentagon Reservation parking facilities. A thorough review and understanding of AI 88 is required for all employees and visitors who elect to participate in the Pentagon parking program.

Each DOD component has a Component Parking Representative (CPR) who administers their respective Component Parking Program (the Navy's CPR is located at 5E148). Moreover, most offices and directorates have a collateral-duty parking coordinator who liaises with the Parking Office to manage the permits allotted to their team. Of note, temporary vehicle parking clearance is available for employees who receive Metro subsidies for a period not to exceed five calendar days or temporary duty not to exceed one week. Temporary vehicle parking permits are obtained from the PMB. Driving directions and detailed Pentagon Parking Reservation information is available for authorized Common Access Card (CAC) holders on the Washington Headquarters Service Employee and Customer Resources pages (www.whs.mil).

ENTERING THE BUILDING

Employees and visitors can enter the Pentagon through one of six entrances. People arriving by mass transit enter through the Metro Entrance, which is located on the east side of the Pentagon near the Pentagon Metro Station and Pentagon Transit Center (adjacent bus terminal). There are three additional entrances—the South Parking Entrance, the North Parking Entrance near the Pentagon Library and Conference Center, or the Mall Entrance near the Pentagon Athletic Center (PAC)—for employees who drive and park. Two additional entrances are located on the north and west side of the Pentagon—the River Entrance and the Corridor 5 entrance, respectively.

Every entrance to the Pentagon is electronically controlled. CAC electronic entry is linked to DOD employees who are authorized CAC holders. In concert with the Pentagon Force Protection Agency (PFPA), the Pentagon Access Control Branch (PACB) manages employee access to the Pentagon. PACB is located near the Metro Entrance in Room 1F1084 and is open weekdays.

Visitors to the Pentagon enter through the Pentagon Visitor Entrance, which is open during the week and is located directly adjacent to the

Pentagon Metro Entrance. Pentagon visitors fall into one of three categories: Pentagon tour participants, government and DOD CAC holders who lack "swipe-in" Pentagon access, and other personnel without authorized access. PFPA-administered visitor access is meticulously managed and requires strict adherence to visitor registration and sponsorship guidelines. Unescorted entry for approved visitors (typically uniformed military or government civilians who work at another installation and are visiting on business) requires a special badge. Pentagon visitors without unescorted approval require an authorized badge holder escort at all times. Additionally, Pentagon employees with an authorized CAC may sponsor up to ten guests. To minimize sponsorship approval time, PFPA strongly encourages registration of guests at least one business day in advance since walk-in visitors who are not preregistered may experience longer process times. Additional information concerning Pentagon access is available online (www.whs.mil and www.pfpa.mil).

NAVIGATING WITHIN THE BUILDING

It is not uncommon for new or even returning Pentagon employees to wander the hallways of the Pentagon as they futilely search for a meeting location. Indeed, every servicemember has suffered embarrassment at some point or another during his or her first several weeks in the Building while attempting to navigate from one point to another. It is generally accepted that it takes six months or so for a person to gain a full sense of navigational certainty at the Pentagon. Even then, it is advisable to carry a small map of the Pentagon in the event you lose your way.

The Pentagon—affectionately known as the "Five-Sided Puzzle Palace"—contains five concentric rings labeled A through E from the inside out. The outer E-ring has the greatest circumference and requires the most time to circumnavigate. If traveling to the opposite side of the Pentagon to an outer ring, it is usually more efficient to navigate along the A-ring to the desired corridor and move outward to the desired ring. Weather permitting, traversing through the center courtyard can also reduce distance and travel time between locations.

Every ring contains seven floors made up of a basement, mezzanine, and five aboveground floors, all of which are accessible by elevators and staircases throughout the building. Ten corridors spaced equally apart perpendicularly bisect each ring from A to E, allowing easy cross-ring

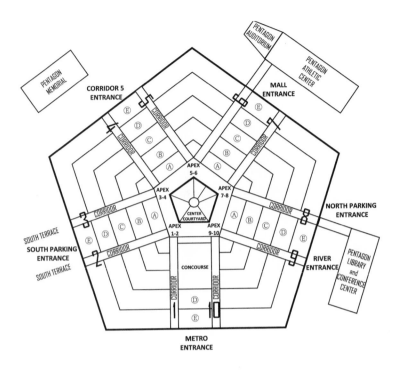

HOW TO FIND A ROOM

FLOOR
RING
CORRIDOR
ROOM NUMBER

Figure 2-2. Map of the Pentagon

access to interior spaces. The convergence of two corridors is known as an "apex" and the Pentagon contains five apexes. Apexes are a convenient meeting place and are home to various exhibits, ceremonial sites, and food and beverage options. Several corridors also contain historical exhibits, ceremonial sites, and additional dining choices.

Finding a particular room in the Pentagon requires deconstruction of a simple five- to six-character alphanumeric code separated into four parts: the first digit placeholder denotes the floor number (B, M, or 1–5); the second digit is the letter corresponding to the ring (A–E); the third (and, possibly, fourth) digit indicates the corridor number (1–10); the final two digits denote the room number (01–99). The following examples illustrate how to decipher a Pentagon room location.

The Pentagon is immense; it contains 131 stairways. *DOD photo by Sgt. Amber I. Smith/Released*

4E384	4th Floor, E-ring, 3rd Corridor, Room 84
5D245	5th Floor, D-ring, 2nd Corridor, Room 45
3B1024	3rd Floor, B-ring, 10th Corridor, Room 24
BE922	Basement, E-ring, 9th Corridor, Room 22

On certain occasions, you may find yourself navigating to a room that seems to break with the convention above. Some rooms are located in passageways halfway between corridors (called "half corridors") or in less familiar parts of the building. It is always wise to allow ample walking time when attending meetings in a new or unfamiliar part of the Pentagon. Time permitting, taking a different route back to your office following a meeting is a great way to discover new exhibits, learn more about fellow services and other nonmilitary DOD agencies, broaden your understanding of the Pentagon, and possibly even run into friends or colleagues.

TAKING A TOUR

The Pentagon is home to more than 140 permanent and rotating exhibits, ceremonial sites, memorials, and special collections. The rich history of our military is showcased in professionally crafted displays devoted to a broad array of military-related subjects. Every ring, corridor, and floor provides countless opportunities to learn about a person, place, or time as a byproduct of simply moving around in the Pentagon. Both formal and self-guided tours are available for servicemembers interested in learning more about the Pentagon and our armed forces—past, present, and future.

THE FORMAL PENTAGON TOURS PROGRAM

First established in 1976, the Pentagon tours program hosts more than 106,000 visitors annually and is operated and managed by the Assistant to the Secretary of Defense for Public Affairs (ATSD[PA]). The Pentagon tours program showcases the missions and history of the five armed services, the Office of the Secretary of Defense (OSD), and the Joint Staff (JS). Tour length is approximately sixty minutes spread across nearly one-and-a-half miles throughout the Pentagon. The approximately thirty tour guides are specially selected active-duty personnel from the National Capital Region's military ceremonial units. Their yearlong tour guide assignment is preceded by an extensive course of instruction and on-the-job training. All guided tours of the Pentagon are free to the public and are available to schools, civic and educational organizations, and other select groups by reservation only. Group size is limited to sixty people.

Tours are available to the general public on weekdays. Reservations are accepted as early as ninety days from the requested date and are required at least fourteen days in advance. Reservations are not accepted outside of ninety days or within thirteen days of the requested date. Tours book quickly and it is recommended visitors reserve space early. Visitors should plan to arrive at least thirty minutes before the start of a scheduled tour to facilitate entrance and processing time.

Pentagon visitors should not expect access to reservation parking or shuttle services. Visitors can park at the Pentagon City Mall (for a fee) and walk less than five minutes to the Metro Entrance by way of a pedestrian tunnel. At least one form of identification is required for visitors eighteen years of age and older to enter the Pentagon, while no identification is required for visitors seventeen years of age and younger when accompanied by an adult possessing a DOD building pass or authorized form of identification. Ramp access is available, and accommodations are offered for hearing and visually impaired visitors with two weeks' notice. Visitors should review security guidelines and additional detailed tour information online (https://pentagontours.osd.mil/Tours).

SELF-GUIDED TOUR

A self-guided tour offers flexibility and a more intimate view of the Pentagon tailored to fit busy work and family schedules. It is also a convenient way for Pentagon employees or people with building access to familiarize themselves with the building. A self-guided tour brochure guides visitors along a route that highlights thirteen exhibits, including:

- Australia—New Zealand—U.S. (ANZUS) Security Treaty Corridor
- Prisoners of War/Missing in Action (POW/MIA)
- GEN Douglas MacArthur Corridor
- Marine Corridor
- Navy Aviation Corridor
- Coast Guard
- Air Force Display Cases
- Humanitarian Corridor
- North Atlantic Treaty Organization (NATO) Corridor
- Soldiers and Signers of the Constitution Corridor
- 9/11 Memorial
- Center Courtyard
- The Hall of Heroes

Of note, the outdoor 9/11 Memorial is open to the general public and does not require a visitor's badge or authorized Pentagon entrance for access. The self-guided tour begins and ends at the Metro Entrance and a convenient brochure is available to inform your tour. Though knowledge of building navigation—corridors, apexes, and rings—can expedite your movement around the Pentagon, a self-guided tour is one means of helping new Pentagon employees to familiarize themselves with the mysteries of the Five-Sided Puzzle Palace.

FOOD AND BEVERAGE OPTIONS

Nearly every floor, corridor, and apex offers some sort of eating option for Pentagon employees and visitors ranging from quick snack to more formal sit-down dining. Three main categories of dining choices are available in the form of food courts, stand-alone restaurants, and snack bars. In addition, vending machines are conveniently located in nearly every corridor around the Pentagon to grab a quick snack in between meetings.

The Pentagon boasts five different food courts that are home to more than twenty vendors, including national restaurant chains. (Note: Like the Pentagon itself, which is ever-changing, specific dining choices may come and go, so be sure to check with co-workers and try a few different locations yourself during the early part of your tour.)

Corridors 3 and 4 (2nd Floor, C-ring; Monday through Friday 0600–1500)

- Qdoba Mexican Grill—Mexican food
- Starbucks—coffee, tea, and food
- Peruvian Chicken—rotisserie-style Peruvian chicken with variety of sides
- Freshens—soft-serve yogurt and variety of salads

Corridors 7 and 8 (2nd Floor, C-ring; Monday through Friday 0600–1700)

- Baskin Robbins—ice cream
- Dunkin' Donuts—coffee, donuts, bagels, and sandwiches
- KFC Express—chicken meals, assorted sides, and beverages
- McDonald's—traditional fast-food dining
- Panda Express—Chinese-inspired dishes
- Taco Bell—Mexican-inspired fast-food dining

Corridor 7 (3rd Floor, B-ring; Monday through Friday 0600–1700)

- Five Star Espresso—hot coffee and espresso
- Sbarro—Italian-inspired dishes, pizza, and salads

Concourse Food Court

- Baskin Robbins—ice cream
- Burger King—traditional fast-food dining
- Dominic's of New York—sandwiches for breakfast, lunch, and dinner
- Dunkin' Donuts—coffee, donuts, bagels, and sandwiches
- Popeye's Louisiana Kitchen—Louisiana-inspired chicken dishes and sides
- Rollerz—personalized sandwiches
- Starbucks—coffee, tea, and food
- Subway—fresh sandwiches and salads
- Surf City—smoothies and healthy wrap-style sandwiches
- Auntie Anne's— beverages and freshly baked soft pretzels

Pentagon Conference Center (Monday through Friday 0600–1700)

- Farmer's Market Café—healthy breakfast, lunch, and dinner options
- Five Star Espresso—hot coffee and espresso

Stand-alone restaurants provide an additional dining option that allow employees to enjoy a more relaxing meal experience (time and schedule permitting.)

Center Court Café (Center Courtyard; Monday through Friday 0600–1500)
- Breakfast and lunch sandwich specialties and outdoor dining options during warmer months

Dominic's of New York (Basement Level; 8th Corridor, C-ring; open 24/7)
- Sandwiches for breakfast, lunch, and dinner

Five Star Espresso
- 5th Floor, Apex 3 (Monday through Friday 0600–1500)
- 5th Floor, Apex 7 (Monday through Friday 0600–1400)

Market Basket (Pentagon Concourse; Monday through Friday 0630–1730)
- Cafeteria-style food buffets where customers pay by weight, hot and cold breakfast and lunch bars including sandwiches, sushi, and other grocery items (catering services available)

Subway
- 4th Floor, 3rd Corridor, B-ring (Monday through Friday 0600–1600)
- 5th Floor, Apex 5 (Monday through Friday 1030–1430)

Snack bars provide flexibility and on-the-go options:

Larry's Snack Bar—sandwiches, snacks, beverages
- 2nd Floor, 10th Corridor, B-ring (Monday through Friday 0630–1600)

Lorraine's Snack Bar—sandwiches, snacks, beverages
- 2nd Floor, 3rd Corridor, D-ring (Monday through Friday 0500–1830; Saturday 0600–1300; Sunday 0700–1300)

Maurice's Snack Bar—sandwiches, snacks, beverages
- 2nd Floor, 2nd Corridor, B-ring (Monday through Friday 0600–1800)

Patrick's Snack Bar—sandwiches, snacks, beverages
- 1st Floor, 8th Corridor, B-ring (Monday through Friday 0500–1515)

The Pentagon Concourse Food Court is the most frequented mealtime location. It is located a short distance from the Metro Entrance between Apexes 1–2 and 9–10 immediately adjacent to the Center Courtyard and is home to a variety of dining options identified above. Relatively plentiful seating offers Pentagon employees and visitors a place to eat and socialize. Moreover, the Pentagon Concourse Food Court is an ideal location for meeting other governmental employees and visitors who do not require an escort for building access. Coffee shops throughout the building serve as another venue for collaboration and networking outside the office. Additional dining and nutrition information is available for authorized CAC holders on the Washington Headquarters Service Employee and Customer Resources web pages (www.whs.mil).

STAYING FIT

The Pentagon Athletic Center (PAC) is a first-rate fitness facility that provides a respite from work so you can focus on your physical and mental health. The PAC is a non-appropriated fund actively supported by the Support Services–Washington under the Office of the Administrative Assistant to the Secretary of the Army. The PAC is accessed via the Mezzanine Level, Corridor 7, G-ring by elevators 73, 74, or 75, and is located on the Basement Level between Stairwell 64 (Corridor 6) and Stairwell 74 (Corridor 7). Additionally, exterior entrance is available from the north parking lot. The PAC is open early (0530) and closes late (2130) to provide employees significant scheduling flexibility.

The PAC offers a wide array of facilities and fitness resources, including:

- Courts—squash, racquetball, handball, wallyball, badminton, and volleyball
- Full-line strength-training equipment
- Full-line cardio training equipment
- Functional fitness workout area
- Group exercise classes
- Heavy bag/speed bag
- Six-lane, twenty-five-meter lap swimming pool
- Indoor track (three lanes)
- Stretching areas
- Two large spas
- Saunas & steam rooms

- Towel services
- Physical fitness specialists

All active-duty military and DOD civilians in the National Capital Region are eligible to become members. Dues are paid annually or semi-annually, and initial payment includes a $25 processing fee. A no-fee membership program is available for active-duty personnel who work in the Pentagon, Taylor Building, and Mark Center. Non-assigned lockers are available for daily use on a first-come, first-served basis. Permanently assigned lockers are available but members can expect a lengthy waiting period due to limited numbers (locks are not provided). For further questions, contact the Membership Desk, (703) 614-9998.

PERSONAL CONSUMER SERVICES

Like any small city, the Pentagon is home to a variety of personal and consumer services. Most of these amenities are located in the Pentagon Concourse, which facilitates easy access when arriving and departing the building via the Metro Entrance. These convenient features and services, such as on premise shoe care and dry cleaners, can be valuable time savers but be aware that locations and businesses do change over the years.

- Armed Forces Hostess Association—Area Transition Services (2E1087)
- Virginia Department of Motor Vehicles (2C1049)
- United States Post Office (2E1041)
- Pentagon Federal Credit Union (2D1043)
- Navy Federal Credit Union (2D152)
- Bank of America (2D1076)
- CVS Drug Store (2B1080)
- David Mann Jewelers (2D1083)
- Dental Office (2E1073)
- Fort America (Pentagon/military memorabilia) (2D1075)
- Greensleeves (florist) (2C1087)
- H&R Block (open mid-January to April 15 at designated location)
- Hair Care Center (2D1069)
- Lynch Collection Clothier (2D117)
- Pentagon Customer Assistance Center (2E122)
- Pentagon Laundry & Cleaners (2E1076)
- Pentagon Luggage and Leather (2C115)
- Pentagon Vision Center (2C113)

- WHS Parking Office (2D1039)
- Velatis (Belgian chocolate and other assorted sweets) (2E117)

Additional personal consumer services information is available for authorized CAC holders on the Washington Headquarters Service Employee and Customer Resources pages (www.whs.mil).

CONCLUSION

Duty at the Pentagon promises a challenging but rewarding experience that offers participation in unique social and cultural aspects of the National Capital Region. At first glance, simple facets of daily life in the Pentagon may seem daunting. However, through preparation and familiarization you will find the Pentagon a welcoming environment of nearly 30,000 dedicated uniformed and civilian professionals working together toward a common goal: defense of the United States. Indeed, the collegial environment of the Pentagon—which combines the work of those in uniform, senior civilian executives, analysts, and even diplomats and academics—exemplifies the Greek philosopher Thucydides' observation, "The Nation that makes a great distinction between its scholars and its warriors will have its thinking done by cowards and its fighting done by fools." Best of luck as you chart your course!

LCDR Jonathan "Shank" Lushenko is a 2005 Distinguished Honor Graduate of the U.S. Naval Academy. A plankowner of Helicopter Maritime Strike (HSM) Squadron SEVEN ONE, he participated in the first operational deployment of the MH-60R and served as a department head/officer in charge of the Navy's only forward-deployed HSM expeditionary squadron, HSM-51, stationed at NAF Atsugi, Japan. Lieutenant Commander Lushenko served as an ISR capabilities analyst on the OPNAV staff (N810), was the DESRON TWO TWO Air/Future Operations Department head, and served as the executive assistant to the 84th and 85th Commandant of Midshipmen and the 14th company officer at the U.S. Naval Academy. He holds a master's of professional studies in leadership education and development from the University of Maryland, College Park.

PART II
KEY ORGANIZATIONS

3

THE NAVY (OPNAV) STAFF

LCDR DOUG ROBB, USN

I n much the same way that technology has transformed American society, so too has the U.S. Navy (USN) undergone myriad "reinventions" over the past two centuries. Wooden ships have given way to steel hulls; sails have been lowered in favor of turbines and nuclear-generated steam; and cannon balls have been stowed as long-range, precision strike missiles now fill weapons magazines. But these seismic technological advancements did not just miraculously materialize, nor were they developed in a vacuum. Indeed, they were conceived by teams of military and civilian professionals answering to the highest echelon of naval leadership adapting to new challenges.

This chapter explores how and why that team emerged and how it has evolved over the past century; the current organization's purpose, construct, and functions; and the military and civilian professionals who—to modify a command issued during a traditional ship commissioning ceremony—"man this staff and bring it to life."

BRIEF HISTORY OF THE NAVY STAFF

Despite being the leader of the naval service, a job steeped in statutory and symbolic importance, the Chief of Naval Operations (CNO) and the office he leads—called the Navy Staff, or simply OPNAV—are relative newcomers to the American naval tradition and both have evolved markedly. From the time of its founding through the nineteenth century, presidents and Navy secretaries saw little need for a uniformed advisor with resident executive authority. Instead, the Navy Department relied on the Board of Navy Commissioners, who advised the cabinet-level civilian secretary although they lacked the operational or administrative authority necessary to command forces, organize the Navy, and pursue the requisite tools, tactics, and training their era demanded.

As the United States' entrance into World War I drew near, President Woodrow Wilson recognized that the Navy Department—whose role would be instrumental in securing critical sea lanes and shuttling hundreds of thousands of soldiers to the front lines—was not organized to conduct the efficient and effective wartime operations. In 1915, he signed a law authorizing the creation of the office of the CNO charged with the "preparation and readiness of plans for [the Fleet's] use in war."

During the 1920s–30s, CNOs had a daunting but important task: to reduce the size and scope of the Navy in accordance with agreements negotiated in Washington and London while maintaining a force that could defend the nation and satisfy other international commitments. During World War II, the CNO's scope of responsibility and authority increased markedly so that a singular uniformed "commander in chief" could plan and execute a two-ocean war. FADM Ernest J. King thus assumed the dual titles of commander in chief, U.S. Fleet (COMINCH), charged with overseeing the combined operations of three fleets: the Atlantic, the Pacific, and the Asiatic (Philippines); and Chief of Naval Operations, responsible for manning, training, and equipping the naval forces for war. More than a decade after the war's conclusion, in 1958, Congress passed the Department of Defense Reorganization Act, which shifted fleet operational command and control from the CNO to unified commands (the forefather of the combatant command) and to lower-echelon Navy commanders.

In the 1960s, Secretary of Defense Robert McNamara instituted the Planning, Programming, and Budgeting System (PPBS), an analytical method of budget construction involving systematic warfighting requirement determinations and precise resource allocations that largely persist today. This new process emphasized the Navy Staff's administrative role in resourcing—rather than operating—the fleet, and McNamara's obsession with centralized authority further subordinated OPNAV to his staff within the OSD and the Joint Staff. The contributions of both the Army and the Air Force during the Cold War and the Vietnam conflict seemed intuitive to policymakers, but the Navy's role in the national defense was less certain. To better advocate for resources and defend investments, the then–CNO ADM Elmo Zumwalt reorganized OPNAV's "OP" office coded directorates such that each division was responsible for a clearly defined programmatic, budgetary, or warfare portfolio.

The 1986 Goldwater-Nichols Act further clarified the relationship between operational commanders and administrative service chiefs by creating a customer-provider dynamic in which the service branches provide forces to those executing military operations. Consequently, as CAPT Peter Haynes, USN (Ret.), noted in his Naval Postgraduate School (NPS) doctoral dissertation, the President and SECDEF determined the *ends* (the objectives that should be accomplished), the combatant commands formulated the *ways* (the processes and methods to accomplish those goals), while the services furnished the *means* (the tools and personnel). Despite leadership and occasional organizational changes, and though not immune to outside pressures, the CNO and Navy Staff have done just that.

PURPOSE OF THE NAVY STAFF

Since its introduction in 1915, the CNO and the Navy Staff have worked, in the words of RADM Samuel Cox, USN (Ret.), Director of the Naval History and Heritage Command, "to ensure our globally deployed Sailors have all the tools and training necessary to successfully achieve their missions and return home safely."

Since 1915, the Chief of Naval Operations has been the uniformed leader of the entire U.S. Navy, including the Navy Staff in the Pentagon. Pictured here in December 1964, Secretary of the Navy Paul Nitze (*left*) and ADM David McDonald (*second from right*) look at the newly authorized CNO personal flag with Dr. Thomas McKnew of National Geographic, who suggested the design, and then-CAPT (and future CNO) Elmo Zumwalt. *Naval History and Heritage Command*

As the Navy's service chief—and, by definition, the senior most ranking admiral—the CNO is charged with manning, training, and equipping the naval force; in short, executing the service's administrative authority as outlined in Title 10 Section C of the U.S. Code. The Navy Staff by extension exists to support the CNO in his management of the fleet and report on issues ranging from personnel policy to maritime strategy to budget preparation. Additionally, and complementary to this core function, the CNO is responsible for:

- Creating the service's annual five-year budget (Future Years Defense Program, or FYDP) for submission and defending the resourcing investment decisions
- Devising long-term maritime strategies and operational concepts of employment for emerging technologies and systems
- Advising the Chairman of the Joint Chiefs of Staff (CJCS), Secretary of Defense, President, and Congress on naval matters
- Determining fleet and shore establishment organizational composition and structure to support operational and administrative duties and demands
- Communicating the "Navy's story" to the general public

ORGANIZATIONAL FUNCTIONS AND TITLES

Like the personnel of a ship, submarine, or squadron, OPNAV is a team of individuals whose dedication, coordination, and collaboration are critical to the broader organization's (in this case, the Navy's) success. Together, its members plan, develop, negotiate, purchase, produce, test, integrate, man, field, operate, and maintain the equipment and systems on which the naval force relies to accomplish its mission. Additionally, the CNO trusts to OPNAV to represent the Navy's interests at the highest levels of government, which it does by executing unique responsibilities that are codified by law or Navy instruction:

- Conduct strategic planning and programming for the Navy's budget submission, known as the Program Objective Memorandum (POM).
- Perform assessments to determine capability gaps and identify the programs, resources, and investments necessary to mitigate those gaps.
- Monitor fleet readiness to ensure naval forces can meet combatant command demands.
- Execute operational test and evaluation (T&E) for new fleet systems and concepts.

- Manage Navy recruiting and the reserve force.
- Align actions of Navy organizations, subordinate commands, and lower echelons to support the other services, Joint Staff, OSD, interagency work, allies, and partners.

ADM Frank Kelso is credited with shaping the modern OPNAV staff during his tenure as CNO in the early 1990s. Structurally, he transformed OP office codes into "N-codes" to better align with Joint Staff and unified command staff "J-code" naming convention. Though seemingly superficial, this nomenclature change was a savvy way to align Navy portfolios to their joint counterparts, which strengthened relationships within the Pentagon and facilitated collaboration.

These OPNAV N-code directorates are three-star admirals with flag officer-equivalent civilian senior executive service (SES) deputies who act in a sense as the CNO's department heads. Leadership titles include: Deputy Chief of Naval Operations for (Directorate), Special Assistant for (Subject), or Director of (Division). Directorates have subordinate offices, called "divisions," which are typically led by a one- or two-star admiral or SES whose title is Director or Deputy Director.

Divisions are identified by two-digit office codes where the first digit denotes its parent N-code. For example, the Director, Surface Warfare Division (OPNAV N96) reports to the Deputy Chief of Naval Operations for Warfare Systems (OPNAV N9) (OPNAV N2/N6 is the exception as it relies on alphabetic suffixes to denote divisions, for example, N2/N6F). Divisions are then further subdivided into branches (usually led by an O-6 or GS-15) and sections (led by an O-4/5 or GS-14/15) responsible for a defined portfolio of similar programs, systems, or capabilities.

OPNAV PRINCIPAL OFFICERS

By instruction, "OPNAV Principal Officers (OPOs) are individuals in charge of major OPNAV directorates, or serving as Special Assistants to the CNO." These include the VCNO and Director of the Naval Nuclear Propulsion Program (both four-stars); the Director of the Navy Staff and Deputy CNOs (three-stars); and a group of other one-, two-, and three-star flag officers who maintain dual reporting responsibilities to both the CNO and SECNAV.

The unclassified *OPNAV Operations and Organization Manual (OOOM)* governs the missions, functions, and structure of staff directorates and subordinate divisions. Given OPNAV's preeminent role in

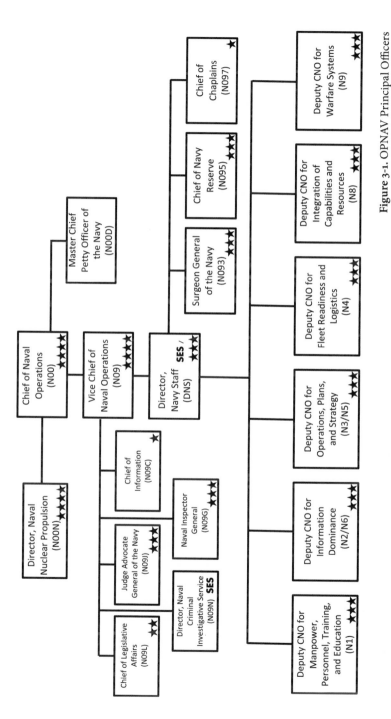

Figure 3-1. OPNAV Principal Officers

OPNAV REORGANIZATIONS

"THE ONLY CONSTANT IS CHANGE"

Just as any organizational leader—from the most junior division officer aboard ship to the senior-most four-star admiral in the Pentagon—seeks to create a team that will support and complement his or her agenda, so too have CNOs historically aligned (and re-aligned) OPNAV to meet their needs and to better advocate for their priorities. In its 2010 study entitled, "Organizing OPNAV (1970–2009)," the federally funded research center CNA noted, "Reorganization has been a conspicuous and continual phenomenon in OPNAV.... Some reorganizations have been massive; some have been small; but some degree of organization churn has been constant."

Though every staff reshuffle seeks to achieve certain goals, reasons for past organizational changes have included:

- To complement the sitting CNO's professional background or personal desires
- To fill a professional void so the CNO can accomplish things he cannot do himself
- To create efficiencies in an effort to execute priorities
- To respond to seminal events or strategic demands
- To conform to geopolitical and budgetary realities
- To implement direction of senior government leaders, such as the SECNAV, the SECDEF, the POTUS, or Congress
- To better position the Navy Staff relative to the other services inside the defense establishment

The CNO must manage tension among strategy, requirements, and resources, and past reorganizations have traditionally sought to strike an optimal balance as the time period dictates. Management skills and the ability to delegate take on greater importance. Given the glacial pace of some changes that must navigate the Pentagon bureaucracy, staff reorganization can represent a "quick win" for CNOs looking to deliver results. Perhaps not surprisingly then, nearly every decade has been distinguished by at least one administrative "sea change."

determining requirements and integrating the annual budget, many (though not all) N-code divisions act as resource sponsors—the entity responsible for determining the investment strategy of a specific Navy system, program, or concept.

While reorganizations may change the exact office numeric code or title, the general functions of these principal officers remain relatively constant over time. The following section details the main functions of OPNAV's directorates and some of their primary divisions, as well as other offices with direct reporting responsibilities to the CNO. Though not all-encompassing, officers assigned to the Navy Staff will likely serve with or within one of the following offices.

VICE CHIEF OF NAVAL OPERATIONS (OPNAV N09)

Like the vice chiefs of the other services, the VCNO is the CNO's principal assistant and sounding board. With approval from the SECNAV, CNO may delegate certain authority to the VCNO; orders then issued by the VCNO then hold equal weight to those issued by the CNO. Occasionally, CNO may assign specific projects or topics for the VCNO to lead or oversee—this is especially common in instances in which the CNO and VCNO's professional backgrounds or experiences differ. Like the CNO, the VCNO has a contingent of officers, enlisted personnel, and civilians supporting the "front office": executive assistant (EA), deputy executive assistant (DEA), aide, legal counsel, speechwriter, flag secretary, and scheduler.

DIRECTOR, NAVAL NUCLEAR PROPULSION PROGRAM (N00N)

The descendent of the organization founded by the "father of the nuclear Navy," ADM Hyman Rickover, in 1949, the Naval Nuclear Propulsion Program (synonymously named Naval Reactors, NR, or NAVSEA 08) is led by a four-star admiral who serves an eight-year tour and is responsible for the safety of naval nuclear propulsion aboard submarines and aircraft carriers. NR oversees the entire life span of naval nuclear technology, including research, development, design, procurement, construction, installation, certification, testing, overhaul, refueling, standard operating procedures, maintenance, sustainment, and disposal. NR also manages training programs for officer and enlisted accessions, as well as midgrade and senior officers returning to tours aboard nuclear vessels. In addition to his or her Navy reporting responsibilities, the director also serves as the deputy administrator for Naval Reactors in the Department of Energy's National Nuclear Security Administration.

DIRECTOR, NAVY STAFF (DNS)

The third-ranking officer in OPNAV based on positional authority, DNS functions as the Echelon I Chief of Staff—with an emphasis on *of Staff*. ADM Vern Clark, the twenty-first century's first CNO (and, importantly, the first CNO to hold a master's in business administration), elevated DNS from a one-star admiral to a three-star, thus creating a "chief operating officer" and natural intermediary between the three-star deputy CNOs (called DCNOs) and the CNO and VCNO. Occasionally filled by a senior civilian, DNS also serves as the principal liaison between the two four-stars and the lower echelon commands over which the CNO exercises administrative control, thus ensuring that guidance from the CNO reaches the staff and the fleet. One forum he uses to communicate to the staff is the B-code meeting DNS chairs ("B-code" is the colloquial Pentagon term for the civilian SES or one- or two-star flag officers who serve as deputies to the principal officers and whose alpha-numeric designation ends in the letter B, for example, N3/N5B or N80B).

Additionally, among other responsibilities, DNS manages the electronic "tasker" system that tracks the status of requests for information or briefings that may originate from within OPNAV or from an external organization and must be coordinated and traced; organizes senior-level meetings in which the CNO or VCNO will participate; plans CNO-hosted conferences with flag officers, U.S. government officials, and foreign dignitaries; and establishes—in coordination with the VCNO and DCNOs—the Navy Staff's annual budget submission timeline, milestones, and briefings. DNS is also the USS *Constitution*'s immediate superior in command (ISIC). To discharge these duties, teams of people are organized into multiple "DNS codes" (e.g., DNS-1 Executive Secretariat, or DNS-D Civilian Personnel & Policy).

DCNO FOR MANPOWER, PERSONNEL, TRAINING,
AND EDUCATION (MPTE) (N1)

This three-star admiral, who is also known as the Chief of Naval Personnel (CNP), is responsible for performing the analysis, creating the strategies, and overseeing the policies governing fleet personnel issues. These include manpower recruitment, accessions, and promotions, as well as professional education and training curricula ranging from the Naval Reserve Officer Training Corps (NROTC) to enlisted "A" and

"C" schools. CNP also exercises administrative command (ADCON) over the Naval Education and Service Training Commands (NETC/NSTC), as well as the Naval Personnel Command (NPC) in Millington, Tennessee, where the two-star commander also holds the title of Deputy CNP. CNP also reports to the Assistant Secretary of the Navy (ASN) for manpower and reserve affairs (ASN[M&RA]), the political appointee responsible to the SECNAV for nearly all military and civilian employee personnel issues.

Director, Financial Management Division (N10). This division within OPNAV N1 manages the Military Personnel, Navy (MPN) appropriation to include coordinating programming, developing, and integrating budget inputs; and performing active-duty officer and enlisted end-strength planning and projections.

Director, Total Force Manpower, Training, and Education Requirements Division (N12). Led by a senior civilian, N12 implements manpower requirements policies, planning, and programming; and determines the associated manpower, training, and education requirements of new or proposed platforms, systems, or capabilities.

Director, Military Personnel Plans and Policy Division (N13). Traditionally led by a two-star admiral, N13 is the primary Navy Staff point of contact for military personnel matters. As a result, it is the division with which most Pentagon action officers will work if there are personnel considerations or issues affecting their portfolio. N13 purview extends over training, education, reserve component, compensation, diversity, and family support.

Director, Twenty-First Century Sailor Officer (N17). Created in 2013 and led by a one-star admiral, the Twenty-First Century Sailor Office focuses on building resilience in the force by integrating and applying Navy policies and objectives relating to equal opportunity, sailor personal and family readiness, physical fitness, substance abuse prevention, suicide prevention, sexual assault prevention and response, hazing prevention, and transition assistance.

Director, Flag Officer Management and Development (PERS-00F). Often referred to as "flag matters," this team manages aspects of flag officer selection, assignments, and administration.

DCNO FOR INFORMATION WARFARE (N2/N6)

OPNAV N2/N6 is a three-star Information Dominance Corps (IDC) flag officer who acts as the lead advocate and resource sponsor for a broad portfolio of systems and concepts, including information technology (IT) and network security; command and control (C2) systems; intelligence, surveillance, and reconnaissance and targeting (ISR-T); positioning, navigation, and timing (PNT); electronic warfare (EW); unmanned and automated capabilities; meteorology, oceanography, and climate change; space-based systems; and offensive and defensive cyber capabilities. Additionally, N2/N6 serves as the Department of the Navy's Deputy Chief Information Officer (CIO) and the Director of Naval Intelligence (DNI).

Director, Oceanography and Navigation Division (N2/N6E). This one-star meteorology and oceanography (METOC) admiral is the resource sponsor for naval weather, GPS, navigation, timing, and maritime domain awareness programs and policies. Additionally, this flag officer commands the Naval Meteorology and Oceanography Command splitting time between Washington, DC, and Mississippi's Stennis Space Center.

Director, Warfare Integration Division (N2/N6F). When OPNAV N2 (Intelligence) combined with OPNAV N6 (Communications Networks) in 2009, many of N6's programs-of-record were nestled under N2/N6F. These include satellite communications systems, ISR-T assets, battlespace awareness tools, and platform-based sensors. N2/N6F also sponsors "integrated fires," a series of concepts and programs for ships, submarines, and aircraft to conduct electronic and information warfare (EW/IW) missions. Consequently, and because of their charter to integrate capabilities, N2/N6F is a primary interface point of contact for action officers and requirements officers in other directorates.

Director, Navy Cyber Security Division (N2/N6G). This team, led by a one-star information warfare admiral, determines Navy cyber requirements, formulates mandates for cyber program compliance, and creates department-wide cyber policies.

Deputy Director of Naval Intelligence (N2/N6I). N2/N6I is the principal assistant supporting OPNAV N2/N6's concurrent responsibilities as DNI, the Navy's principal representative to the broader intelligence community (IC). In this capacity, this SES-led division determines the service's intelligence requirements and serves as the Department of the Navy's liaison to the Office of the Undersecretary of Defense for Intelligence (OUSD[I]).

N2/N6I also generates intelligence policies, oversees the employment of intelligence assets, and conducts intelligence assessments that inform department strategy and underpin requirements analysis and assumptions.

DCNO FOR OPERATIONS, PLANS, AND STRATEGY (N3/N5)

Unlike the Joint Staff or combatant commands, which typically divide their J-3 and J-5 into directorates dedicated to covering current operations and future planning, respectively, OPNAV combines these functions into a single three-star directorate. OPNAV N3/N5 serves as the CNO's "lead strategist" charged with planning the laydown and employment of naval forces around the globe. Additionally, N3/N5 coordinates with the U.S. Marine Corps and U.S. Coast Guard to formulate and implement the Maritime Strategy, and fosters international ties with allies and partners. To assist OPNAV's administrative duties, the strategic assessments that N3/N5 produces are used to inform CNO investment priorities and formulate annual budget guidance (called CNO guidance, or CNOG). Moreover, N3/N5 is the community sponsor for the foreign area officer (FAO) community, and the manager for the Navy's political-military (pol-mil) strategist, operational planner, and Federal Executive Fellowship (FEF) programs.

Director, Operations and Plans Division (N31). Typically led by a one-star admiral, OPNAV N31 monitors current naval operations and advises N3/N5 and the CNO on global force management (GFM), anti-terrorism and force protection (AT/FP), and current or emergent operations. In addition to operating the Navy Operations Center (NOC), a watch floor in the Pentagon manned around-the-clock, N31 assists in preparing and presenting daily operations briefs to the CNO and other senior leaders.

Director, Strategy Division (N50). Led by either a one-star admiral or a senior civilian, N50 prepares future strategy, concepts of employment, force-shaping guidance, and joint doctrine recommendations.

Director, Global Integration and Engagement Division (N5I). Created during a reorganization in 2018, "N5-eye" coordinates OPNAV meetings with foreign officials, CNO-hosted international conferences, personnel exchanges, staff talks, security cooperation, bi- and multilateral maritime exercises, technology transfers, foreign disclosures, and professional military education (PME). It also handles strategic laydown and unit/squadron homeporting plans, and conducts war games and other operational- and strategic-level analysis.

DCNO FOR FLEET READINESS AND LOGISTICS (N4)

OPNAV N4 is a three-star admiral whose background and experiences are traditionally steeped in shore facility management or Navy regional command. This expansive portfolio encompasses the expertise of multiple URL, restricted line, and staff corps communities.

Director, Logistics Programs Division (N41). A Supply Corps flag officer, OPNAV N41 oversees supply chain management of parts, ordnance, fuel, and expeditionary medical treatment facilities in support of afloat operating forces and shore establishments.

Director, Strategic Mobility and Combat Logistics Division (N42). Working with the Military Sealift Command (MSC), OPNAV N42 serves as the resource sponsor for sea-based combat logistics force (CLF), including fleet oilers, ammunition ships, and hospital ships.

Director, Energy and Environmental Readiness Division (N45). Typically led by a one- or two-star Civil Engineer Corps (CEC) flag officer, OPNAV N45 creates policies and oversees implementation for Navy environmental programs in order to minimize the impact of afloat and ashore naval operations on the surrounding area. N45 also directs Navy energy programs to promote efficient use of resources in an effort to reduce operating costs.

Director, Shore Readiness Division (N46). In close coordination with Commander, Naval Installations Command (CNIC) and the Naval Facilities Engineering Command (NAVFAC), OPNAV N46 is responsible for shore services, and serves as the resource sponsor for shore facility military construction (MILCON), base operations and infrastructure support, and base realignment and closure (BRAC). N46 also supervises numerous family readiness programs and issues, including child and youth programs; commissaries; galleys; housing and lodging; and morale, welfare, and recreation (MWR) programs.

DCNO FOR WARFIGHTING DEVELOPMENT (N7)

Writing in *A Design for Maintaining Maritime Superiority, Version 2.0* released in December 2018, ADM John Richardson announced his intent to establish a new three-star position on the OPNAV staff "responsible for coordinating and aligning the Navy's education, experimentation, exercise, and analytic efforts" to synergize how the Navy learns and fights.

DCNO FOR INTEGRATION OF CAPABILITIES AND RESOURCES (N8)

The Navy Staff's primary responsibility is assisting the CNO in developing, integrating, and submitting the Navy's budget (called the Program Objective Memorandum, or POM). OPNAV N8 leads this monumental undertaking. This three-star admiral, who has likely spent the better part of his or her career in financial management, programming, assessments, or requirements tours, is charged with conducting operational and strategic assessments on current or planned programs; integrating the manpower, facilities, operations, and systems requirements submitted by the other "N-heads"; balancing all Navy investments across the Future Years Defense Program (FYDP), a budget projection that extends out five fiscal years; allocating resources as part of the Planning, Programming, Budgeting, and Execution (PPBE) system; and defending Navy strategic investment decisions to Congress. Though you will learn more about their exact role in chapter 7, it is safe to say that any OPNAV officer assigned a resourcing program or action officer portfolio will work, in some capacity, with the OPNAV N8 organization.

Director, Programming Division (N80). OPNAV N80 builds and balances the Navy's POM submission. To accomplish this immense task, this one- or two-star admiral relies on a large team of programming analysts and action officers—known colloquially in the Pentagon as "the Bullpen"—to create funding strategies to meet CNO's and broader department funding priorities. Once the POM is assembled, N80 advocates for Navy investments before OSD during DOD-wide budget deliberations (referred to as "endgame"). Not surprisingly, N80 is intimately involved in requirements discussions and milestone development, and is a key participant in the Navy Capabilities Board (NCB), which evaluates current programs-of-record (POR), proposed investments, and emerging technologies.

Director, Assessments Division (N81). N81 is OPNAV's lead analytic organization, responsible for providing the CNO and other directorates with (often classified) assessments on key warfighting capabilities and capability gaps. This analysis then informs spending priorities, where the objective is targeting investments to mitigate potential or projected warfighting shortfalls. Typically led by a one- or two-star flag officer with an academic background or professional experience in the field of operations research, N81 works with think tanks, academia, and federally funded research and development centers (FFRDC; described in chapter

17) to identify and assess capabilities that could positively affect how the Navy fights in localized battles or larger campaigns. N81 also maintains a library of research from which action officers can draw in determining warfighting needs. Additionally, N81 coordinates with the Joint Staff and OSD on assumptions and objectives for strategic assessments, and manages the Navy Munitions Requirements Program (NMRP), the analytic process that monitors and plans ammunition quantity needs.

Director, Fiscal Management Division (N82). Whereas N80 formulates the future Navy budget, N82—known as FMB—executes the current budget. This two-star director has dual reporting responsibilities to both the CNO (via N8) and to the SECNAV (via the Assistant Secretary of the Navy [Financial Management and Comptroller]). In this latter role, FMB also holds the title of Deputy Assistant Secretary of the Navy (Budget); among other things, this involves integrating the Marine Corps' budget submission into the Navy's POM to create the unified Department of the Navy budget submission (referred to as "the DON"), which is subsequently sent to OSD. FMB monitors programmatic obligations and expenditures and makes recommendations to Navy, OSD, Office of Management and Budget (OMB), and congressional leadership to adjust or reallocate resources when needed. Additionally, as you will learn in chapter 14, the Office of Appropriations Matters (FMBE) develops legislative strategy and coordinates all Navy engagements with congressional appropriators and committee staff.

Director, Fleet Readiness Division (N83). The lead organization for monitoring, analyzing, and advocating for fleet readiness issues, this division identifies and validates aviation, ship, submarine, and naval expeditionary requirements for operations, maintenance, and associated support required to meet fleet operations and achieve expected service life of warfighter equipment. N83 also assesses needs for, and advises resource sponsors and stakeholders on, ship steaming days and aviation flight hours, training ranges and targets, ship maintenance and aviation depot maintenance, and contractor logistics support, as well as other personnel, equipment, supply, training, ordnance, networks, and infrastructure (PESTONI) issues.

DCNO FOR WARFARE SYSTEMS (N9)

Created in 2012, OPNAV N9 is the organizational descendent of the three-star "warfare barons"—a small group of senior flag officers who for decades controlled nearly every aspect of surface ship, submarine, and aviation warfare requirements generation and resourcing from platforms to weapons to personnel. OPNAV N9 is responsible for determining warfighting requirements, resourcing priority programs, integrating systems across warfare domains, and balancing warfighting capability investments during POM development. To meet this tasking, N9 assumed responsibility for the manpower, training, sustainment, modernization, and procurement needs associated with each program—functions that were previously spread across the other OPNAV directorates (echoing CNO Kelso's move to split the now-defunct N7 requirements directorate from N8). Additionally, N9 works with numerous outside organizations, including industry; the acquisition community to develop strategies for emerging technologies by funding research, development, test, and evaluation (RDT&E); and both U.S. Fleet Forces Command and the three-star type commanders (naval surface/submarine/air forces, the de facto community leader) to identify warfighting capability gaps refine requirements solutions. N9's two-star divisions, which are staffed by line officers representing the various warfare communities, serve as the CNO's principal advisor for their respective warfare area and are known collectively as the "High-9s."

Director, Warfare Integration Division (N9I). "N9-eye" serves as N9's primary focal point for prioritizing and integrating the myriad requirements and capabilities that exist across the warfighting spectrum. In addition to shepherding official requirements documentation through the formal approval process, N9I works to balance investments across all warfare areas. Unlike the other divisions, which are staffed almost exclusively by officers of a particular warfighting designator, the N9I staff maintains a blend of warfighting backgrounds and expertise. N9I also hosts the Digital Warfare Office (DWO) to execute near-term pilot projects—developing new technologies and also applying innovative concepts or nonmaterial solutions—in an effort to mitigate warfighting gaps.

Director, Innovation, Technology Requirements, and Test and Evaluation Division (N94). Dual-hatted as the Chief of Naval Research (CNR) and leader of the Office of Naval Research (ONR), N94 serves as the resource sponsor for Navy science and technology (S&T) accounts—initiatives and demonstrations in the nascent stages of development—and is the OPNAV principal responsible for test and evaluation (T&E).

Director, Expeditionary Warfare Division (N95). By law, N95 is led by a Marine major general—the only general officer on the OPNAV staff. N95's resource sponsor portfolio includes large amphibious ships and associated small boats, naval special warfare (SEAL), explosive ordnance disposal (EOD), mine warfare, riverine forces, and Marine Corps expeditionary capabilities and integration.

Director, Surface Warfare Division (N96). N96 acts as the resource sponsor for surface combatants (cruisers, destroyers, frigates, littoral combat ships, and future ships), surface-launched weapons (missiles and guns), shipboard sensors (radars and navigation), combat systems, ballistic missile defense, surface fleet manpower and training, operations and steaming days, and maintenance and modernization.

Director, Undersea Warfare Division (N97). N97 is the resource sponsor for submarine development and procurement, sea-based strategic deterrence, tactical systems (weapons and seasons), and unmanned underwater vehicles (UUV).

Director, Air Warfare Division (N98). N98 resources aircraft carrier construction and overhaul, rotary-wing and fixed-wing (strike and maritime multi-mission) aircraft, unmanned aerial vehicles (UAV), air-launched weapons, training, logistics and readiness, flight hours, aviation depot maintenance, and air traffic control issues.

Director, Special Programs Division (N9SP). Led by a civilian SES who serves concurrently as the Department of the Navy's special access program coordinator (DON SAPCO), N9SP oversees the planning, management, budgeting, administration, and security for special access programs and sensitive activities for both OPNAV and the Navy Secretariat.

SURGEON GENERAL OF THE NAVY (N093)
As the head of the Navy's Bureau of Medicine and Surgery (BUMED)—which includes the Medical Corps, Dental Corps, Medical Service Corps, and Nurse Corps—this three-star flag officer advises the CNO on health care issues for eligible Navy and Marine Corps recipients, formulates health care policy, oversees medical training, and manages medical treatment facilities.

CHIEF OF NAVY RESERVE (N095)
As the three-star commander of the Navy Reserve Force, the Chief of Navy Reserve (CNR) is responsible for mobilization readiness, training and education, recruitment policies, and other budget issues for reserve personnel, equipment, and facilities. Additionally, CNR coordinates with the CNO, Commandant of the Marine Corps, and Joint Staff on the formulation and execution of plans requiring reserve support.

CHIEF OF CHAPLAINS (N097)

This one- or two-star admiral serves as the CNO's principal advisor for religious issues, and assists the Commandant of the Coast Guard on religious matters in which Navy chaplains are supporting. The chief's one-star deputy is dual-hatted as the Chaplain of the Marine Corps. Additionally, the chief of chaplains is responsible for officer and enlisted (religious program specialist, RP rating) manning, training, and education, as well as developing policies to deliver timely ministry services around the globe.

MASTER CHIEF PETTY OFFICER OF THE NAVY (N00D)

The Master Chief Petty Officer of the Navy (MCPON) is the CNO's primary advisor on enlisted personnel matters. The MCPON represents the enlisted community at senior leadership and ceremonial events and maintains liaison with enlisted family readiness, spouse, and ombudsman organizations. The MCPON—working through fleet, force, and command master chiefs—helps shape training and personnel issues across the enlisted community. Additionally, MCPON ensures guidance from the Navy's senior leaders reaches senior enlisted leaders in units around the globe.

In addition to the "N-heads" listed above, other Echelon I and II organizations have direct reporting responsibilities to the CNO (and, in some instances, to the SECNAV, as well):

- Special Assistant for Public Affairs Support (also known as the Chief of Information [CHINFO]) (N09C)
- Special Assistant for Safety Matters (Commander, Navy Safety Center [NAVSAFCEN]) (N09F)
- Special Assistant for Inspection Support (Navy Inspector General [IG]) (N09G)
- Special Assistant for Legal Services (Judge Advocate General of the Navy [JAG]) (N09J)
- Special Assistant for Legislative Support (Chief of Legislative Affairs [CLA]) (N09L)
- Special Assistant for Naval Investigative Matters and Security (Director, Naval Criminal Investigative Service [NCIS]) (N09N)
- Special Assistant for Material Inspection and Surveys (President, Board of Inspection and Survey [INSURV]) (N09P)

WORKFORCE COMPOSITION

Like other major tenant commands within the Pentagon, the Navy Staff comprises a diverse mix of active-duty officers and enlisted sailors, government civilians, and civilian contractors. Those who have not served previously in Washington or in a fleet concentration area may be surprised at the relative seniority of uniformed personnel working within the Pentagon. Mid-grade officers ranging from O-3 to O-4 make up a large portion of the active duty component, serving in a diverse range of action officers and front office billets. Senior officers in the rank of O-5 to O-6 are more common in OPNAV than on the waterfront; they typically serve as division deputies or branch heads and are often entrusted to represent their division flag or general officer at meetings or briefings.

The majority of the OPNAV workforce comprises of civilians who fill important administrative, support, action officer, and managerial roles. Civilian workers tend to remain in a specific job longer than their military counterparts; consequently, they provide continuity within program portfolios and can become repositories of knowledge and institutional history.

There are two types of civilian employees: "government civilians" and "contractor support." Government civilians are federal government employees responsible for a portfolio or who serve in a leadership position within a division or branch—sometimes even as a deputy for a mid-grade or senior officer. These employees typically maintain security clearances and are often included in sensitive or proprietary discussions with industry, military, or congressional leadership.

Similar to a military rank, government civilians earn promotions along the Office of Personnel Management's (OPM) general schedule (GS) pay scale. Some government civilians attain flag officer-equivalent positions in the senior executive service (SES); they are accorded many of the same flag officer privileges and it is common to address them more formally in conversation than their junior GS counterparts (e.g., Mr./Ms. Smith). The *OPNAV Protocol Handbook* includes a comparison between military and civilian paygrades (see table 3-1).

In contrast, contractor support employees do not work directly for the federal government. Instead, they work for private companies that compete for contracts to support the federal workforce. These contracted employees offer subject matter expertise not resident within the federal government and are often embedded within offices working side by side with military

Table 3-1. Military and Civilian Pay Grades

Military Grade	Civilian Grade
O-7 to O-10	SES 1-6
O-6	GS-14/15
O-5	GS-13/14
O-4	GS-12
O-3	GS-11
O-2	GS-7/9
O-1	GS-7
E-7 to E-9	GS-6
E-5 to E-6	GS-5
E-4	GS-4
E-1 to E-3	GS-1-4

and government civilian workers. However, on average, turnover among support contract personnel tends to be higher than their government civilian counterparts—largely because their parent company must periodically compete for support contracts awards, a process that can create long-term employment uncertainty. Though their portfolios may require them to have a security clearance, contractors may be excluded from sensitive meetings or those sessions in which the outcome is not yet ready for public release (colloquially referred to as "predecisional" meetings). Importantly, while contractors can be involved in planning and deliberations, they do not have the authority to make decisions on behalf of the federal government.

Every organization within the federal government—including the Navy Staff—relies on civilian workers to accomplish the mission. Writing in the *NavCivGuide: A Handbook for Civilians in the United States Navy*, LCDR Thomas J. Cutler, USN (Ret.), captured the vital contributions of the Navy's civilian workforce:

> The success of the U.S. Navy in its more than two centuries of existence is due not only to the essential contributions of Sailors on active duty and in the Reserve, but also to that other vital arm of the Total Force triad, the civilians who have worked as part of the Navy since its earliest days. In March 2004, Secretary of the Navy Gordon England told the U.S. Senate, "A large part of the credit for the Navy's outstanding performance goes to our civilian workforce. These experienced and dedicated craftspeople, researchers, supply and maintenance specialists, computer experts, service providers and their managers are an essential part of our Total Naval Force concept."

CONCLUSION

Since its creation in 1915, the role of the CNO and the OPNAV staff has evolved for many reasons and in response to both external pressures and internal Pentagon dynamics. CNOs rely on the staff for a variety of reasons, namely to execute strategic priorities in support of building the Navy's budget. Despite these changes, OPNAV's mission has remained constant: to ensure the fleet is manned, trained, equipped, and ready to deploy in support of the nation.

LCDR Doug Robb is a surface warfare officer who has served two tours in the Pentagon on the Navy Staff and one on Capitol Hill.

4

THE NAVY SECRETARIAT

SARANDIS PAPADOPOULOS, PhD

T he naval services provided by warships, skilled crews, and well-
trained ground and air units, backed by dockyards, communications networks, hospitals, depots, and bases, are the most intricate
organizations one can imagine. Since their establishment in 1775, the U.S.
Navy and the U.S. Marine Corps (USMC) have been complex organizations to operate. To manage such matters, in 1798 President John Adams
appointed Benjamin Stoddert as his first secretary of the newly formed
Department of the Navy (DON). Constitutionally, presidents of the United
States command the armed services. Starting with Stoddert and continuing
until 1946, Navy secretaries turned the presidents' policies into orders that
were conveyed to commanders at sea; they also supervised the building
of ships and, later aircraft, recruitment of Marines and sailors, as well as
supplying and paying the services' personnel. Collectively, these duties are
commonly summarized by the phrase taken from Title 10 of the United
States Code to "man, train, and equip."

What follows is a synopsis of the Secretariat's history since 1797. Readers
should bear in mind that roles and responsibilities, especially the division
of labor between the Secretary of the Navy and Undersecretary of the Navy,
will vary depending on the personalities of the senior leaders involved.
Following that outline, a short summary of the current Secretariat offices
completes this explanation.

THE HISTORIC OFFICES SUPPORTING THE SECRETARY OF THE NAVY

THE NINETEENTH CENTURY

The nineteenth-century Navy and Marine Corps were small services,
growing only in wartime, but secretaries used them to spread American
influence, build trade, and develop new solutions to problems. Under Stoddert's direction, the Navy fought French Caribbean privateers who stole

American cargoes during the Quasi-War of the 1790s. In that successful effort the Navy was joined by the Revenue Cutter Service, predecessor to the U.S. Coast Guard (USCG). Later, Marines launched an amphibious assault at Veracruz during the Mexican-American War tenure of Secretary John Y. Mason, and the Navy served off both Mexican coasts. Technology also made an impact during the Civil War, when Secretary Gideon Welles oversaw the Navy adding ironclads to the fleet, such as the USS *Monitor*. Welles sent his squadron commodores to enforce a blockade that strangled the Confederate economy. With the help of Gustavus V. Fox (the only Navy assistant secretary before 1890), America had the world's second-largest fleet by 1865, but the next two peacetime decades saw that strength fall.

Throughout their history the Marine Corps and the Navy also played diplomatic roles; they have been forward-deployed from their very creation. Operations against Barbary pirates meant a full squadron of ships stayed in the Mediterranean, except during the War of 1812. In 1821, Secretary Smith Thompson ordered the U.S. Navy to embargo the African slave trade, a role that lasted four decades. The Mediterranean Squadron remained a key focus, as in 1849 when Secretary William B. Preston assigned the USS *Constitution* to deliver American diplomats to the Holy See in Rome. In 1854, Secretary James C. Dobbin similarly ordered CDRE Matthew C. Perry to lead the U.S. Pacific Squadron to Tokyo, with the assignment to open diplomatic and trade relations with Japan. These efforts durably linked America to the world, an effort managed by naval forces.

In the 1840s Secretary Abel P. Upshur formed bureaus (for yards and docks; construction, equipment, and repairs; provisions and clothing; ordnance and hydrography; medicine and surgery) to professionalize administration, and founded an engineer corps for the steam Navy. The bureaus' expertise allowed the Office of the Secretary to remain quite small in size, even during the Civil War, with a total staff (including the bureau chiefs) of about 90, for a Navy Department numbering 62,000 sailors and Marines. Numerous boards also complemented the bureaus' expertise for specialized tasks. These organizations remained in place until 1966, when they were succeeded by the Navy's systems commands. Today, just the Bureau of Medicine and Surgery, commonly referred to as BUMED (founded in 1842); the Bureau of Naval Personnel, or BUPERS (an organization named in 1942); and the Board of Inspection and Survey, or INSURV (created in 1868), continue to use their traditional names.

Also in the 1840s, Secretary George Bancroft established the Naval Academy at Annapolis to educate Navy and Marine Corps officers. Secretary William E. Chandler created the Naval War College in 1884 to teach mid-career officers the art of strategy and senior command. Despite those institutions, however, the Navy's bureaus remained highly autonomous from the fleet, especially in the absence of a service chief admiral supported by a staff. Instead, after 1890, the assistant secretary only held management responsibility for Navy shore facilities and civilian personnel. In that era only a dynamic secretary or a strong-willed assistant secretary, such as Theodore Roosevelt (1897–98), could mandate real administrative changes.

THE TWENTIETH CENTURY

After 1900, Secretary John D. Long created the General Board for senior service members' advice on ship design, war plans, basing, and personnel policy; this board reported directly to Long. Its first chair was ADM Thomas Dewey. That organization helped the secretary compose war plans and manage new fleet technology, especially steel ships, steam turbines, long-range guns, armor, torpedoes, and communications gear. The Marine Corps made its own changes, introducing custom-built transport ships (purchased by the Navy) for amphibious landings and beginning its first "small wars" in the Philippines, actions that continued for decades in the Caribbean. In 1909 Secretary George von Lengerke Meyer created the Naval Postgraduate School to spread professional skills to officers, especially in engineering.

The war in Europe prompted more changes. Seeing technical complexity continue to rise as aircraft and submarines joined the fleet, in 1915 Secretary Josephus Daniels created a senior admiral's billet, the Chief of Naval Operations (CNO); the position of Commandant had existed throughout the Marine Corps' history. The Navy's enlisted force also experienced a technical transformation under Daniels. Although Secretary Daniels misguidedly limited the role African Americans could play in the fleet, on the plus side of the ledger he envisioned that petty officers and chiefs would focus on mechanical specialization in a fleet that was ever more dependent on modern technology. To help find the people to man the fleet and force, Daniels created the Navy and Marine Corps Reserve; this meant that America entered both world wars with a larger pool of trained uniformed personnel.

Between the world wars aviation assumed greater importance, leading to the creation of the position of Assistant Secretary (Air). Hard fiscal times during the Depression meant the position went unfilled for most of that decade. Despite the lack of a civilian leader, the sea services remained the world's professional leaders in the field of aviation, developing aircraft and tactics for new missions such as torpedo delivery, dive bombing, and long-range reconnaissance. These roles were vital to the fleet, which was restricted in size by international treaty—and limited congressional appropriations—after 1921. The DON's prowess stretched as far as experimenting with dirigibles for scouting, only to dispense with them quickly as better search airplanes and new signals intelligence technology replaced them. Throughout the 1930s and '40s the U.S. Navy remained the world's second-largest fleet, and the Marine Corps counted nearly twice as many servicemembers as it had before American entry in World War I.

A second innovation of the 1920s was a Navy Information Section, established in 1921. An outgrowth of an earlier World War I public relations activity, this predecessor to the Chief of Information, resided inside the Office of Naval Intelligence. It was created to share details with the public about what the service did, as well as to review requests for movie support from filmmakers; only later did this public affairs group directly support recruiting as well. The Marine Corps established its own Publicity Bureau during World War I for the same purposes. These offices started the strategic communication role for the Navy Department, a crucial support for manning and equipping the sea services.

WORLD WAR II

Threat of another world war brought Frank Knox to the post of secretary in 1940 and that same year he appointed the first Undersecretary of the Navy, James V. Forrestal. Knox confronted the widening conflict in the North Atlantic, with German submarines attacking civilian merchant vessels and (then–neutral) U.S. Navy ships, sinking one destroyer in October 1941. Starting a month later, after the devastating Pearl Harbor attack, Knox oversaw the Navy and Marine Corps rapidly growing to nearly four million uniformed personnel, backed by 750,000 more civilian employees, with six Marine divisions, tens of thousands of airplanes, and over 6,000 ships and other craft. After Knox's death in 1944, Secretary Forrestal witnessed the amphibious landings at Normandy, as well as those at Iwo Jima, overseeing the department's greatest wartime victories across the globe.

Managing the immensity of World War II and the rapid growth of the sea services demanded a larger departmental Secretariat, which numbered over 51,000 people at the conflict's end. The new undersecretary quickly became too busy to oversee the contracts needed to equip the services, so a new office—the Procurement Legal Division—began reporting to Forrestal in July 1941. Renamed the Office of the General Counsel in 1944, this agency strove to certify the best use of taxpayers' money, while ensuring compliance with local, state, federal, and international regulations. Given the vast scale of the department, a new organization to evaluate its practices was also needed. In particular, the accidental sinking of the French ocean liner *Normandie* in New York harbor prompted Congress to recommend centralizing naval investigative agencies. As a result, the inspector general's office was established in May 1942.

THE COLD WAR

By federal law, the Secretary of Defense is tasked with transmitting presidential orders to operating forces. Navy secretaries' duties were strictly limited to recruiting, organizing, supplying, equipping, training, and administering the fleet and force. A new activity, the Office of Naval Research (ONR), was added to the mix in 1946; it consolidated a wide variety of research and development tasks at academic institutions, overseas, and at the Naval Research Laboratory (NRL) based in Washington, DC. Since then, the NRL has gone on to develop the Global Positioning System (GPS), among other methods of supporting the sea services and improving national security.

Those evolving roles meant more Secretariat focus on deploying new systems. The first Cold War decade saw Secretary Dan A. Kimball sponsor the introduction of the world's first nuclear-powered submarine, the *Nautilus*, in 1955. His successor, Secretary Charles S. Thomas, oversaw creation of the large *Forrestal* class of aircraft carriers, the Marine Air-Ground Task Force (MAGTF) concept, and ballistic missiles for nuclear deterrence. These were not easy tasks to accomplish, particularly while the Navy and Marine Corps fought a war in Korea between 1950 and 1953. That conflict, and the Cold War need for continuous overseas deployment of large numbers of ships and Marines, poised for any eventuality, drew much of the services' talent and resources.

Subsequent broad U.S. policy changes reshaped defense planning. After President John F. Kennedy's election, Secretary of Defense Robert S.

Secretary of the Navy Dan Kimball's Pentagon office, 1953. *Official U.S. Navy photo, now in the collections of the National Archives*

McNamara changed the national military strategy from "massive retaliation"—which met aggression by any means necessary, including nuclear weapons—to one of "flexible response." The new strategic method meant that American and North Atlantic Treaty Organization (NATO) military reaction to an attack would now be scaled proportionally. Such an approach led to all the U.S. military services placing greater emphasis on general-purpose forces whose creation demanded higher fiscal outlays. Throughout the 1960s, making that investment while modernizing the aging fleet's ships (both attempted while mobilizing to fight the Vietnam War) challenged the skills of Navy Secretary Paul H. Nitze. In the end, ship modernization and repair suffered.

DEFENSE REFORMS OF THE 1960s

After 1960, the Navy Department assumed the structure we recognize today. The successor to the Assistant Secretary of the Navy (Aeronautics) (ASN[Air]), was redesignated as ASN (Research and Development) in 1959. He was responsible for equipping the services with aircraft and other systems. Going forward, in addition to the secretary and undersecretary, a total of four assistant secretaries and the general counsel rounded out the Senate-confirmed senior leaders of the department. The four ASNs continued the backbone functions of department: financial management and the budget, personnel and reserve issues, and installations. Their duties also included a combined portfolio for shipbuilding and logistics, to ensure that recruiting, training, and equipping took place.

Beginning in 1963, Navy secretaries also relied on the Office of Program Appraisal (OPA), an organization comprising uniformed members of the Marine Corps and Navy, headed by an admiral. Created by Secretary Fred Korth, this special office added rigor to the department's budget submissions in response to the Office of the Secretary of Defense's new Planning, Programming, and Budgeting System (PPBS, now PPBE, described in chapter 7 of this volume). Advanced by Defense Secretary McNamara, PPBS used "systems analysis" to match operational needs to the funding for them by assessing requirements in distinct phases, all to support allotting resources over a dynamic five-year period in the Future Years Defense Program (FYDP). If done correctly, these steps would cut duplicated efforts across the services and save money.

The early 1960s justified making these changes. In that period, the U.S. armed services added technological improvements that swamped the pace of previous eras. The Marine Corps and Navy completed the adoption of helicopters, supersonic tactical aircraft, guided missiles, nuclear weapons, and advanced communications, while the Navy had also embraced satellites and nuclear propulsion. The scale of that last effort deserves emphasis: for half a decade before 1964, the Navy annually purchased a dozen nuclear-powered ballistic missile (the *Polaris* boats) or attack submarines, plus surface combatants. Each successive Secretary of the Navy struggled to find the resources to pay for this build-up, a fiscal challenge worsened by a growing need to support forces fighting in South Vietnam. Crewing nuclear warships also strained the personnel system. PPBS was meant to help balance these challenges.

In practice, while improving budgeting, PPBS emphasized programming more than all other functions and made OSD, not the services, defend priorities to the President. In essence, the service chiefs—and department secretaries—no longer stressed their most important weapon investments. As a result, since the 1960s secretaries of defense can and have overruled the advice and recommendations of uniformed leaders. While consistent with the U.S. Constitution, which mandates civilian control of the military, politicians can change priorities quickly. For example, one 1960s program resulting from this new responsiveness was the TFX, started as a joint Air Force–Navy effort to purchase a variable-geometry tactical fighter. Despite the program's intent to save money by buying the planes on a larger scale, over time it became so mired in problems and rising costs it eventually became the Air Force (only) F-111, at great cost to the Navy Department's credibility.

Such policy changes meant the Department of the Navy needed OPA to make the strongest possible justifications to the Office of the Secretary of Defense. In 1966, the department redesignated its bureaus as "systems commands," such as NAVAIR (for aircraft), NAVSEA (ships), and NAVMAT (for logistics). NAVMAT was dissolved in 1985, with its functions spread among the other commands. In general, this environmental shift has lasted for the past fifty-five years. Practically speaking, these restrictions in departmental autonomy meant Navy secretaries needed OPA to scrub DON budget submissions, support the preparation of testimony, sponsor studies, and offer program analyses through 2010 (when the office was disbanded).

Since the 1960s the assistant secretaries' duties have carried on, although offices have been renamed. Three assistant secretaries' offices are mandated by Congress, the largest of which is the ASN for Financial Management and Comptroller (FM&C); its staff needed to write the annual departmental budget and oversee the services' spending. Next in size is the ASN for Manpower and Reserve affairs (M&RA), responsible for setting policy for personnel, including departmental civilians. The assistant for Research, Development, and Acquisition (RD&A) has held increasing responsibility for purchasing large items (ships, aircraft, vehicles) for the department, especially after 1990. That change witnessed the end of the Navy's internal shipbuilding capability by 1970. The construction of warships shifted to contractors while the services' yards assumed responsibility for performing repairs. To more closely manage acquisition, after 1990 RD&A set up program executive offices (PEOs) for major systems. To oversee the extensive shore infrastructure of the department, the assistant for installations and environment (I&E) was also added. This position, which was created at the discretion of the Secretary of the Navy, saw its portfolio enlarged to include energy, becoming ASN(EI&E). All of the assistant secretary offices are staffed by a mix of military and civilian personnel.

Despite the rising importance of the Office of Secretary of Defense, one role Navy secretaries retain is to nominate officers to senior flag rank and general officer positions, prior to their confirmation by the Senate. That manning role means secretaries fundamentally shape the leadership of the Marine Corps and the Navy. For example, in 1970 Secretary John Chafee exercised his authority to reach deep into the Navy officer corps and recommend VADM Elmo Zumwalt for the position of Chief of Naval Operations. Zumwalt's appointment and confirmation by the Senate made him the youngest CNO in history; Chafee was committed to making the Navy more closely reflect American society (with particular sensitivity to race relations).

The main military change of the 1970s was the end of Selective Service and its replacement by the All-Volunteer Force (AVF). Secretary of Defense Melvin Laird spearheaded the effort at the behest of President Richard Nixon. The draft's ultimate end in 1973 marked a return to the traditional American practice of only conscripting for wartime service. Advocates anticipated the AVF would cost less, recruit better-educated service-members, and halt the perceived inequities of the thirty-three-year-old Selective Service system, especially those observed in the Army during the Vietnam War. In this same period (1972) and as a result of détente, Secretary John Warner signed an agreement to prevent incidents between U.S. and Soviet Navy ships on the high seas.

The national economy worsened after 1973, and this meant constrained resources had to match wider commitments, including those in the Arabian Gulf, stretching the Navy and Marine Corps to the limit. Worse still, President Jimmy Carter's priority was strengthening NATO's land forces, which translated to limiting funds for shipbuilding. Carter emphasized that choice by vetoing funding to construct a nuclear-powered aircraft carrier early in 1978. A worsening of Cold War relations with the Soviet Union soon pressed Secretary Edward Hidalgo to make difficult choices to rebalance the sea services toward the Middle East after the dual threats of the Iranian Revolution and Soviet invasion of Afghanistan in 1979. During the previous 140 years, only a few components from the Navy Department had deployed to the Gulf. Following President Carter's announcement of a Rapid Deployment Force (forerunner to today's Central Command), the United States started reinvesting in the Marine Corps and Navy, as well as the other armed services.

THE REAGAN AND LEHMAN ERA

After the election of President Ronald Reagan in 1980, Secretary John Lehman managed a growing flow of resources to rebuild the Navy and Marine Corps, equipping and training them to outlast the Warsaw Pact's forces. Procurement of equipment such as the Aegis combat system, *Los Angeles*–class submarines, AV-8B Harrier vertical and/or short takeoff and landing (VSTOL) aircraft, and F-14 Tomcat fighters had started before his term. But Secretary Lehman accelerated delivery of the new gear and launched a series of exercises to demonstrate their effectiveness. These new systems, with America projecting the will to use them, conveyed a Navy and Marine Corps oriented to deter the Soviet Union or defeat it, if necessary.

Crucial to Lehman's effort was the drafting of the so-called Maritime Strategy, cosigned by the Commandant and Chief of Naval Operations. The document was initially intended to provide internal guidance for coordinating the Navy's policies and making its case on Capitol Hill. The Maritime Strategy relied on intelligence sources to link the ends, ways, and means of confronting the USSR. The 1986 public version of the policy explained how the services used sea power to manage the entire continuum of operations in peacetime, crises, and war. Vitally, that version of the document compellingly argued for expanding the fleet to six hundred ships, including fifteen aircraft carriers; it enjoyed support from the leadership of all three sea services, who used it to show how they could and would deter the Soviet bloc.

After uncovering a set of operational and procurement problems in the Defense Department, Congress divided responsibilities further, which once again challenged secretarial talent. For example, the 1986 Goldwater-Nichols Defense Reorganization Act (1986) oriented the armed services to fight as parts of joint commands. But the same legislation also narrowed the Department of the Navy's role in procuring equipment, as two secretaries, James Webb and Sean O'Keefe, discovered. Thereafter, operational requirements (set by uniformed service members) became more distant from the process of acquiring weapons, a process managed mostly by Navy civil servants. The change also led to the amalgamation of ASN (Shipbuilding and Logistics) with ASN (Research, Engineering, and Systems) to become ASN (Research, Development, and Acquisition).

Similarly, after 1988, attempts to realign homeports for ships or to cut unneeded bases became more politically sensitive. A long period that began in 1969 had seen no major facilities changes taking place; this forced both the Marine Corps and the Navy to support much unwanted overhead. From the late 1980s such infrastructure changes were renewed, but were now managed under what became a series of five Base Realignment and Closure Commissions (BRAC) that were overseen by Congress. This inflexible process again limited the Secretary of the Navy's choices. At the departmental level the details of these changes were managed by the ASN (Installations and Environment) (EI&E), which set up a dedicated BRAC office as needed.

A DIFFERENT WORLD

The 1989 end of the Cold War saw a reduction of both Navy and Marine Corps strength, although these services remained even busier handling smaller-scale conflicts and long-lasting missions. Following the 1991 Iraq War, the last decade of the century saw the sea services move away from a strategy to deter or fight against a similarly organized opponent. Instead, in the post-1991 world their operational focus has shifted to civil wars, ethnic strife, regional despots, and terrorism. Service thinking changed, too. For example, Secretary O'Keefe signed the *From the Sea* document in 1992 that showed how Marine Corps and Navy persistence, mobility, steady access, and flexibility could help counter the wide array of challenges facing the nation in the 1990s.

Since 1991, the number of staff in the Secretariat's offices has remained fairly constant. The secretary's front office usually comprises eight people, including a political appointee senior executive service (SES) assistant, one or two Marine Corps or Navy aides, a scheduling staff of four, plus several enlisted or rated personnel on the main desk. Beyond that office is the secretary's administrative staff, which includes uniformed public affairs personnel, a speechwriter, protocol officers, and a correspondence section, as well as other support staffs of civil servants, including the Executive Mess staffed by sailors and Marines. While the first responsibility of these offices is to the secretary, they also offer support to the undersecretary's office, as well as to the broader departmental activities of the headquarters.

One final change occurred late in the 1990s. With the looming concern of digital data loss at the turn of the millennium—the "Y2K challenge"—the Department of the Navy created a Chief Information Officer (DON CIO) as required by Congress. That official and his or her staff set policies and provided oversight of the department's data and the electronic systems that contain it.

THE TWENTY-FIRST CENTURY

Following the September 11, 2001, attacks on New York City, Pennsylvania, and the Pentagon, both services engaged in wars in Afghanistan and Iraq. As a measure of the demands of combat, the department kept one-third of its active-duty Marine Corps expeditionary forces in the two theaters for almost thirteen years, continuously backed up by dozens of Navy ships and aircraft, as well as thousands of individual augmentee (IA) sailors on the ground. When combined with regular global forward-presence commitments, the demand stretched the services to their utmost as the Navy struggled to fight halfway around the world. In 2007, *A Cooperative Strategy for 21st Century Seapower* explained the full range of these maritime missions. Like its 1986 predecessor, this document enjoyed Secretarial, Navy, Marine Corps, and U.S. Coast Guard support.

As these wars dragged on (Afghanistan is now considered the longest war in American history), three Navy secretaries—Gordon England, Donald Winter, and Ray Mabus—ensured the services could keep fighting overseas. New equipment included the *Gerald R. Ford* class of aircraft carriers, *Virginia*–class submarines, F-35B and F-35C Lighting II fighters, the MV-22 tilt-rotor Osprey, and a family of mine-resistant vehicles (MRAPs). All were needed in Iraq and Afghanistan. As a notable marker, the first female Undersecretary of the Navy, Susan M. Livingstone, also helped lead the department between 2001 and 2003. Her job had its risks, for on 9/11 she helped lead a large group of survivors trapped in the Pentagon to safety.

To answer congressional mandates for better business controls, the department has tasked undersecretaries (after 2009—these included Robert Work, Janine Davidson, and Thomas Modly) as its Chief Management Officer (CMO). Likewise, the deputy undersecretary's position split in two, divided between policy and management roles. The former briefs department leaders and provides information to OSD, while the latter is the DON deputy chief management officer. Shifting part of the 3rd Marine Expeditionary Force (MEF) from Okinawa meant creating an office to station Marines and sailors on Guam. To streamline the headquarters, again at congressional behest, the assistant for administration (DON/AA) launched a series of efficiencies to centralize more responsibilities. Another mandate, to ensure the department could pass an audit, mandated the growth of the ASN(FM&C) office. And to accelerate the pace of problem-solving, Secretary Mabus created an Office of Strategy and Innovation in 2015, focusing on delivering unmanned systems, using data for decision-making, and bringing additive manufacturing to the fleet and force.

TODAY

In 2018, the seventy-sixth secretary, Richard V. Spencer, oversaw an undersecretary, the offices of four assistant secretaries, and the General Counsel. To build greater agility and craft quicker decisions, while maintaining accountability, in March of that same year the Secretariat staff was reorganized. These changes ended the tenure of one of the deputy undersecretary's offices, replacing it with the Office of the Chief Management Officer (OCMO). That organization will work as a set of cross-functional teams to improve departmental responsiveness in recruiting, training, equipping, and support. The same changes eliminated the Strategy and Innovation office and reordered the Chief Information Officer function.

In mid-2019 Secretary Spencer and Undersecretary Modly are supported by a Secretariat that numbers approximately 1,100 people, although the number is set to drop to meet major headquarters' staff reductions set by Congress. Their key mandate remains to support the Chief of Naval Operations and Commandant of the Marine Corps in building and maintaining

Secretary of the Navy Richard V. Spencer at a Pentagon briefing with Chief of Naval Operations ADM John Richardson and Commandant of the Marine Corps Gen Robert Neller on May 2, 2018. *U.S. Navy photo by MC1 Raymond D. Diaz III/Released*

the sea services. In the early twenty-first century the 900,000 sailors, Marines, and civilians charged with planning and organizing America's maritime defense rely on Secretary Spencer's advocacy and guidance to create success. No other military organization can boast the depth and breadth of capabilities maintained by today's Department of the Navy, which is the product of over two centuries of devoted and talented leadership.

CURRENT DEPARTMENT OF THE NAVY OFFICES

Each of the assistant secretaries as well as the General Counsel are accorded respect equivalent to three-star flag officers or general officers. The Secretary of the Navy and the Undersecretary of the Navy, both also confirmed by the Senate, are considered equivalent to four-star officers.

ASSISTANT SECRETARY OF THE NAVY, ENERGY, INSTALLATIONS, AND ENVIRONMENT (ASN[EI&E])

Responsible for the bases and shore infrastructure of the department, this organization also manages the safe management of natural resources, along with programs designed to reduce fleet and force dependence on fossil fuels. It is the smallest ASN office.

ASSISTANT SECRETARY OF THE NAVY, FINANCIAL MANAGEMENT AND COMPTROLLER (ASN[FM&C])

As the budget-submitting entity for the entire Navy Department, the Financial Management and Comptroller transmits the documents that request funds for programs across the services. Since 2015, one of its subsidiary offices has also assumed responsibility for ensuring the audit readiness of the department.

ASSISTANT SECRETARY OF THE NAVY, MANPOWER AND RESERVE AFFAIRS (ASN[M&RA])

This office sets policies for the recruitment and readiness of active-duty and reserve service members of the Navy and the Marine Corps. The ASN(M&RA) also oversees the DON Office of Civilian Human Resources, a distributed organization that recruits and hires civil servants in conformity with relevant federal laws and regulations.

ASSISTANT SECRETARY OF THE NAVY, RESEARCH, DEVELOPMENT, AND ACQUISITION (ASN[RD&A])

With lead responsibility for equipping and arming the U.S. Marine Corps and the Navy, this office manages acquisition, matches funds to

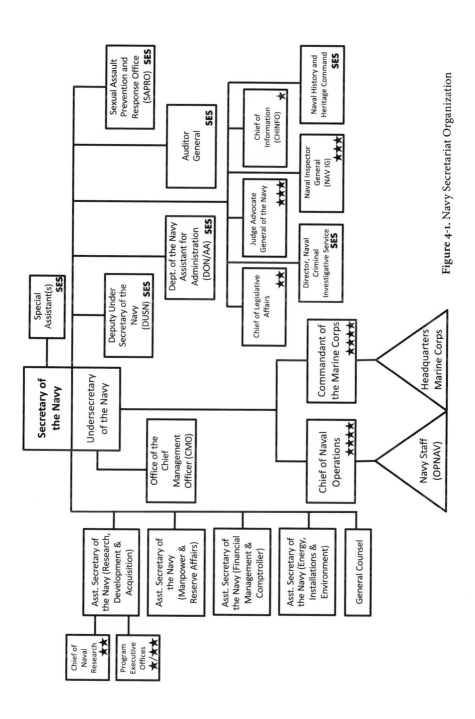

Figure 4-1. Navy Secretariat Organization

requirements, oversees research (including the Chief of Naval Research [CNR] and program executive offices [PEO]) to create new capabilities, and supports design changes in conjunction with industry.

CHIEF OF NAVAL INFORMATION (CHINFO)

The Chief of Naval Information is responsible for the messaging of the department Secretariat and of the Navy, and with coordination of all public affairs officers across the Navy, this comparatively large uniformed and civilian office is headed by a rear admiral (lower half).

DEPARTMENT OF THE NAVY ASSISTANT FOR ADMINISTRATION (DON/AA)

The office takes care of the headquarters functions of the department, including budget submissions for the entire Secretariat, as well as the full range of human resources support, facilities, historian, information technology, records management, the executive dining room, and other activities.

DEPUTY UNDERSECRETARY OF THE NAVY FOR POLICY (DUSN)

In direct support of the secretary and undersecretary, this senior executive-headed organization helps the leaders of the department with international engagement briefings, preparing congressional testimony, as well as offering security and other specialized support.

NAVAL AUDIT SERVICE

Distinct from the audit function residing in ASN(FM&C), this is an independent organization that tracks risks inside the Navy Department, seeking to build efficiency, tighten accountability, and improve program effectiveness.

NAVY INSPECTOR GENERAL (NAV IG)

Headed by a vice admiral, and with a staff drawn from across the fleet backed by civilians, this office builds public confidence in the department. It routinely investigates conditions and processes across the Navy, and fields complaints involving potential waste, fraud, and abuse inside the department.

NAVY JUDGE ADVOCATE GENERAL (JAG)

Headed by a vice admiral, this office manages the community of uniformed attorneys that provides military advice to commanding officers, as well as providing judges and trial lawyers for cases in military courts.

OFFICE OF THE CHIEF MANAGEMENT OFFICER (OCMO)

Created in 2018 and reporting to the undersecretary, this predominantly civilian office works to improve the Navy Department's data, business systems, education, and reform processes. It is the successor to the Deputy Undersecretary of the Navy (Management) organization.

OFFICE OF THE GENERAL COUNSEL OF THE NAVY (OGC)

The General Counsel of the Navy oversees the careers of all attorneys across the department, individuals who offer commands and offices a comprehensive range of legal services. In the Pentagon, its personnel offers advice to the Secretariat on acquisition and legislative questions.

OFFICE OF LEGISLATIVE AFFAIRS (OLA)

Headed by a rear admiral (upper half), this largely military office provides answers to congressional inquiries, as well as preparing the Navy Department leadership for testimony on Capitol Hill.

OFFICE OF THE SECRETARY OF THE NAVY (SECNAV)

This is a comprehensive administrative office managing the secretary's outside engagements, speeches, protocol, correspondence, and public affairs roles. Headed by an executive assistant (sometimes referred to as a "military assistant"), usually a captain or commander, it is the inner office of the Secretariat.

OFFICE OF THE UNDERSECRETARY OF THE NAVY (UNSECNAV)

The deputy chief of the Navy Department's leadership, the Undersecretary of the Navy is a political appointee typically delegated responsibility for management issues of special interest, as well as standing in as the departmental executive when the SECNAV is on travel.

SEXUAL ASSAULT PREVENTION OFFICE (SAPRO)

A small policy office headed by a civilian executive, it aims to lower incidence of criminal sexual assault, and provides education and resources to create an improved working environment for all members of the department.

FURTHER READING

Barlow, Jeffrey G. *From Hot War to Cold: The U.S. Navy and National Security Affairs, 1945–1955* (Palo Alto: Stanford University Press, 2009).

Bruns, Sebastian. *U.S. Naval Strategy and National Security: The Evolution of American Maritime Power* (London: Routledge, 2017).

Buderi, Robert. *Naval Innovation for the 21st Century: The Office of Naval Research since the End of the Cold War* (Annapolis, Md.: Naval Institute Press, 2013).

Chisholm, Donald. *Waiting for Dead Men's Shoes: Origins and Development of the U.S. Navy's Officer Personnel System, 1793–1941* (Palo Alto: Stanford University Press, 2001).

Coletta, Paolo E., ed. *American Secretaries of the Navy.* 2 volumes (Annapolis, Md.: Naval Institute Press, 1980).

Furer, J. A. *Administration of the Navy Department in World War II* (Washington, DC: GPO, 1959).

Goldberg, Alfred, et al. *Pentagon 9/11* (Washington, DC: GPO, 2007).

Kuehn, John T. *America's First General Staff: A Short History of the Rise and Fall of the General Board of the Navy* (Annapolis, Md.: Naval Institute Press, 2017).

Nemfakos, Charles, Irv Blickstein, Aine Seitz McCarthy, and Jerry M. Sollinger. *The Perfect Storm: The Goldwater-Nichols Act and Its Effect on Navy Acquisition* (Santa Monica and Arlington: Rand, 2010). Accessed February 6, 2018. https://www.rand.org/content/dam/rand/pubs/occasional_papers/2010/RAND_OP308.pdf.

O'Connell, Aaron B. *Underdogs: The Making of the Modern Marine Corps* (Cambridge, Mass.: Harvard University Press, 2012).

Secretary of the Navy Instruction 5430.7Q. "Assignment of Responsibilities and Authorities in the Office of the Secretary of the Navy." August 17, 2009.

Dr. Sarandis Papadopoulos is the Secretariat Historian, Department of the Navy. His history degrees include a BA from the University of Toronto, MA from the University of Alabama, and PhD from the George Washington University. He was principal coauthor of the book *Pentagon 9/11*, published under the auspices of the Historian's Office, Office of the Secretary of Defense.

5

THE JOINT STAFF

COL DOUG DOUDS, USMC (RET.)

A BRIEF HISTORY OF THE JOINT STAFF

The United States has always needed "jointness"—interservice coordination and cooperation. The U.S. Constitution provides for the War Department and the Navy Department, and the President, in his or her role as Commander in Chief, to coordinate their activities. While there have been brief historical glimpses of successful joint operations, a distinct lack of interservice cooperation characterized their interaction through the Spanish-American War. In 1903, the Joint Army and Navy Board was created to address "all matters calling for cooperation of the two Services." Lacking authority, it was a planning and deliberative body that failed to resolve or adjudicate joint matters satisfactorily.

It was the United States' growth into a global power during World War II that produced the nascent roles of the Joint Chiefs of Staff, the Chairman of the Joint Chiefs, and the Joint Staff. The JCS was created in January 1942 to fight a global conflict and facilitate wartime planning and coordination with the British. The heads of the Army, Navy, and Army Air Forces made up the JCS; President Roosevelt's representative, ADM William Leahy, guided this body that consisted of GEN George Marshall, ADM Ernest King, and GEN Henry "Hap" Arnold representing the three services, respectively. Without a formal charter and reporting directly to the President, their broad national security strategy formulation and liaison powers were immense. However, this early JCS never became a fully functioning staff; it was a committee of coequal service chiefs.

The 1947 National Security Act provided the statutory birth of the JCS under the direction, authority, and control of a secretary of defense. It also codified JCS duties to corporately advise the President, SECDEF, and National Security Council (NSC). Service disagreements over roles,

The Joint Chiefs meet over lunch, 1943. *Official U.S. Navy photo, now in the collections of the National Archives*

missions, and the allocation of funds at the start of the Cold War with the Soviet Union, led Congress to create the position of CJCS. In 1949, GEN Omar Bradley became the first chairman. Without service responsibilities and with the prestige of being the nation's senior military officer, the CJCS coordinated JCS activities, attempted to minimize interservice rivalry, and enabled JCS corporate military advice. Law, executive action, and practice continued to expand the CJCS's role. During this time, the CJCS regularly attended NSC meetings and became the de facto spokesman for the armed forces. Yet the CJCS remained merely the first among JCS equals, and the inefficiencies of generating service chief consensus to provide military advice remained a concern.

The 1986 Goldwater-Nichols Department of Defense Reorganization Act attempted to address that concern and others by greatly expanding the CJCS's role and responsibilities. Goldwater-Nichols defined the CJCS role as the principal military advisor to the President, SECDEF, and NSC. It also strengthened the CJCS's role in the national security policy-strategy formulation structure. To support the CJCS's new authorities, the Joint Staff became the Chairman's staff. It bears noting that, in a profession where command and authorities matter and in an environment like Washington, DC, where the ability to budget and fund often determine relative power, the chairman possesses little of either. Rather, a chairman's ultimate success depends on conceptual competency and interpersonal skills. As an action officer (AO), you will help expand and deepen what the Chairman needs to be successful by thinking, leading, communicating, and building the relationships necessary to keep the nation, in the words of President Harry Truman, "free from coercion."

JOINT STAFF FUNCTIONS

The Joint Chiefs of Staff consists of the Chairman of the Joint Chiefs; Vice Chairman of the Joint Chiefs (VCJCS); Chief of Staff, U.S. Army (CSA); Chief of Naval Operations; Chief of Staff, U.S. Air Force (CSAF); Commandant of the U.S. Marine Corps; and Chief of the National Guard Bureau (CNGB). The CJCS may also invite the Commandant of the U.S. Coast Guard to participate in meetings and discuss matters of mutual interest.

While the CJCS is the principal military advisor to the President, National Security Council (NSC), Homeland Security Council (HSC), and SECDEF, the other members of the JCS are also military advisors and may submit to the CJCS advice or opinions that diverge with the Chairman's view. When providing advice, it is the Chairman's responsibility to provide the JSC's consensus view together with any alternative perspectives. The advice-giving capacity of the service chiefs and CNGB takes precedence over all of their other duties. Notably, after informing the SECDEF, a member of the JCS may provide recommendations to Congress.

The Joint Staff (JS) supports the JCS and constitutes the immediate military staff of the SECDEF. Under the exclusive authority, direction, and control of the chairman, the JS assists the CJCS and JCS carry out their responsibilities. Proportional numbers from the Army, Navy, Air Force, Marine Corps, and Coast Guard comprise the Joint Staff. The interservice makeup of the JS facilitates coordination among the services and combatant command (CCMD) staffs. Joint Staff activities are functionally aligned to J-coded staff sections (e.g., J-3: Operations Directorate). Like the other staffs housed in the Pentagon, the size, organization, and functioning of the JS often reflect the personality of the CJCS who leads and manages it. By law, the CJCS cannot command forces nor can the Joint Staff operate or organize as an overall armed forces general staff.

THE CHAIRMAN OF THE JOINT CHIEFS OF STAFF (CJCS)

The President of the United States, with the consent of the Senate, appoints the CJCS for a four-year term. An officer generally cannot serve as both chairman and vice chairman if the length of combined service exceeds six years, though the President can seek an exception for up to eight years if it is deemed in the national interest. There is no limit to the number of reappointments in a time of war.

Like the JCS and Joint Staff, the chairman's specific roles and responsibilities have grown over time. Concurrently, the CJCS's role waxes and wanes as a function of the domestic and international context and the personalities of the President, SECDEF, and CJCS. While a principal military advisor, the CJCS is subject to the authority, direction, and control of the President and the SECDEF. Informally, CJCS and Joint Staff serve five broad roles. The functions overlap, and there are specific documents that correspond to many of these functions. Broadly, the chairman, supported by the Joint Staff, must

Advise—convey formal counsel to the President, SECDEF and NSC:

- Consult with and seek advice from the JCS and combatant commanders (CCDRs)
- Evaluate the strategic environment
- Recommend requirement priorities, programs, and budget proposals
- Participate in National Security Council meetings

Assess—across missions, domains, functions, and time:

- Readiness through the Chairman's Readiness System (CRS)
- Risk of executing the National Military Strategy (NMS) through the Chairman's Risk Assessment (CRA)
- Sufficiency through the Capabilities Gap Assessment (CGA)
- Validate military requirements through the Joint Requirement Oversight Council (JROC)
- Joint Military Requirements through the Chairman's Program Recommendation (CPR)
- Budget and Chairman's Program Assessment (CPA)

Direct—transmit presidential and SECDEF guidance:

- Strategic direction through the NMS and guidance to the joint force (JF)
- Strategic planning through the Joint Strategic Capabilities Plan (JSCP) and Joint Staff Planning System (JSPS)

CCDR VS. CCMD VS. COCOM

These acronyms are often confused and misused. Functional and geographic combatant commanders are also referred to as CCDRs. They are responsible for combatant commands. The authority they uniquely wield over assigned forces is combatant command (COCOM), which sits at the height of command authorities that includes operational control (OPCON), tactical control (TACON), and administrative control (ADCON). The confusion on this issue stems from informal use, such as when CCDRs call themselves COCOMs. *They are not authorities.* While one could argue, "If we are all wrong, we are all right," that is not the standard. Moreover, as national security professionals, we should use properly the language of our profession and more fundamentally, we should understand that words are powerful—so be precise.

- Joint doctrine, training, and education
- Exclusive direction of the Joint Staff

Execute—implement presidential and SECDEF guidance:

- Oversee and manage the Adaptive Planning and Execution (APEX) system
- Operate the National Military Command Center (NMCC)
- Produce execution orders (EXORDS)
- Produce planning orders (PLANORDS)
- Other matters as directed by the President

Communicate—share or exchange information and ideas:

- Facilitate communications between the National Command Authority (NCA) and combatant commands
- Share the armed forces' story

From this panoply of functions, you can garner that the CJCS uniquely stands at the nexus of a study in tension between service chiefs and CCDRs. Chiefs are primarily responsible for organizing, manning, training, and equipping their respective component of the armed forces. They build readiness, own the risk to the force, and are force providers for CCDRs. Conversely, geographic and functional CCDRs are predominantly joint-focused; they are responsible for planning and accomplishing specific missions either globally or in specific geographic areas of responsibility (AORs). They manage readiness and own the risk to the mission. The CJCS has one foot in both worlds—critical perspectives that inform and enable "best military advice."

JOINT STAFF ORGANIZATION AND TITLES

The Joint Staff's organization is constantly evolving in response to crisis, opportunities, and direction from the SECDEF, Congress, and the CJCS. The form and function of JS directorates and personnel assigned to them also changes with each new JS refinement. Likewise, the number of JS personnel fluctuates: at the tail end of the Cold War, the staff size numbered around 1,600. In 2002, in response to call for staff size reductions, that number dropped to around 1,100. Later, with the disbanding of Joint Forces Command (JFCOM) in 2011, the JS subsumed many of those uniformed and civilian employees, and the staff swelled to more than 2,300.

The CJCS approved your selection to serve on the Joint Staff. Your assignment is probably to a specific standard joint duty assignment list (S-JDAL) billet; however, while assigned to a specific billet, there is no guarantee that you will remain there. Personnel move throughout the Joint Staff all the time. You may start in your JDAL assigned billet, but the needs of the JS may dictate that you move to another office or directorate; for example, you may become an aide, an executive officer, or a member of the Chairman's Action Group (CAG).

The Joint Staff uses unified command, functional J-codes to organize its activities. Generally, three-star general officers/flag officers (GO/FOs) lead the Joint Staff Directorates (J-Dirs). There are exceptions to this rule; for example, a one-star leads the J-1 and a two-star runs the J-2. Additionally, each J-Dir has a civilian, flag-level senior executive service (SES) deputy that provides continuity to that directorate. Beneath the J-Dirs are two-digit deputy directorates (DDs) that tend to be led by a one-star GO/FO. In turn, DDs subdivide their responsibilities to divisions and branches led by O-6s. J-Dirs perform the majority of the Joint Staff's tasks and missions, and most AOs fill billets within them.

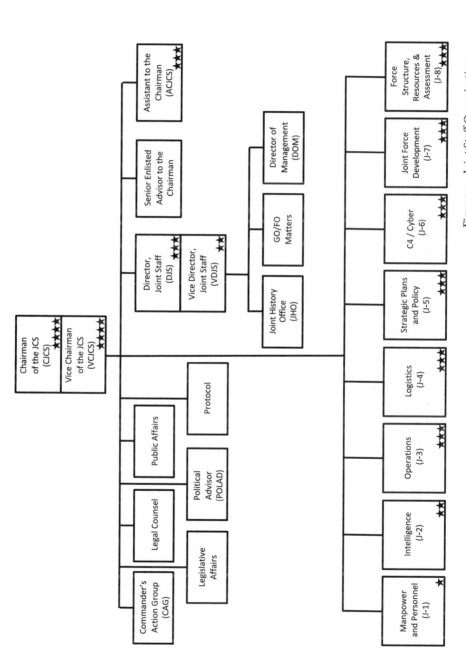

Figure 5-1. Joint Staff Organization

JOINT STAFF PRINCIPAL OFFICERS

The senior leadership of the JS is called the "Top 5." These include the CJCS, the VCJCS, the Assistant to the Chairman of the Joint Chiefs of Staff (ACJCS), the Director of the Joint Staff (DJS), and the Vice Director of the Joint Staff (VDJS).

VICE CHAIRMAN OF THE JOINT CHIEFS OF STAFF (VCJCS)

The Goldwater-Nichols DOD Reorganization Act of 1986 created the position of VCJCS as the second highest-ranking member of the armed forces. Appointed by the President, the VCJCS serves as the acting chairman during the absence or disability of the CJCS. The VCJCS serves as a trusted CJCS advisor and confidant. In particular, the VCJCS is a member of the NCS Deputies Committee and can represent the Chairman at NCS principals meetings. The VCJCS chairs the JROC; he or she also serves as the Vice Chairman for the Defense Acquisition Board (DAB), and is a member of the Senior Readiness Oversight Council (SROC).

ASSISTANT TO THE CHAIRMAN OF THE JOINT CHIEFS OF STAFF (ACJCS)

The ACJCS, a three-star GO/FO and CJCS advisor, is a liaison to external governmental agencies. The ACJCS's particular focus is on international relations, politico-military concerns, and homeland security matters, and he or she represents the CJCS and VCJCS at all levels within interagency forums.

DIRECTOR JOINT STAFF (DJS)

The three-star DJS serves as the de facto Joint Staff chief of staff. In this capacity, the director supervises, coordinates, supports, and administers JS work and guides specialized JCS activities. The DJS oversees the Joint Staff Inspector General, general officer/flag officer matters, and Joint Staff history offices. Additionally, the DJS chairs a body known as the Operations Deputies of the Joint Chiefs of Staff (OPSDEPs). The OPSDEPs are service, three-star chiefs of operations who meet periodically to consider issues best resolved in a joint council. They also screen issues to ensure the Joint Chiefs' time is spent effectively.

VICE DIRECTOR JOINT STAFF (VDJS)

The VDJS is typically a two-star GO/FO who works for the DJS and oversees both JS daily operations and the Director of Management (DOM)—the JS administrative support directorate. Additionally, the VDJS chairs a group known as the Deputy Operations Deputies, JCS (DEPOPSDEPs). These two-star service directors of plans meet to consider issues of importance that must be settled or forwarded to the OPSDEPs.

SENIOR ENLISTED ADVISOR TO THE CHAIRMAN OF THE JCS (SEAC)

On October 1, 2005, CSM William J. ("Joe") Gainey became the first senior enlisted advisor to the Chairman of the Joint Chiefs of Staff (SEAC). GEN Richard Myers established the position of the SEAC. The SEAC advises the SECDEF and CJCS on all enlisted matters involving joint and combined total force integration, utilization, health of the force, and joint development. Appointed by the CJCS, the SEAC is the senior noncommissioned officer (NCO) in the U.S. armed forces and serves term(s) consistent with the Chairman's tenure.

JOINT STAFF ORGANIZATIONS AND DIRECTORATES

As stated earlier, the Joint Staff evolves with law, practice, and principal personalities. The specific designations of the following organizations may change; however, the enduring role of the CJCS and JS demands that the following organizational functions will remain relatively unchanged and the broad descriptions of their roles constant. The following descriptions provide a snapshot of these J-Dirs and deputy directorate roles.

OFFICE OF THE CJCS

The "front office" that provides specialized support to the CJCS—including public affairs, protocol, legal counsel, legislative affairs, communications, history, and staff surgeon. Additionally, there are a bevy of subject matter experts that advise the CJCS. While the number and nature of these individuals can change, there is normally a foreign policy and scientific advisor. The Chairman's Action Group—established by GEN Peter Pace in 2006 as a "council of colonels" representing each service provides a think tank–like capability that informs and advances the chairman's thinking—is also part of this collection of offices.

DIRECTORATE OF MANAGEMENT (DOM)

The VDJS oversees the offices of the military secretariat, JS comptroller, the Joint Staff's support services, and JS security. Collectively, the two hundred DOM employees assist the chairman by managing, planning, and directing administrative services that include budget and finance, action management and archiving, records and research management, security, and all aspects of staff and information security.

J-1 MANPOWER AND PERSONNEL DIRECTORATE

A one-star GO/FO oversees the J-1 and works with service detailers, personnel specialists, and J-Dirs to coordinate and fill JS assignments. Functions within this directorate include joint personnel readiness, manpower management, policy guidance, personnel programs, and joint specialty officer (JSO) career guidance (GO/FO personnel issues are handled separately). The J-1 divisions include personnel readiness; human capital; and military, and civilian and reserve programs. Additionally, the Joint Staff chaplain resides in the J-1 and advises the CJCS on religious affairs.

J-2 INTELLIGENCE DIRECTORATE

The J-2 is the primary Defense Intelligence Agency (DIA) office to deliver direct, all-source intelligence support to the SECDEF and CJCS. J-2 also supports CCMDs and advocates for their intelligence requirements. The J-2 coordinates, integrates, and synchronizes the intelligence planning activities of combat support agencies (CSAs), services, and other defense intelligence enterprise organizations. Additionally, the J-2 coordinates and develops joint intelligence doctrine and architecture. Finally, the J-2 operates the intelligence watch teams' component of the National Joint Operations and Intelligence Center (NJOIC) as part of the NMCC to provide global situational awareness and warning. A two-star GO/FO guides this directorate and oversees six deputy directors.

National Joint Operations and Intelligence Center (NJOIC). During the 2008 Russian invasion of Georgia, ADM Michael Mullen sought to maintain situational awareness of the fast-moving crisis and help inform the military advice he was providing to senior leaders throughout the government. The NJOIC was created and exists today as part of the NMCC. At various times in response to emergent events, the Joint Staff will stand up ad hoc organizations to mirror the NJOIC's original construct. This is both an opportunity and a curse: maintaining situational awareness of a developing crisis is the opportunity; however, J-Dirs must supply the AOs to staff these temporary teams, yet still retain their day-to-day work load (the curse). Ad hoc organizations can live for days, months, or more. In each instance, it serves as an inflection point for the JS to evaluate its organizational construct to best support the CJCS, the JCS, and Joint Staff missions.

J-3 OPERATIONS DIRECTORATE

The J-3 provides guidance to CCMDs and relaying communications between the President, SECDEF, CJCS, and CCDRs regarding current operations and plans, thus aiding the chairman as he advises, directs, executes, and communicates. The J-3 is a large directorate, led by a three-star GO/FO who oversees a Vice Director (VDJ-3), a Deputy (DDJ-3), and six DDs. The DJ-3 and VDJ-3 serve as CJCS points of contact for a near-real-time picture of operations and current plans. They also represent CCDRs' views to the CJCS and SECDEF. The J-3 serves as the lead agent for developing and executing the global force management (GFM) process to align force allocation, assignment, and apportionment between the services and CCMDs.

J-32 Deputy Director for Intelligence, Surveillance, Reconnaissance Operations. The J-32 provides the SECDEF and CJCS expertise on DOD airborne and maritime intelligence, surveillance, and reconnaissance (ISR) platforms/sensors. They provide oversight for the allocation and deployment of DOD airborne and maritime surface/subsurface collection platforms in support of the CCMDs and National Command Authority. They monitor the status of DOD ISR platforms, sensors, and associated processing and exploitation systems.

J-33 Deputy Director for Nuclear, Homeland Defense, and Current Operations. The J-33 enables command and control (C2) at the highest levels of national security, regardless of circumstance. They manage the policy, planning, and operations of the National Military Command System (NMCS) and enable the CJCS's continuity of operations. The J-33 provides for global national and nuclear C2 policy and procedures and manages the security and reliability of the nuclear stockpile. They provide policy, planning, and operations oversight for protection of DOD's critical infrastructure. An element of the J-33 supports the CJCS in planning, coordinating, and monitoring homeland defense (HD), theater security cooperation, and defense support to civilian authorities. Part of J-33's broad tasks includes managing the worldwide global command and control system that supports situational awareness and deployment planning, employment, and redeployment processes. It accomplishes this role in part through the NMCC.

DD for Operations: National Military Command Center (NMCC). J-3 operations teams (OTs) provide the NMCC expertise to ensure worldwide monitoring, crisis response, and strategic watch. Five OTs staff the NMCC on a revolving 24/7/365 around-the-clock schedule; an NMCC OT is usually the first organization alerted to a crisis outbreak. A one-star deputy director of operations (DDO) supervises each OT. The DDO oversees the immediate crisis response and interfaces with the interagency to ensure continuity of operations (COOP) and continuity of government (COG). As an AO, you may be assigned to work in the NMCC, a responsibility comes with an extensive amount of training. Once assigned to an OT, you will work on a rotating shift schedule including weekends and holidays; however, the nature of the mission generates minimal take-home work and provides a dependable schedule.

J-35 Deputy Director for Regional Operations and Force Management. In broad terms, the J-35 monitors and responds to potential crisis situations. Working with CCMDs, they help prepare military options for presidential/ SECDEF consideration. The J-35 leads the GFM policy and process. Specifically, they identify and recommend the most appropriate and responsive force or capability to meet CCDR requirements. Functionally, they help the CJCS execute by processing EXORDS and deployment orders (DEPORDS) for the movement of forces to support CCDR requirements as approved by the President or SECDEF. In conjunction with the JS J-5 and CCMDs, the J-35 reviews existing military plans. This team also provides DOD leadership with joint force readiness evaluations and insights on near-term strategic risk.

J-37 Deputy Director for Special Operations and Counter Terrorism. The J-37 advises the J-3 and CJCS on all special operations, counterterrorism, and worldwide detainee matters.

J-39 Deputy Director for Global Operations. The J-39 advises the CJCS on information operations (IO), special technical operations (STO), sensitive DOD support to/from non-DOD government agencies, military information support operations (MISO), offensive and defensive computer operations, counter proliferation, and unified collection strategies.

J-4 LOGISTICS DIRECTORATE
The J-4 assists joint force commanders (JFCs) in generating and sustaining force employment across a range of military operations. This mission includes engineering, mobilization, and medical responsibilities. The J-4 leads the Joint Logistics Enterprise (JLEnt) by developing and integrating joint logistics capabilities and crafting joint logistics doctrine. This team oversees joint logistics readiness and mans the Joint Logistics Operations Center (JLOC) that monitors and reports logistical aspects of current and future operations. The J-4 divides work among two DDs and a vice

director of the Joint Staff surgeon, a special staff officer who advises the Chairman on medical issues.

J-5 STRATEGIC PLANS AND POLICY DIRECTORATE

The Joint Staff J-5 proposes strategies, plans, and policy recommendations to the CJCS. It is a large directorate whose vast responsibilities drive regular JS organizational change and alignment. A three-star GO/FO serves as the J-Dir. A Vice Director and multiple DDs are also GO/FOs.

Specifically, the J-5 develops recommendations on strategy, strategic concepts, required military capabilities, and politico-military matters. It prepares, in collaboration with the rest of the JS, joint strategic plans and documents, strategic studies, and staff work on current and future military strategy and policy. This office reviews and comments on the National Security Strategy (NSS), the National Defense Strategy (NDS), the Global Employment of the Force (GEF), and those JS planning system documents assigned to it. The J-5 prepares the CJCS's National Military Strategy (NMS), a biennial comprehensive review, and the annual Chairman's Risk Assessment that examines the military's ability to execute the NMS.

Transregional Threat Coordination Cell. The Transregional Threat Coordination Cell assists in the development and coordination of policy, strategy, and plans for the war on terrorism. In conjunction with the Office of the Secretary of Defense (OSD), it facilitates coordination between CCMDs, the NSC staff, and other federal agencies. It includes elements that develop strategy to counter and eliminate the ideological base of extremism.

DD for Global Policy and Partnerships. A broad portfolio that includes acting as the JS point of contact for all policy aspects of security assistance and experts on stability operations. This team also provides analysis and recommendations on policies relating to U.S. arms control, and counter-proliferation and nonproliferation of weapons of mass destruction (WMD).

DD for Politico-Military Affairs. "Pol-mil" DDs are divided region-ally and represent Asia, Europe/NATO/Russia/Africa, the Middle East, and the Western Hemisphere. Focused on geographical areas, they work with CCMDs and prepare recommended positions regarding U.S. policy and politico-military matters relating to individual countries, regional organizations, and international organizations.

DD for Strategic Planning. A forward-looking office that produces many of the national security documents required by law of the CJCS. It also formulates and recommends national space and missile, nuclear weapon, and biological and chemical weapons policy.

J-6 COMMAND, CONTROL, COMMUNICATIONS, AND COMPUTERS/CYBER DIRECTORATE

The J-6's current construct was established in 2012 to guide joint force command, control, communications, and computer (C4)/cyber capabilities. It helps develop C4/cyber capabilities to deliver a sustained information advantage, enable decision and action at the speed of the problem.

The J-6 is composed of four DDs. One advises the CJCS regarding joint C2 requirements, which includes the interoperability of legacy and future C2 capabilities, ISR, joint close air support, and combat identification mission areas. Another division handles all positioning, navigation, and timing (PNT) capabilities for joint/coalition operations, and develops doctrine and policies for terrestrial, surface, aerial, and space PNT systems. A third division secures the JS enterprise networks to ensure that information is secure, accurate, and relevant. A fourth DD keeps the JS information systems configured, responsive, and running.

J-7 JOINT FORCE DEVELOPMENT DIRECTORATE

Led by a three-star GO/FO, the J-7 synchronizes joint training, doctrine, concept development, education, lessons learned, and experimentation. Two vice directors—one of whom is permanently assigned to the J-7 facility in Suffolk, Virginia, former home of the Joint Forces Command from which the JS J-7 assumed much of its portfolio—and four GO/FO-led DDs compose this directorate. They develop and deliver officer and enlisted joint professional military education (JPME). Additionally, they are responsible for senior leader education via the CAPSTONE, KEYSTONE, and PINNACLE programs.

Additionally, the J-7 team manages and oversees the joint doctrine development process, which creates new joint concepts to improve future joint force effectiveness. The J-7 also collects, analyzes, and disseminates joint lessons and best practices to institutionalize them across the DOD. Working with the J-5 and OSD, an element within J-7 ensures force development implications are carried into strategic level processes and documents. Finally, an element of the J-7 focuses on JF readiness to execute irregular warfare tasks and meet emerging threats.

J-8 FORCE STRUCTURE, RESOURCES, AND ASSESSMENT DIRECTORATE

The J-8 develops capabilities, conducts studies, analysis, and assessments, and evaluates plans, programs, and strategies for the CJCS. The Director of J-8 (DJ-8) serves as the JROC secretary and Joint Capabilities Board (JCB) chairman. Both roles testify to the J-8's principal role orchestrating the capabilities development process through the Joint Capabilities Integration and Development System (JCIDS) and the Functional Capabilities Board (FCB). Four GO/FOs serve as DDs for the following divisions: Requirements; Resources and Acquisition; Simulations and Analysis; and Force Protection.

DD for Requirements. The DD for Requirements orchestrates the JCIDS process, coordinates FCBs, validates urgent and rapid acquisition requirements, and conducts CGAs. Through these processes, CCDRs and services identify and develop material and nonmaterial solutions (material solutions include those that necessitate a new system or technology; nonmaterial solutions include changes in doctrine, organization, training, matériel, leadership and education, personnel, and facilities [DOTMLPF]). This group resolves cross-service requirements issues, ensures interoperability, and promotes economies of scale. These processes also assist the chairman in assessing the priority of joint military requirements and acquisition programs to meet the NMS, and they inform SECDEF's budgetary recommendations to the services through the CPR.

DD for Resources and Acquisition. This officer oversees the programming and budgeting process and aids the CJCS in assessing strategy, CCDR activities, and service acquisition programs. Many service AOs working on acquisition programs interact with this DD's Program and Budget Analysis Division (PBAD).

DD for Simulations and Analysis. The DD for Simulations and Analysis conducts joint, bilateral, and multilateral wargames and simulations. It also maintains and improves the models and techniques used by the JS and CCMDs to conduct studies and analysis. These efforts consider the challenges and opportunities in the current and future national security environments to shape future force sizing constructs and identify existing or potential capability gaps.

DD for Force Protection. The DD for Force Protection evaluates, assesses, and develops joint operational concepts and capabilities related to chemical, biological, radiological and nuclear (CBRN) defense and protecting the force and critical infrastructure. He or she also identifies, reviews, and develops air and missile defense requirements and interoperability through the Joint Integrated Air and Missile Defense Organization (JIAMDO).

JOINT STAFF RELATIONSHIP TO THE OFFICE OF THE SECRETARY OF DEFENSE

OSD helps the SECDEF plan, advise, and carry out the nation's security policies as directed by both the SECDEF and POTUS. Essentially, OSD has four main managerial focus areas: ideas (policy), money (finance), people (force readiness), and material (purchasing). These wide-ranging mission areas have abundant and clear linkages to Joint Staff efforts. They drive constant, deep, and professional collaboration between the SECDEF, CJCS, and their staffs.

This cooperation is statutorily directed: "All elements of the JCS shall cooperate fully and effectively with appropriate offices of the OSD." This pre–Goldwater-Nichols Act language captures the urgency and need for cooperation, coordination, and collaboration between the Joint Staff and OSD. Likewise, Joint Staff J-Dirs are directed to maintain active liaisons with appropriate OSD leaders. Similar direction is provided to the heads of OSD offices. These mutually beneficial liaisons facilitate the sharing of information, technical advice, and guidance.

WORKING ON THE JOINT STAFF

WORKFORCE COMPOSITION
The Joint Staff is composed of active- and reserve-duty military members, government civilians, and contractors. The military members of the Joint Staff tend to be field grade (O-4 and above, though most are O-5s and O-6s). In this sense, it is a senior staff. This is not to say that there are no junior officers on the JS, there are, but their numbers are few and their duties vary from aides to subject matter experts (SMEs). Additionally, there are educational fellows "stashed" throughout the JS gaining insights and experience. Enlisted military members also serve on the JS, though they tend to be senior and are usually technical experts.

Government civilians provide the continuity of the Joint Staff. The most senior are members of the senior executive service (SES), civilians with GO/FO rank equivalent who should be accorded proper respect. On the JS, SESs serve as J-Dir deputies and DDs. Like the government services/general schedule (GS) civilians, they provide corporate knowledge and long-term perspectives that balance the two- to three-year outlooks of rotational military members. Civilians also provide administrative support and subject matter expertise of the formal processes, models, and applications necessary to support the JS mission. Additionally, there are contractors who usually provide technical expertise or fulfill specific needs for notionally shorter periods of time. While many contractor functions are enduring, more frequent turnover is commonplace as different companies bid on those positions as the contracts expire.

You may find yourself working for an SES or GS civilian, for a military officer, or leading them. Regardless, everything you already know about professionalism, good work ethics, and effective leadership applies. However, it may be novel to you to oversee contract civilians. First, talk to your leadership to learn from their experience. Second, look at the statement or scope of work (SOW) in their contract. The scope of work explains what they are contractually obligated to perform and should accurately reflect what the government requires. A good SOW should specify in detail the expected quantity and quality of work and the delivery schedule—that is, when the work is to be performed. The SOW provides some boundaries as to how, when, and what contractors can be asked to do. Understanding those boundaries will help you and them be successful. Finally, if you have questions, talk to them. As technical experts, they are professionals, too. They can provide you valuable insights into the limits and flexibility of their assignments.

THE JOINT STAFF ACTION PROCESS (JSAP)

Work flows through the JS via the Joint Staff Action Process (JSAP), and understanding this system is one of an action officer's prime responsibilities. This formal coordination process—spanning CCMDs, the services, and CSAs with equities in the JSAP topic—ensures staffing effectiveness, transparency, input, and a detailed record of the action taken. The coordination process identifies critical issues and presents them to leadership for direct decisions.

As an AO, you will conduct research and develop responses that, in many cases, are CJCS positions on national security issues. Actions vary widely in importance, but all must reflect the best possible military advice or guidance. You will build JSAP packages, provide input, or comment on others' JSAPs (depending on the issue). Based on tasks from the Joint Staff or CCMDs, JSAPs may require you to prepare executive summaries, letters, memoranda, information papers, or decision papers.

As an AO assigned a JSAP, always look at the suspense date to assess the urgency with which you must prioritize that JSAP's issue. Ultimately, you must balance the objective of producing the "the perfect action" against the need to complete work promptly. Your responsibility for the action continues until the final decision has been made and implemented documents dispatched.

Upon checking into the JS, you will get some formal education about the JS and its processes to include handling JSAPs. Depending on your billet, you will become more or less familiar with them throughout your time on the JS. If you are required to build a JSAP package, read pertinent instructions and ask people who have compiled them before to help you grind through the process.

JOINT QUALIFIED OFFICER REQUIREMENTS

DOD policy directs that officers be educated, trained, and experienced in joint matters to enhance the joint warfighting capability of the United States. The Joint Qualification System (JQS) provides a path for active and reserve officers to earn joint qualification on the completion of requisite joint professional military education and a full tour of duty in a joint assignment. JQS is a points-based system that accounts for the intensity of each joint activity that ultimately identifies you as being proficient in joint matters. Four levels of joint qualification recognize the accumulation of joint knowledge, skills, and abilities throughout a career. Depending on your service and the billet to which you are assigned, joint credit requires either two or three years' service in a JDAL billet unless your service requests a waiver. Approved waivers require a minimum of twenty-two months of service in a JDAL billet to receive joint credit. Importantly, not every billet at joint command is "coded" for joint credit so work closely with your detailer, personnel specialist, and/or office to verify.

OFFICE OF THE JOINT CHIEFS OF STAFF IDENTIFICATION BADGE

Your nomination to work on the Joint Staff means that you are considered to be one of your service's most outstanding members. However, do not expect to be issued a joint officer purple leisure suit! Daily, you will wear your service equivalent uniform. To identify you as a member of the JS, you will be presented an Office of the Joint Chiefs of Staff identification badge during check-in. This temporary badge will be authorized for permanent wear on your uniform once your Joint Staff service exceeds one year for active duty or two years as a reservist.

CONCLUSION

The greatest myth uttered by any Joint Staff AO working some issue—grand or obscure—is, "If I could only get five minutes of the CJCS's time, I would know how to think about this issue and where it should go." The bottom line is that the Chairman and Joint Staff principals have most likely not thought about your issue. That is why they have you! The time to think is now. It has been said, "In times of crisis, we must rely on thinking that we have already done." Think critically, share, refine, and think anew in preparation for the moment the Chairman, the joint force, and the nation needs it. And take heart, your challenge is not new.

The United States' founders created an Army and a Navy. Ever since, there has been a need for growing degrees of deconfliction, coordination, integration, synchronization, and interdependence. The addition of an Air Force, an independently represented Marine Corps and Coast Guard, and increasingly vital interaction with interagency and intelligence community partners have heightened that need. Combined with a global presence and mission set and a vast interagency that works with other instruments of national power, the need for a JCS, CJCS, and Joint Staff has grown. In your time on the Joint Staff, you will contribute to informing and advancing the ability of the JCS to provide the best military advice to our civilian leadership. Moreover, you will enhance the capability, capacity, effectiveness, and efficiency of the joint force to engage and respond to today's and tomorrow's threats and opportunities. Your joint skills and knowledge will grow. You will build lifelong relationships with fellow members of the profession of arms. You will prepare yourself for your next assignment at the highest levels and along the way, sew your story into the fabric of the Joint Staff. Go get 'em!

FURTHER READING

DOD Directive 5100.1 Function of the Department of Defense and Its Major Components.

DOD Directive 5158.1 Organization of the Joint Chiefs of Staff and Relationships with the Office of the Secretary of Defense.

Joint History Office. *The Chairmanship of the Joint Chiefs of Staff 1949–2012* (Washington, DC: 2012). http://www.jcs.mil/Portals/36/Doucments/chairman-shipjcs49_12.pdf.

JSM 5100.01E Organization and Functions of the Joint Staff.

Locher, James, III. *Victory on the Potomac: The Goldwater-Nichols Act Unifies the Pentagon* (College Station: Texas A&M University Press, 2002).

Rearden, Steven L. *Council of War: A History of the Joint Chiefs of Staff 1942–1991* (Washington, DC: NDU Press, 2012). http://www.detic.mil/doctrine/history/councilofwar.pdf.
Title 10 United States Code (10 U.S.C. 5 Sections 151-155).

Col Doug Douds, USMC (Ret.), is a U.S. Army War College faculty member teaching the Advanced Strategic Art Program seminar. An F/A-18 pilot, he commanded a squadron in Iraq prior to serving as a strategist and senior speechwriter to the Chairman of the Joint Chiefs of Staff. He is currently working on his PhD in military history. He is an avid historian and a licensed Gettysburg battlefield guide and enjoys leading educational tours of Civil War battlefields.

6

THE OFFICE OF THE SECRETARY OF DEFENSE

CAPT THANE CLARE, USN

Since 1947, the presidentially appointed, Senate-confirmed Secretary of Defense has been charged by law to serve as "the principal assistant to the President in all matters relating to the Department of Defense." The SECDEF is the nexus between the armed forces and the policies, decisions, and statutes that govern their activities. The Secretary of Defense provides his or her best advice to the President and ensures that the President's orders are executed faithfully and in keeping with the law.

Advising the President on weighty matters of defense strategy and planning, working with Congress, directing the armed forces in war, and steering a department that encompasses four services and nearly three million active-duty, guard, reserve, and civilian personnel is a job of such breathtaking scope and responsibility that defense scholar Charles A. Stevenson has dubbed it "nearly impossible." Indeed, as former Secretary of Defense James Schlesinger noted, "the list of secretarial responsibilities is so imposing that no single individual can totally fill them all." Every SECDEF therefore needs a strong team to assist in the execution of his or her duties. This chapter describes the history, purpose, and structure of that team: the Office of the Secretary of Defense as of mid-2018, while making note of several ongoing and anticipated organizational changes specified in the National Defense Authorization Acts (NDAAs).

BRIEF HISTORY OF THE OFFICE OF THE SECRETARY OF DEFENSE

As the United States and its allies fought their way to victory in World War II, two Presidents, Franklin D. Roosevelt and Harry S. Truman, relied on a team of trusted advisors to help them execute their responsibilities as Commanders in Chief. It is a testimony to the wartime presidents' leadership that they could focus and distill the contributions of these extraordinarily capable (yet frequently contentious) subordinates into a common vision for U.S. and allied military strategy.

Following the Allied victory, the gathering storm clouds of the Cold War convinced President Truman that the United States would need a streamlined organization that reduced the presidential burden of adjudicating disagreements among military advisors. The experience of global war in World War II highlighted the challenges of mobilizing and integrating national resources, and in establishing command structures to marshal the efforts of a world-spanning military amid the services' competition for resources and influence. The United States could ill afford to ignore these hard-won lessons, particularly in an era when, to quote Defense Department historians Roger Trask and Alfred Goldberg, "The critical and revolutionary effect of nuclear weapons clearly indicated that control and policymaking must come from the highest government authority." Thus, in December 1945, President Truman called on Congress to consolidate the disparate elements of the national defense into a single department.

The result was the National Security Act of 1947, signed into law by President Truman on July 26 of that year. The act created a "National Military Establishment" in which the Department of the Army (formerly the Department of War), the Department of the Navy, and the newly created Department of the Air Force—along with the Joint Chiefs of Staff— were subordinated to a Secretary of Defense who would now serve as the President's principal advisor on all national security matters. (The act also created the National Security Council and the Central Intelligence Agency, and codified the role of the JCS into law as "the principal *military* advisers to the President and the Secretary of Defense.") Former Navy Secretary James V. Forrestal was appointed the nation's first Secretary of Defense.

Perhaps surprisingly, the National Security Act of 1947 did not yet establish a single "Department of Defense" in its own right. Instead, the Secretary of Defense was charged only with "general direction, authority, and control" over the armed forces, without meaningfully abridging the service secretaries' prerogatives within their own departments. The Office of the Secretary of Defense had correspondingly humble beginnings. The act allowed for only three special assistants to the secretary, and Forrestal's small staff consisted of just forty-five people he had brought with him from the Navy Department. Forrestal initially intended OSD to be primarily a policy-making group, with detailed management delegated to the services. However, this proved insufficient to the task of managing three powerful departments that often had competing purposes when it came to policy, planning, and procurement. At the same time, the three service secretaries were full members of the NSC, complicating SECDEF's ability to act as the principal voice in defense policy debates.

Against these powerful crosscurrents, OSD's modest size did little to help the secretary establish effective control over the armed forces. Forrestal therefore requested an amendment to the act, subsequently signed into law in 1949, which replaced the National Military Establishment with a full-fledged Department of Defense. The 1949 amendment solidified SECDEF's authority and control over the military by reducing the three service departments from cabinet-level to subordinate elements of DOD. It also strengthened OSD by establishing a deputy secretary of defense and several assistant secretaries, including a comptroller, through whom SECDEF could reinforce his control over the department-wide budget. Forrestal's successor, Louis A. Johnson, was the first secretary to serve under the amended National Security Act.

OSD continued to expand in subsequent years with President Dwight D. Eisenhower advocating forcefully for more centralization of power in OSD. This lobbying led Congress to enact legislation in 1953 and 1958 that further strengthened SECDEF's authority.

Secretary of Defense Robert McNamara (*right middle, with glasses*) meets with his assistant secretaries and the Joint Chiefs of Staff while Chief of Naval Operations ADM Arleigh Burke (*third from left wearing service dress blues*) speaks. *Naval History and Heritage Command*

The Defense Department and, by extension, the OSD continued to evolve over the years. Notably, the Goldwater-Nichols Act of 1986 catalyzed further organizational developments. For example, in addition to elevating military "jointness" to new levels, the legislation established OSD as a distinct entity rather than simply a collection of political appointees and their staffs subordinate to SECDEF. The SECDEF's responsibilities and authorities have also evolved, which has forced OSD to continue to adjust its size and structure to help support the secretary. This trend has been acutely observed recently as the demands of the Cold War gave way to the exigencies of the war on terrorism and today's reemergence of great power competition. To meet these security challenges, secretaries of defense have depended on the assistance of their OSD teams to help them carry out their "nearly impossible" duties.

PURPOSE OF OSD

The purpose of the Office of the Secretary of Defense (as established by law in Title 10 U.S. Code, Section 131) is "to assist the secretary of defense in carrying out the secretary's duties and responsibilities and to carry out such other duties as may be prescribed by law." The practical implications of this seemingly straightforward definition are best understood by first examining SECDEF's duties and then by observing how OSD fits into the overall organizational structure of the Department of Defense.

The secretary's duties can be divided into three broad categories. First, with the advice and assistance of the Chairman of the Joint Chiefs of Staff, he or she assists the President in carrying out the duties of Commander in Chief—that is, providing direction and guidance in the planning and execution of military operations, ranging from warfighting to rendering support to civil authorities in the event of a national disaster or other catastrophic event. Second, to ensure that DOD is best prepared for such operations, SECDEF provides policy and budgetary guidance to subordinate leaders in OSD and throughout the department. In line with overarching presidential policies, including the National Security Strategy, this guidance includes prioritization of military missions and delineation of expected resource levels on which to base planning and budgeting. Third, SECDEF is responsible for the smooth functioning of the entire department. Like the commanding officer of a ship or squadron, SECDEF is ultimately responsible for exercising "authority, direction, and control over the Department of Defense."

THE DEFENSE AGENCIES

Defense Advanced Research Projects Agency
Defense Commissary Agency
Defense Contract Audit Agency
Defense Contract Management Agency
Defense Finance and Accounting Service
Defense Health Agency
Defense Information Systems Agency
Defense Intelligence Agency
Defense Legal Services Agency
Defense Logistics Agency
Defense POW/MIA Accounting Agency
Defense Security Cooperation Agency
Defense Security Service
Defense Threat Reduction Agency
Missile Defense Agency
National Geospatial Intelligence Agency
National Reconnaissance Office
National Security Agency/Central Security Service
Pentagon Force Protection Agency
Space Development Agency

THE DEFENSE FIELD ACTIVITIES

Defense Media Activity
Defense Technical Information Center
Defense Technology Security Administration
DOD Education Activity
DOD Human Resources Activity
DOD Test Resource Management Center
Office of Economic Adjustment
Washington Headquarters Services

Having reviewed the daunting responsibilities of the Secretary of Defense, it is useful to briefly look at the organization that SECDEF leads. As set forth in Title 10, Section 111 and DOD Directive 5100.01, the major components of the Department of Defense are:

- The Office of the Secretary of Defense
- The Joint Chiefs of Staff
- The Joint Staff
- The Office of the DOD Inspector General
- The combatant commands
- The military departments
- The defense agencies and field activities (see inset)
- Such other offices, agencies, activities, and commands as may be established or designated by law or by the President

OSD is the critical node that links these components of DOD, and the "connective tissue" that translates the secretary's direction and guidance into action by the far-flung elements of the department. Though the Chairman of the Joint Chiefs of Staff, the combatant commanders, and the secretaries of the military departments report directly to the Secretary of Defense (meaning that no element of OSD has independent authority over them), in practice there is close and continuous coordination between OSD and these senior subordinates' staffs. Moreover, OSD also assists SECDEF in carrying out his or her outward- and upward-facing duties, such as working with the National Security Council, other parts of the U.S. government, foreign governments, and international organizations. Subordinate leaders within OSD also perform direct oversight of the defense agencies and DOD field activities.

THE STRUCTURE OF OSD

The top tiers of OSD are composed of civilian leaders appointed by the President and confirmed by the Senate. Indeed, while uniformed officers serve in OSD as action officers, military assistants, and (in rare instances, at the flag/general officer level, and generally in an "acting" capacity) as deputy assistant secretaries of defense, Title 10 specifically prohibits the Secretary of Defense from establishing a "military staff" within OSD—a deliberate injunction that reflects the foundational importance of civilian oversight of the U.S. military. Congress takes an active hand in directing the shape and structure of OSD, providing a minimum organizational

The Office of the Secretary of Defense has evolved markedly since its creation in the wake of World War II. Pictured here: former Secretary of Defense James Mattis (*left*) and the Chairman of the Joint Chiefs of Staff. *DOD photo by Lisa Ferdinando*

foundation on which SECDEF can build his or her team. Title 10 Section 131 sets out those organizational requirements (and, for interested readers, provides a fascinating glimpse of history in the form of a list of amendments detailing how OSD has evolved over the years). Figure 6-1 provides an overview of OSD's organizational structure (as of early 2019).

The senior member of OSD is the Deputy Secretary of Defense—DOD's second in command. Like any good executive officer (XO), DEPSECDEF ensures that DOD is operating effectively and efficiently to carry out the secretary's priorities, with a particular focus on management and business practices within the department. (In fact, Title 10 specifies that nominees for Deputy Secretary of Defense are to have "appropriate management experience.") More than simply a manager-in-chief, however, DEPSECDEF—as codified in law and DOD Directive 5100.01—"has full power and authority to act for the secretary of defense and to exercise the powers of the secretary of defense upon any and all matters concerning which the secretary of defense is authorized to act pursuant to law."

The senior leaders who report directly to SECDEF and DEPSECDEF are called principal staff assistants (PSA). By law and DOD instruction, the PSAs include the undersecretaries of defense and a range of other

Office of the Secretary of Defense

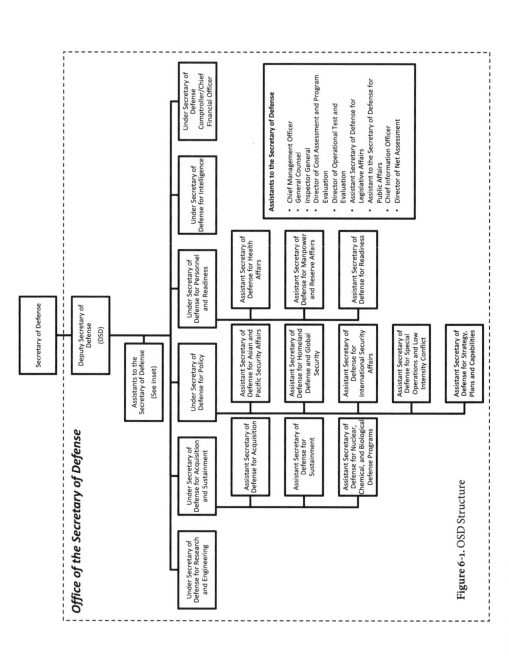

Figure 6-1. OSD Structure

assistants to the Secretary of Defense (such as the chief management officer and the general counsel; see inset "Assistants to the Secretary of Defense" in figure 6-1). The structure and titles may differ in other cabinet or individual military departments; however, OSD's secretariat hierarchy is generally as follows, in descending order: secretary; deputy secretary; undersecretary; assistant secretary; deputy assistant secretary.

The PSAs are responsible for advising the secretary on the formulation of policies, programs, and budgets for the implementation of national security objectives, and then ensuring that SECDEF's decisions are properly executed. Each PSA has a team of subordinate leaders and action officers who assist the principal in carrying out his or her duties. The composition of each team varies depending on the PSA and his or her particular portfolio and responsibilities. Each PSA has a "principal deputy"—for under secretaries, these are known as deputy undersecretaries of defense, or DUSDs (see inset)—and undersecretaries of defense also typically have a team of assistant secretaries of defense (ASDs), as shown in figure 6-1. Each ASD, in turn, has a principal deputy and a team of deputy assistant secretaries of defense (DASDs). Military officers detailed to OSD are typically assigned as military assistants to these leaders' front offices or executive secretariats, or as action officers working for a DASD or another OSD civilian leader of similar seniority.

OSD PRINCIPAL STAFF ASSISTANTS

Like the department heads and executive assistants within a Navy command (albeit holding the equivalent of a three- or four-star rank), the principal staff assistants provide advice to, and help execute the decisions of, their "CO"—the Secretary of Defense. As noted earlier in this chapter, the secretary's scope of responsibility is nothing short of breathtaking. Accordingly, each PSA shoulders a substantial load in helping to fulfill those heavy responsibilities. This section briefly describes each PSA's duties.

UNDERSECRETARIES OF DEFENSE

UNDERSECRETARY OF DEFENSE FOR ACQUISITION AND SUSTAINMENT
While each military department and various other elements of DOD enjoy broad latitude to develop, defend, and execute their procurement and sustainment priorities, Undersecretary of Defense for Acquisition and Sustainment (USD[A&S]) is responsible for preparing the overarching policies that govern technology acquisition and sustainment across the

DEPUTY UNDERSECRETARIES OF DEFENSE

Figure 6-1 lists no deputy undersecretaries of defense (DUSDs) distinct from the principal assistants to the USDs—which could be seen as an organizational oddity considering that OSD leadership titles generally mirror those in the Navy Secretariat, which features several DUSNs. Five DUSDs were initially established by law; however, by 2009 the total had reached twenty-eight, many created by secretarial fiat. As a result, the Senate Armed Services Committee expressed concern that "the proliferation of DUSDs at multiple levels of the organization could muddy lines of authority and may not be in the best interest of the Department of Defense." Indeed, as former DEPSECDEF William J. Lynn III conceded the evolution of DUSD positions over time had generated "inconsistencies and confusion with the perceived rank and stature of officials within OSD."

Consequently, Congress eliminated the DUSD position in FY 2010, and DOD responded by changing some DUSDs to chiefs of staff, renaming others as directors, and in some cases elevating DUSDs to assistant secretaries of defense. In the FY2018 NDAA, congress restored the title DUSD and bestowed it upon the principal deputies to each of the five USDs. These changes demonstrate that OSD is a continually evolving organization, congress wields the power to shape the executive branch, and what is old may become new again!

entire department. Established by the FY 2017 NDAA in a congressionally mandated reorganization of the former Office of the Undersecretary of Defense for Acquisition, Technology, and Logistics (USD[AT&L]), the USD(A&S) provides central direction and oversight to ensure that DOD material programs are aligned to SECDEF's strategic objectives. Assisting USD(A&S) in these efforts are and Assistant Secretary of Defense for Acquisition, an ASD for Sustainment, and an ASD for Nuclear, Chemical, and Biological Defense Programs.

A&S oversees the following defense agencies and DOD field activities on behalf of the secretary:

- Defense Contract Management Agency
- Defense Logistics Agency
- Defense Threat Reduction Agency
- Office of Economic Adjustment

UNDERSECRETARY OF DEFENSE FOR RESEARCH AND ENGINEERING

The FY 2017 NDAA directed DOD to split the office of USD(AT&L) into two separate organizations: USD(A&S), and an Undersecretary of Defense for Research and Engineering, or USD(R&E). The aim of this change was to "elevate the mission of advancing technology and innovation within the Department" and "foster distinct technology and acquisition cultures to better deliver superior capabilities" for an era of increasing worldwide military competition. The USD(R&E), in short, is to "drive innovation and accelerate the advancement of our warfighting capability," while the USD(A&S) is to "deliver proven technology into the hands of the Warfighter more quickly and affordably." As shown in figure 6-1, USD(R&E) does not have any Assistant Secretaries. Instead, USD(R&E) is supported in his or her duties by two primary assistants who serve in a similar role to that of an ASD: the Director, Defense Research and Engineering for Research and Technology, and the Director, Defense Research and Engineering for Advanced Capabilities.

Additionally, R&E oversees the director, Strategic Capabilities Office, or SCO (which was a PSA prior to the FY 2017 reorganization). A relative newcomer to OSD, SCO was established as a "black" (classified) organization in 2012 and was not recognized publicly until 2016. SCO director Dr. William B. Roper Jr. described the organization's mission in his 2016 testimony before the Senate Armed Services Committee, where he said SCO seeks to create "trick plays [for our military by] . . . reimagining its strengths—ships, submarines, aircraft, armored vehicles—by using them in unforeseen, and hopefully uncontested, ways" in an attempt to deceive and surprise potential adversaries and maintain a competitive combat advantage.

USD(R&E) oversees the following agencies and field activities:
- Defense Advanced Research Projects Agency
- Missile Defense Agency
- DOD Test Resource Management Center
- Defense Technical Information Center
- Space Development Agency

UNDERSECRETARY OF DEFENSE FOR POLICY

The USD(P) is SECDEF's principal advisor for the development of national security and defense strategies, and for the preparation of the DOD policies that implement them. In addition, USD(P) represents the secretary in interactions with the National Security Council as DOD's member of the NSC Deputies Committee, and works closely with the Department of State and other U.S. government departments engaged in the formulation of security policies. USD(P) manages DOD's foreign affairs portfolio, from developing technology transfer guidelines and arms control policy positions to overseeing alliance activities and representing DOD in negotiations with foreign partners. To manage this broad portfolio, USD(P) relies on assistant secretaries for international security affairs (ISA) and Asian and Pacific security affairs (APSA). By law, USD(P) assists the secretary in providing war planning guidance and reviewing the planning efforts of the combatant commanders. USD(P) is also responsible for "the activities of the Department of Defense for combating terrorism," assisted in this role by an Assistant Secretary of Defense for Special Operations and Low-Intensity Conflict (SO/LIC). USD(P) oversees the Defense Security Cooperation Agency, Defense POW/MIA Accounting Agency, and Defense Technology Security Administration.

UNDERSECRETARY OF DEFENSE FOR PERSONNEL AND READINESS

While USD's acquisitions directorate oversees the development and procurement of the *things* that DOD needs to fight and win, USD(P&R) is responsible for ensuring the *people* of DOD—both uniformed and civilian—are ready to execute their missions in peace and in war. USD(P&R)'s policy and oversight responsibilities encompass all aspects of "total force management," ranging from personnel accession and training across all of the services (including the Reserve Component and National Guard); to dependent support and education; equal opportunity; and morale, welfare, and recreation (MWR) affairs. In addition, USD(P&R) is required by law to monitor the operating tempo (OPTEMPO) and personnel tempo (PERSTEMPO) of the armed forces, and to establish reporting systems to capture this data in support of programs that promote the long-term health and readiness of the force. USD(P&R) oversees the Defense Commissary Agency, Defense Health Agency, DOD Education Activity, and DOD Human Resources Activity. Per the FY 2017 NDAA, and reflecting its core responsibilities, USD(P&R) is to be renamed Undersecretary of

Defense for Personnel and Health, or USD(P&H). At press time, this change had not yet been made.

UNDERSECRETARY OF DEFENSE FOR INTELLIGENCE

The USD(I) is SECDEF's principal advisor on all matters concerning intelligence, counterintelligence, security, and other sensitive activities under DOD's purview—to include planning, programming, and budgeting for these critical responsibilities. As part of this portfolio, USD(I) oversees the activities of DOD's wide-ranging intelligence apparatus, from National Security Agency cryptanalysts and hackers to Defense Intelligence Agency human intelligence (HUMINT) operators and National Geospatial-Intelligence Agency (NGA) imagery analysts. Additionally, USD(I) serves as the advisor to the director of national intelligence (DNI) on defense intelligence matters, thus playing in important role in the broader intelligence community.

USD(I) oversees the following defense agencies:
- Defense Intelligence Agency
- Defense Security Service
- National Geospatial Intelligence Agency
- National Reconnaissance Office
- National Security Agency/Central Security Service

UNDERSECRETARY OF DEFENSE (COMPTROLLER)

Responsible for a budget of over half a trillion dollars per year, SECDEF requires a diligent chief financial officer to assure careful stewardship of taxpayer dollars. The DOD comptroller—USD(C)—fulfills that critical role, managing every aspect of the departmental budget from planning through execution, and ensuring that corresponding accountability measures are in place. Just as USD(P) is DOD's "external face" for strategic, interagency, and foreign matters, the comptroller is DOD's interlocutor within the broader U.S. government fiscal structure, including the Office of Management and Budget (OMB) and Congress.

The Comptroller oversees the Defense Contract Audit Agency and Defense Finance and Accounting Service.

OTHER PRINCIPAL STAFF ASSISTANTS

The *Chief Management Officer* (CMO) assists the SECDEF and his or her deputy in managing and improving DOD business practices. Formerly the *Deputy Chief Management Officer*, the CMO was elevated by the FY

2017 NDAA—consistent with congressional and presidential intent to
"improve the quality and productivity of the business operations of the
department, thereby reducing the costs of those operations" and supporting "the President's goal of improving the efficiency, effectiveness,
and accountability of the executive branch." The CMO will also become
DOD's chief information officer as of January 2019 (more on this below).
Additionally, when you report for duty in OSD you will quickly become
acquainted with the two organizations for which the CMO has oversight
responsibilities: the Pentagon Force Protection Agency, whose personnel
maintain the security of the Pentagon; and Washington Headquarters
Services, the DOD field activity that provides administrative and facilities
support to OSD and other DOD agencies in the national capital region.

The *Inspector General of the Department of Defense* (IG) is responsible
to the secretary for providing an independent assessment of activities and
programs throughout DOD—including the military departments—to
identify and eliminate fraud, waste, and abuse, and propose corrective
actions when necessary. Similarly, the IG holds a mandate to monitor and
provide guidance on DOD-wide law enforcement and criminal justice
activities. In executing these two roles, the IG interfaces as required with
the Government Accountability Office (GAO) and the Department of
Justice (DOJ). The IG is also responsible for managing hotline and whistle-
blower programs that promote early identification of problems within
the department, and for moving aggressively to investigate allegations of
reprisal against whistleblowers.

The *General Counsel of the Department of Defense* is the chief legal officer
for DOD. Besides advising SECDEF and other members of OSD on legal
matters internal to DOD, the GC coordinates the department's legal position on issues ranging from executive orders and congressional legislation
to international agreements. (Future OSD staff officers take note: because
so many OSD staff actions are intimately connected to matters of U.S. and
international law, you will generally want to coordinate your analysis and
recommendations with the GC's office early and often!) Additionally, the
GC oversees the Defense Legal Services Agency.

The *Director of Cost Assessment and Program Evaluation*, more commonly known as CAPE, provides management discipline to the planning,
programming, budgeting, and execution (PPBE) process, and analytic
expertise to probe deeply into the costs of—and alternatives to—DOD

acquisition programs. A linear descendent of the Office of Systems Analysis established by Secretary of Defense Robert McNamara in 1961, CAPE provides SECDEF an independent assessment of program cost performance and how operational requirements might be met through more efficient or effective approaches.

The *Director of Operational Test and Evaluation* (DOT&E) provides independent assessments and recommendations to the Secretary of Defense regarding the effectiveness of DOD warfare systems under operational and live-fire testing conditions. When necessary, DOT&E may recommend that SECDEF direct the services to perform additional testing and evaluation to ensure that a system is suitable for combat use and/or operational employment.

The *Assistant Secretary of Defense for Legislative Affairs* (ASD[LA]) oversees all aspects of DOD interactions with Congress. In addition to assisting SECDEF and OSD leaders in their testimony and briefings on "the Hill," coordinating responses to congressional inquiries, and generally ensuring smooth lines of communication with Congress, ASD(LA) is responsible for the development of DOD's overall strategy for engagement with Congress on key legislative and policy goals.

The *Assistant to the Secretary of Defense for Public Affairs* (ATSD[PA]) is the secretary's primary advisor and executive agent for all public communications, serving as the department's principal spokesperson and (as codified in DOD instruction) ensuring "a free flow of news and information to the news media, the general public, the internal audiences of the DOD, and other applicable forums." ATSD(PA) also leads internal communications within DOD, spearheads the department's community relations initiatives, and oversees the Defense Media Activity.

The *DOD Chief Information Officer* (CIO) advises SECDEF on all matters related to DOD information systems, from network standards and cyber security to command and control and positioning, navigation, and timing systems. The DOD CIO's responsibilities include oversight of the Defense Information Systems Agency. As noted above, the CIO's business system and management-related duties will become vested in the CMO as of January 2019. A newly created chief information warfare officer will, in addition to the portfolios listed above, be responsible for space, electronic warfare, electromagnetic spectrum management, information assurance, and nuclear command and control communications systems.

The *Director of Net Assessment* (DNA) heads the Pentagon's internal think tank, charged by DOD instruction to set aside the "tyranny of the inbox" in order to conduct long-term "assessments of the standing, trends, and future prospects of U.S. military capabilities and military potential in comparison with those of other countries or groups of countries so as to identify emerging or future threats or opportunities for the United States."

WORKFORCE COMPOSITION

Like the Navy Staff (Office of the Chief of Naval Operations, or OPNAV) and other major staffs in the Pentagon, OSD is made up of a blend of civilian, uniformed, and contract support personnel. The predominant group, however, is composed of appointed officials, career senior executive service personnel, and government service (GS) civilian leaders. Befitting of the principle of civilian control of the military, OSD is a civilian-led organization—from SECDEF down to a majority of the action officers working "in the trenches."

The bureaucratic structure of OSD has been summarized earlier in this chapter, and officers serving in OSD will quickly grasp the staff's internal hierarchy. What may be less obvious at first glance, however, is just how senior OSD leaders are in relation to DOD personnel *outside* OSD by virtue of the position to which they have been appointed or assigned. Table 6-1 provides a brief summary of these leaders' relative seniority, which officers must understand in order to properly coordinate interactions with their bosses' uniformed and civilian counterparts on the service, combatant command, and joint staffs.

This table is derived from the "Order of Precedence" memorandum maintained by OSD's Office of the Chief Management Officer. Readers interested in more details on where OSD leaders rank relative to one another and all other senior DOD leaders, including those on service secretariat staffs, can obtain the memo from https://cmo.defense.gov/About/Organization/OPDS/OPDSLibrary/OPDSOrderPrec.aspx.

Finally, while the service staffs and Joint Staff employ an "army of O-4s," officers assigned to OSD are usually O-5 or senior. Additionally, while a commander or lieutenant colonel assigned to the service staffs or Joint Staff is often a section or branch chief with several action officers in his or her charge, an O-5/O-6 assigned to OSD can expect to be one of the more junior members of the team, typically serving as an action officer (often called an "advisor") and reporting to a GS-15 supervisor who, in turn,

Table 6-1. Comparison between Senior OSD and Military Staff Leadership

Secretary of Defense **Deputy Secretary of Defense**
Senior to all other members of DOD, uniformed or civilian
Under Secretaries of Defense **Chief Management Officer**
Four-star equivalent *Below Chairman of the JCS, but above Vice Chairman, service* *chiefs, and combatant commanders*
General Counsel of the DOD **Director of Cost Assessment and Program Evaluation** **Inspector General of the DOD** **Director of Operational Test and Evaluation** **Chief Information Officer of the DOD** **Deputy Under Secretaries of Defense** **Assistant Secretaries of Defense**
Four-star equivalent *Below service chiefs and combatant commanders, but above* *service vice chiefs and all other four-star officers*
Chiefs of Staff for the Secretary and Deputy Secretary of Defense **Deputy Chiefs of Staff for the Secretary and Deputy Secretary of Defense** **Assistant to the Secretary of Defense for Public Affairs** **Director of Net Assessment** **Directors of Defense Agencies** **Directors of DOD Field Activities** **Deputy Assistant Secretaries of Defense** **Deputy Assistants to the Secretary of Defense**
Three-star equivalent

reports to a deputy assistant secretary of defense or another OSD leader of similar seniority. Alternatively, you may be assigned to front office staff of an assistant or undersecretary of defense. In either case, despite being relatively junior in an OSD context, you will find that serving in OSD is a rewarding experience with plentiful opportunity to influence high-level policy formulation and executive decision-making that affects the entire Department of Defense.

COORDINATION WITH THE SERVICE, JOINT, AND COMBATANT COMMAND STAFFS

By law, the service secretaries, Chairman of the Joint Chiefs of Staff, and combatant commanders report directly to the Secretary of Defense. Their staffs, in turn, support them in preparing their advice to the secretary and in executing decisions relayed down the chain of command. Naturally, this necessitates significant and thorough coordination across staff boundaries, as it is unrealistic to expect the almost inconceivable volume of information entailed by DOD's operations to be channeled through a handful of senior leaders. Thus, officers serving in OSD will communicate frequently with counterparts on the joint, combatant command, and service staffs.

Nevertheless, officers assigned to OSD must recognize that staff coordination does not always yield staff consensus; some difficult or contentious issues will require direct communication between principals. These situations should not be viewed as staff failures; rather, they reflect the reality that the Secretary of Defense, Chairman of the JCS, service secretaries and chiefs, and combatant commanders are collectively dealing in matters of weighty principle—civilian control of the military, the scope and limits of statutory authorities, war planning requirements, and fundamental budget priorities to name only a few. In many cases, these senior leaders are charged with making operational and strategic decisions involving matters of life and death. When such difficult issues arise, your primary responsibility is not to drive to staff consensus but rather to ensure that OSD continues to provide timely, accurate, and independent advice to the Secretary of Defense to make these tough calls.

CONCLUSION

The Office of the Secretary of Defense has evolved considerably in both size and function since its humble beginnings in 1947. From a team of forty-five former Navy Department staffers to today's team of several thousand civilians and service members, OSD has ably assisted more than twenty-five secretaries in guiding DOD through a diverse set of challenges ranging from the Cold War to the war on terrorism and beyond. If you are detailed to OSD, you can look forward to a tour in which you will learn a great deal about decision-making at the highest levels—and make meaningful contributions to our national defense.

CAPT Thane Clare is a surface warfare officer currently assigned to the Office of the Secretary of Defense as a strategic plans adviser. He commanded USS *Mustin* (DDG 89), homeported in Yokosuka, Japan; and Patrol Coastal Crew Delta, embarked in USS *Squall* (PC 7) and USS *Whirlwind* (PC 11), sailing from Norfolk, Virginia, and Manama, Bahrain. Captain Clare also served in strategy, international affairs, and surface ship requirements billets on the Navy headquarters staff. He holds a PhD in international relations from Georgetown University.

PART III
THE PENTAGON AT WORK

7

THE BUDGET PROCESS

CDR ROB NIEMEYER, USN

The Chief of Naval Operations is charged with manning, training, and equipping naval forces; the vehicle he uses to accomplish this monumental undertaking is the Navy's annual budget submission to the Office of the Secretary of Defense. The Planning, Programming, Budgeting, and Execution (PPBE) process guides the Navy Staff in this effort to create and defend the CNO's budget—called the Program Objective Memorandum (POM).

The PPBE process was originally established during the Kennedy administration under Secretary of Defense Robert McNamara and his comptroller, Charles Hitch. McNamara, a Harvard Business School graduate, served as president of Ford Motor Company prior to leading the department, and he brought an analytic and process-focused mindset to the DOD's management culture. McNamara and Hitch realized that the PPBE process enabled OSD to exert centralized control over the services' POM submissions and to better align DOD resourcing decisions to meet the nation's defense needs. Though many components of the Navy's PPBE process are modified each year, the original management philosophy that underpins it has endured. This chapter will describe that process and introduce some of the key organizations that play an active role in it.

THE PPBE PROCESS AND TIMELINE

The disciplined PPBE process ensures that DOD's fiscally constrained resources deliver the optimal mix of manpower, equipment, and support to the combatant commanders in support of the National Security Strategy. As one would expect, submitting a strategy-based, fiscally balanced annual budget to OSD that reflects SECNAV and CNO priorities requires a formidable team effort across the Navy Staff. Considering the large number of billets of all pay grades in the Pentagon that contribute in some way to building the budget, it is essential to understand the PPBE process—its schedule, players, responsibilities, and deliverables that go into delivering a defendable, coherent POM that is aligned with leadership's guidance.

PLANNING/STRATEGY PHASE

Naval strategy and budget formulation guidance, which complement broader defense strategy documents and are produced by OPNAV N3/N5 (Deputy CNO for Operations, Plans, and Strategy), serve as the foundation for the planning stage. The goal of these documents—the National Security Strategy (NSS), National Defense Strategy, Defense Strategic Guidance (DSG), National Military Strategy, and Defense Planning Guidance (DPG)—is to communicate an overarching plan to advance and protect national interests, align the Navy to those central objectives, and allocate limited resources to the most pressing military priorities.

Not surprisingly, a natural tension exists between the fiscally *unconstrained* planning stage and the fiscally *constrained* programming stage. Through the Joint Staff, the combatant commanders have a voice in the planning stage through submission of an integrated priority list (IPL), which is a summation of major capability gaps in their respective areas of responsibility that should be addressed in the budget (similarly, U.S. Fleet Forces Command also submits an IPL to CNO to convey the fleet's capability shortfalls).

PROGRAMMING, REQUIREMENTS ASSESSMENT, RESOURCE INTEGRATION PHASE

The main output of the programming phase is the POM itself, which covers five years of funding, and is known as the Future Years Defense Program (FYDP, or "fih-dip"). Prior to the start of the programming phase, OSD issues schedule and procedural direction for the POM submission and provides fiscal guidance to establish each service's Total Obligation Authority (TOA)—the total funding amount to be allocated over the FYDP. OPNAV N80 orchestrates the programming phase by periodically issuing "POM Serials," which communicate programming directions, timelines, and deliverables.

Although the methodology of building the POM may vary, the objective remains the same: create a defendable Navy program reflecting the best mix of warfighting capabilities and readiness levels within a given level of funding resources. With the strategy, planning, guidance, and POM serials as their guide, the resource sponsors prioritize and program the resources in their portfolio (taking into account requirements for program manpower, operations, maintenance, and interoperability). Resource sponsors work with N80 and N81 (Assessment Division) to communicate the risk to warfighting capability and/or capacity in the event the program is not funded to the levels requested.

After months of programmatic analysis and staff work, resource sponsors brief their collective proposals to Navy leadership and control of the POM database shifts to N8; N80 then must evaluate, validate, integrate, and balance the Navy's POM into a comprehensive, defendable budget submission that aligns with SECNAV and CNO priorities and strategic guidance. At the end of the integration phase, CNO—with help from N8 and N80—adjudicates any outstanding issues before the POM is submitted to SECNAV; it is then redesignated the Department of the Navy budget submission, or DON.

PBIS

OPNAV N80's Program Budget Information System (PBIS) is the electronic financial database that tracks all funding (programming, budgeting, and execution) information for every Navy program element across the FYDP. PBIS records every funding change within each program throughout the budget year as a separate line item (or "issue"), identified by a unique number. Issue numbers document every detail of the funding change—to include the date, time, and individual who that made the change. Some of N80's POM serials will specifically address PBIS database "control" (that is, which organization will own the database and when) and assign a range of issue numbers assignments for each directorate. If your OPNAV assignment includes work as a resource or requirement sponsor, work with your financial manager to learn how to access and interpret PBIS data (one-day tutorial classes are available and are worth your time).

BUDGETING

When the POM programming is complete, N80 hands the reins over to N82/FMB to lead the budgeting phase. The budgeting phase translates DON strategy and programming intent into an appropriations account structure for a non-DOD audience—the OMB and Congress. The budgeting phase sharpens previous, imprecise estimates and properly prices each program in accordance with OMB and OSD fiscal guidance and law.

FMB analysts review budget submission estimates and analyze congressional and OSD adjustments made during the previous budget; program justifications; consistency of the program's funding profile over time; and the program's ability to execute its future funding. If any funding changes or adjustments are made, FMB budget analysts document their rationale in PBIS as a "budget issue," which budget submitting offices (BSOs), resource sponsors, and N80 programming analysts can appeal. If budget issues are not resolved at a lower coordination level, they are forwarded to an FMB-led forum called the Program Budget Coordinating Group (PBCG) for final resolution. The goal of FMB's budget review is to protect the DON's TOA against adjustments from OSD, OMB, and Congress by ensuring every investment can be defended. Once this phase is complete, the SECNAV-approved budget and corresponding justification material is then submitted to OSD. At this point, the DON becomes the BES, or budget estimate submission.

PROGRAM/BUDGET REVIEW PHASE

OSD(CAPE) and OSD(Comptroller) conduct concurrent program and budget reviews (collectively, PBR). The former examines programmatic issues, while the latter analyzes budget issues. During the PBR phase, OSD(CAPE), along with the combatant commanders and the Joint Staff, submits issue papers that can recommend alternatives to the Navy's POM. OSD(CAPE) then forms "issue teams" to review the merits of each approved issue. An N80 programming analyst serves as the Navy's lead issue team member and seeks to clarify and resolve the issue by presenting the Navy's position and programming intent. Each issue is either resolved at the working level or brought to one of two decision bodies for final adjudication: a three-star flag and general officer programming board (N8 is the Navy lead), or the four-star Deputy's Management Action Group (DMAG) decision body (VCNO is the Navy lead).

THE IMPORTANCE OF BUDGET EXHIBITS

Once Congress appropriates the DOD budget, the wording and funding in the budget exhibit—the document that outlines the purpose, funding profile, and timeline for programs of record (POR)—becomes law. Those who help manage a POR should take an active role in reviewing your program's budget exhibits before FMB finalizes them. Additionally, it is important to establish a relationship with your FMB budget analyst (usually a uniformed O-3 to O-5 or government civilian) so they can defend your program in the event it is at risk from being "marked" by Congress (for more on this process, see chapter 14). Year to year cost increases must be justified; if these costs are above published inflation rates (around 2 percent per year) and not adequately explained, the budget authority may be scrutinized by Congress and possibly re-allocated (for either Navy or another department's priorities).

The following checklist can serve as a guide when reviewing budget exhibits before the financial manager approves them:

- Does the budget exhibit reflect requirements?
- Is the funding correct and does it match the PBIS database?
- Have new POM issues been incorporated into the budget exhibit?
- Does the narrative make sense and discuss what the program is doing?
- Is the language specific enough without being overly technical?
- Are costs between similar efforts consistent? If not, are significant differences adequately explained?
- Does the program description accurately depict the program?
- Have there been any changes or anomalies to schedules/contract award since the last budget submission? If so, are they clearly explained?

Reviews end with a program and budgeting direction in an OSD(CAPE) memorandum called a Resource Management Decision (RMD). Fiscally, RMDs can allot additional money (TOA) to fund the decision; direct the service to fund one course of action in favor of another with a net funding change of zero; or direct the funding of a program and the service must fund within existing TOA (that is, at the expense of something else). Because this phase of "end game balancing" is fast paced, it is crucial for action officers to be in constant communication with their N80 counterpart to ensure no last-minute changes have affected their program.

Similarly, OSD(Comptroller) and OMB review the Navy's budget estimate submission to review every appropriation. These hearings are meant to resolve issues across budgetary stakeholders and generally focus on funding estimates, program pricing (fuel, inflation, utilities), compliance with fiscal and legislative guidance, and the ability for the programs to execute their funding (which is affected by research and development, technical maturity, contracting, and testing, among other things). Similar to programmatic changes, budgetary decisions are codified in their own RMD. Many of these issues cross between programmatic issues and comptroller issues through the review process so it is important to monitor both processes.

EXECUTION PHASE
The President's budget (PB) is delivered to Congress each year on or after the first Monday in February. After consideration, the budget is voted on and passed to the President. If signed into law, the execution phase begins in which the Navy manages congressionally appropriated funds to carry out congressionally authorized programs (chapter 14 discusses the differences between appropriations and authorizations in greater detail). The execution process includes apportioning, allocating, allotting, obligating and disbursing program funding. As programs execute their funding, in-progress reviews and reporting requirements measure each program's effectiveness. Based on those ongoing evaluations, funding may be reprogrammed or reallocated to higher priority or emerging requirements. Effective action officers should track their program's actual versus planned performance (as described in the budget exhibits), understand their program's performance metrics (such as obligations and expenditures and how they compare to Navy and OSD benchmarks), and be able to articulate the reasons behind any funding execution discrepancies or schedule slippages.

CONTINUING RESOLUTIONS

When Congress fails to pass an appropriations bill, the federal government must either operate under a short-term continuing resolution (CR) or shut down. A CR typically freezes program budgets at the previous fiscal year's appropriated amount until a new appropriations bill is signed. Continuing resolutions frequently prohibit DOD from funding any new-start programs, production quality increases, and military construction projects. Schedule slips and cost increases are common outcomes under a CR because program managers have less time to execute their funding. Action officers must understand the various program execution implications that a CR inflicts and the domino effect that it can have during mid-year budget reviews and future programming actions.

OVERLAPPING TIMELINES

At any given time, the four phases of PPBE occur simultaneously, creating overlapping periods among them. As a result, during budget discussions it is important to understand *which* budget is being discussed (especially because you are not at liberty to discuss budget specifics with anyone outside DOD until it is formally delivered to Congress). For example, during a single year (such as, FY 20, which runs from October 1, 2019 to September 30, 2020):

- President's Budget (PB) 19 is in execution (signed into law by authorization and appropriations bills)
- PB 20 is delivered to Congress and undergoes congressional review
- POM 21 is in the programming phase
- POM 22 is in the planning phase

While the overarching PPBE process has been consistent over many decades, the finer details of the Navy-specific processes can change based on the current CNO's preferences and management style.

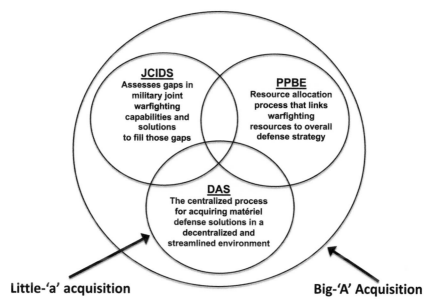

Figure 7-1. Requirements–Budgeting–Acquisitions System Interdependencies

SUPPORTING PROCESSES TO PPBE

In addition to PPBE, two other processes—the Joint Capabilities Integration and Development System (JCIDS) and Defense Acquisition System (DAS)—work together to deliver required capability to the end user: the warfighter. The Defense Acquisition University (DAU), DOD's lead organization for educating acquisitions, contracts, resourcing, and requirements professionals, illustrates the interconnectedness of these three processes—the totality of which is sometimes referred to as "big 'A' acquisition."

JOINT CAPABILITIES INTEGRATION AND DEVELOPMENT SYSTEM

The JCIDS process exists to support the Joint Requirements Oversight Council (JROC, pronounced, "JAY-rock") and Chairman of the Joint Chiefs of Staff responsibilities in identifying, assessing, validating, and prioritizing joint military capability requirements. JCIDS provides a transparent process across all stakeholders to identify capability gaps in the joint force—gaps that are identified by the combatant commanders and validated through the Joint Staff and OSD to confirm they should be resourced. These issues allow the JROC (a four-star body comprising the vice service chiefs and led by the Vice Chairman of the Joint Chiefs of Staff) to balance equities across the services and make informed decisions on the validity and relative priority of existing or emerging capabilities. These capability gaps then inform future resourcing decisions in the program/budget review process in order to mitigate warfighting risk.

DEFENSE ACQUISITION SYSTEM

DAS is the primary process for transforming validated capability requirements into matériel capability solutions—commonly called "little 'a' acquisition." JCIDS documents begin the process by clearly defining the capability gaps and denoting the requirements; the DAS process then guides the development of a matériel solutions, which occurs in five sequential phases: matériel solution analysis (MSA), technology development (TD), engineering and manufacturing development (EMD), production and deployment (P&D), and operating and support (O&S). Each phase has "entry" and "exit" criteria and milestones along the way that ensure the program is on track to deliver.

KEY POM STAKEHOLDERS

Effective action officers must not only understand the processes at work, but also recognize the important organizations that drive them. Indeed, they must have a working knowledge of the three processes (JCIDS, PPBE, DAS) and understand how requirements (resource sponsors), programming (OPNAV N80), budgeting (OPNAV N82/FMB), and acquisition (program offices) depend on and influence each other. In addition, there are numerous stakeholders in the PPBE process both within and outside the Department of the Navy, and knowing *who* is involved during each phase and *why* is fundamental to understanding *how* the POM is built.

STAKEHOLDERS WITHIN THE DEPARTMENT OF THE NAVY

Many of these organizations are covered in detail elsewhere in this book; however, their core functions, responsibilities, and organization as they relate to the budget process are described here.

Secretary of the Navy. Ultimately, the SECNAV is responsible for the Department of the Navy POM submission to OSD, an integrated product that combines both the Navy and Marine Corps' separate POM submissions. The SECNAV will also issue guidance, press releases, testimony, speeches, and priorities that must be carefully considered throughout the planning and programming phases because they can spotlight key focus areas to which leadership intends to allocate resources.

Chief of Naval Operations. The Navy POM is a reflection of CNO's guidance and priorities, which the CNO deliberately communicates to the staff. Routinely monitoring CNO's congressional testimony and speeches, current events, or news releases relating to your program is key to understanding where your equities fit into the larger POM picture.

OPNAV N8. The DCNO for Integration of Capabilities and Resources is the proverbial "center of gravity" in the POM process, responsible for integrating the POM and representing the CNO's viewpoint to internal and external stakeholders during budget deliberations. N8 does not "own" any programs or resources; consequently, the staff is charged to be an honest broker in the POM process—regardless of individual warfare background or specialty biases.

OPNAV N80. The programming division is made up of multiple subdivisions, two of which play a major role throughout the POM cycle. N801 (known as "the Bullpen") is charged with integrating various resource sponsors' POM inputs and balancing the overall POM submission to ensure it fits within the designated "topline" budgetary amount. N801 develops and issues POM strategy guidance (POM Serials) that establishes schedules, fiscal controls, programming guidance, and deliverables to ensure a timely and balanced submission to OSD. Structured to be representative of the Navy as a whole, N801 programming analysts are financial management–coded officers drawn from all warfare specialties responsible for a broad portfolio. Another branch, N804, is an organization comprising uniformed and civilian financial managers who are embedded within the respective resource sponsors' offices (for example, the financial managers in the N9 warfare offices who help build and balance the sponsors' budget submissions officially work for, and have dual reporting responsibilities to, OPNAV N80 via N804). N804 staff members are responsible for daily financial management of resource sponsor programs and are a direct liaison between the resource sponsor and N80.

OPNAV N81. As the lead analytic and assessment organization on the Navy Staff, N81 develops independent assessments on key warfighting capabilities and gaps. This analysis then informs spending priorities in order to invest in programs, capabilities, or technologies that can mitigate potential or projected warfighting shortcomings. N81's major products are the Front End Assessment (FEA) and the Warfighting and Support Capability Assessment (WSCA). The FEA drives endgame balancing for the current POM build and also shapes N80's programming guidance and resource sponsor priorities for the upcoming year's POM development. The WSCA makes programming recommendations to the resource sponsors based on N81's campaign analysis, capability assessments, and wargaming.

OPNAV N82/FMB. OPNAV N82/Financial Management and Budget (FMB) has dual reporting responsibilities in the Navy Staff and the Navy Secretariat. As the director of FMB, he or she is responsible to SECNAV (through the Assistant Secretary of the Navy [ASN] for financial management and comptroller [FM&C]) for the formulation, justification, and execution of the DON budget. As OPNAV N82, he or she reports to the CNO for managing the current year's budget (called the "execution year's budget"). FMB budget analysts ensure the department's investments are defendable to OSD, OMB, and Congress by validating program costs and schedule projections. As a result, close relationships among action officers, program managers, and FMB budget analysts will aid in monitoring important obligation and expenditure benchmarks and identifying areas where program funding may be at risk. FMB is the final budget document check before the DON budget is released. FMB budget analysts ensure that the correct amount of total obligation authority (TOA) is applied to each program under their purview; in other words, they verify there is enough money set aside in the budget to procure, install, operate, sustain, modernize, and maintain each system or program listed in the budget documents.

OPNAV N83. The Fleet Readiness Division is responsible for generating operations and maintenance requirements for the Navy that are informed by, and forecasted using, data models to update cost projections for the POM. Because stakeholders may disagree on the fundamental assumptions on which the models are based, action officers should be involved formulating them.

OPNAV N1. Dually responsible as the DCNO for Manpower, Personnel, Training, and Education and the Chief of Naval Personnel, the N1 staff act as both a resource sponsor and requirements sponsor. As a resource sponsor, N1 programs for all new accessions, and education and training requirements. As a requirements sponsor, N1 oversees the manpower requirements of the other resource sponsors. In this latter role, N1 publishes the manpower baseline assessment memorandum (BAM), which examines all personnel requirements—for which resources sponsors must account in their submissions—throughout POM development.

OPNAV N2/N6. The DCNO for Information Dominance serves as the resource sponsor for a broad portfolio of information warfare capabilities and systems, including cyber; electronic warfare; positioning, navigation, and timing (PNT); and command, control, communications, computers and intelligence, surveillance, reconnaissance, and targeting (C4ISR-T). OPNAV N2/N6 and N9 work closely during the programming phase because many of the capabilities and systems that N2/N6 sponsors are installed or operated by the platforms that N9 controls.

OPNAV N3/N5. The DCNO for Operations, Plans, and Strategy, develops the strategy documents that communicate the CNO's vision and priorities. This direction—called CNO Guidance, or CNOG (pronounced "SEE-nog")—is instrumental in the planning phase because it gives resource sponsors and action officers a sense of how individual programs align with the department's strategic vision. In theory, programs that do not contribute tangibly to broader objectives will be cut, thus creating "trade space"—the ability to consider funding alternative programs that do support strategic goals.

OPNAV N4. The DCNO for Fleet Readiness and Logistics is a resource sponsor for Military Sealift Command vessels, combat logistics force, expeditionary medical services, shore readiness accounts, and environmental programs. N4 also publishes the readiness BAM that defines the funding levels for resource sponsors' maintenance and operations accounts.

OPNAV N9. The DCNO for Warfare Systems is responsible for the integration of manpower, training, sustainment, modernization, and procurement of the Navy's warfare systems. Collectively, the resource sponsors (divisions) within N9—expeditionary warfare (N95), surface warfare (N96), undersea warfare (N97), and air warfare (N98)—maintain the largest programmatic share of the Navy's warfighting assets. As a result, they have "top line authority" to program their resources and, perhaps more than any other stakeholder, influence the overall direction of the Navy's POM. Resource sponsors within N9 conduct yearly program requirements reviews (PRR) for their entire portfolio to propose adjustments based on updated guidance and leadership priorities. These funding profiles are then forwarded to the Warfare Integration Division (N9I), which integrates, prioritizes, and finalizes resourcing decisions across the N9 warfare areas before submitting to N8.

Budget Submitting Offices (BSOs). BSOs are Navy field activity offices (outside the Pentagon) that submit budgets to FMB and execute—that is, spend—program funds. BSOs include U.S. Fleet Forces Command; U.S. Pacific Fleet; Office of Naval Research; Naval Installations Command; Naval Sea Systems Command; Naval Air Systems Command; Naval Supply Systems Command; Naval Facilities Engineering Command; Space and Naval Warfare Systems Center; and the Manpower Personnel Training and Education enterprise.

Headquarters Marine Corps Programs and Resources (P&R). The Deputy Commandant for Programs and Resources is the Marine Corps' equivalent to the OPNAV N8 in the PPBE process. P&R coordinates and integrates the USMC POM for submission to the commandant of the Marine Corps and then to SECNAV. Marine Corps program equities—namely in aviation (N98) and expeditionary shipbuilding (N95)—are represented on the Navy Staff, where there are also Marine liaison officers embedded within N2/N6, N3/N5, and N80. Additionally, you may hear two terms during the POM build that describe the Navy and Marine Corps' budgetary partnership: "blue/green split" refers to the percentage of DON top line authority that is divided between the Navy (blue) and the Marine Corps (green). "Blue in support of green" (BISOG) refers to funding that the Navy executes to support Marine Corps programs, such as aircraft maintenance and operations.

Assistant Secretary of the Navy for Research, Development & Acquisition (ASN[RD&A]). ASN(RD&A) is the Navy's "acquisition executive" and is responsible for the development and acquisition of naval platforms and systems. The program executive office (PEO) flag officers who manage acquisition programs report directly to ASN(RD&A). This individual does not have a formal role in the POM; however, it is critical for the Navy Staff to communicate potential POM adjustments to their acquisition counterparts since programming changes will directly affect a program's cost, schedule, capabilities, and risk.

Assistant Secretary of the Navy (Financial Management and Comptroller). ASN(FM&C) directs and manages all budget formulation and execution of the Navy and Marine Corps financial activities. There are several divisions within the ASN(FM&C) organization, including Financial Management and Budget (FMB), Office of Financial Policies and Systems (FMP), Office of Financial Operations (FMO), Appropriations Matters (FMBE), Fiscal Administrative Division (FMA), and the Naval Center for Cost Analysis (FMB-6/NCCA). As an Echelon I entity, ASN(FM&C) allocates funds to service chiefs and/or heads of major commands, offices, or bureaus. Nineteen Echelon II headquarters comptroller organizations have been established within the DON to manage these funds.

OUTSIDE THE DEPARTMENT OF THE NAVY

Office of Management and Budget (OMB). This office oversees the preparation and submission of the President's annual budget request, which is delivered to Congress each February. The DOD input into the President's budget represents the largest share of governmental discretionary spending.

Secretary of Defense and *Deputy Secretary of Defense (DEPSECDEF).* While SECDEF is overall responsible for the DOD budget (similar to a chief executive officer), the DEPSECDEF's role is analogous to a chief financial officer, who oversees the management of the department's day-to-day budget activities.

OSD Cost Assessment and Program Evaluation. As a principal staff assistant and advisor to DEPSECDEF, OSD(CAPE) evaluates the Navy's POM submission as part of the annual OSD program review. OSD(CAPE) analyzes each service's programmatic decisions to ensure that DOD's overall portfolio complies with presidential and departmental guidance and delivers the optimum capabilities national strategy demands; identifies issues and proposes changes in the Navy's POM; and provides SECDEF with recommendations for final resourcing decisions, which are promulgated through classified resource management decision memos.

OSD(Comptroller). As a principal staff assistant and advisor to DEPSECDEF, OSD(Comptroller) manages the department's budgetary and fiscal matters. The comptroller leads the annual OSD budget review, examining the Navy's compliance with fiscal guidance and proposing budgetary issues. Additionally, OSD comptroller is the final authority on the DOD's budget submission to OMB. Similar to OSD(CAPE), OSD(Comptroller) issues final budgetary decisions in RMD memos.

Joint Staff. The Joint Staff's Force Structure, Resources, and Assessment directorate (J-8) provides analysis and advice to the Chairman and the Joint Chiefs of Staff. Additionally, action officers within the Program and

Budget Analysis Division receive the Navy's POM and work closely with OPNAV N80 programming analysts to understand Navy's resourcing and risk decisions. These J-8 PBAD action officers represent the joint force positions of the chairman and combatant commanders during OSD(CAPE)'s program reviews.

ADDITIONAL RESOURCES

There are a host of formal courses of varying lengths designed to assist new Pentagon action officers with topics covering action officer and requirements officer (RO) fundamentals, introduction to PPBE, and PBIS familiarization. Additionally, DAU's website offers numerous helpful tools to assist action officers working in budgeting, resourcing, or requirements jobs. These include online courses (some of which you may be required to complete depending on your billet), reference library, defense acquisition guidebook, a repository of service-related policies and guidance, and a glossary of terms. Notably, DAU's online "Ask a Professor" function allows action officers to electronically submit routine or time-sensitive inquiries or requests for information to acquisition experts and faculty members for assistance.

CONCLUSION

To be sure, the budget process is complex. However, given the large number of staffs and billets in the Pentagon devoted in some way to building, defending, implementing, and overseeing the budget, it is important to understand the planning, programming, budgeting, and execution process—in place for more than half a century—and the key stakeholders who influence it. There will always be more bills than there is money to pay for them so such insights do more than produce well-informed action officers; they safeguard the service's investments by ensuring funded programs support naval strategy, fill critical warfighting capability gaps, and are grounded in sound analysis. As stewards of taxpayer money, we should expect nothing less.

CDR Rob Niemeyer is a surface warfare officer currently serving in USS *Milius* (DDG 69) in Yokosuka, Japan. At sea, he served on board USS *Coronado* (AGF 11), USS *Thach* (FFG 43), and USS *Pinckney* (DDG 91). Ashore, he served on the Chief of Naval Operations staff, Programming Division (N80) and in the Surface Warfare Directorate (N96) as the deputy branch head for finance. He also served as the officer in charge of the Surface Warfare Officers School's Basic Division Officer Course in San Diego. He holds a BS from the U.S. Naval Academy and an MBA from Harvard Business School.

8

ACTION OFFICERS: THE LIFEBLOOD OF PENTAGON STAFFS

CAPT GRADY MUSSER, USN

M ost officers assigned to the Pentagon will serve at some time as an "action officer"—a catchall title that describes the basic working element of Pentagon staffs. In general, three personnel layers exist on Pentagon staffs: director, branch head, and action officer. Director positions are filled by flag officers/generals or, in some cases, senior executive service civilians; branch head positions are normally filled by a uniformed O-6/captain or GS-15. The AO is often an O-3/lieutenant or O-4/lieutenant commander or, in some cases (depending on the portfolio), an O-5/commander who may be supported by junior officers and/or civilians. He or she oversees specific programs or a functional area within an assigned portfolio.

As described in chapter 7, AOs working in an acquisition or programmatic role are often referred to as requirements officers; they define system performance parameters and oversee the programming, or funding, of their portfolio. Action officers may also be assigned to oversee a functional or geographic area, or a technical capability.

ATTRIBUTES OF AN EFFECTIVE ACTION OFFICER

As other chapters have suggested, the process and workflow in the Pentagon are quite different from the type of work found in operational military tours. So what, then, are the essential attributes of an effective AO? Put simply, you must be able to:

- Work with colleagues in an open, transparent, and collaborative manner to support senior leadership as they frame, make, and execute complex funding or prioritization decisions.
- Write plainly and accurately to convey essential information to senior leaders who may not have a deep background understanding of your portfolio—often on short notice.

- Drive action within your portfolio to accomplish upcoming milestones or other critical activity.

To effectively perform these tasks, you must become a SME on all of the details of your portfolio while also understanding the larger staff processes, dynamics, and variables that may affect it. You must simultaneously work on long-term programmatic issues while remaining flexible and ready to respond to short-fused data calls. You must understand how to use the tools available to work on behalf of the program you oversee. Finally, you must not forget your primary role is to support senior leadership decisions—often with consequential outcomes for our nation's warfighting readiness and lethality.

BECOME THE EXPERT

The most important thing you can do to contribute immediately to your team is to become the expert on your assigned portfolio as quickly as possible. This includes understanding the overarching background and context of your program or issue as well as the application to existing strategy or tactics, funding history, congressional interest, and other details large and small. This subject matter expertise forms the foundation on which your ability to complete nearly every other official task rests.

Where to start? Not unlike what you have done in other jobs or in other tours, use your turnover to acquire and read all relevant documentation that relates to your program or functional area. If you oversee programs, review all requirements documentation along with budgetary and congressional budget exhibit information for your programs. Ensure you have also reviewed all decision memorandums and recent briefs to senior leadership.

Next, develop an understanding of key timelines within your portfolio and identify upcoming milestones or project deadlines. These goals, or "milestones," are often associated with the annual PPBE process cycle. For AOs who oversee a functional area, other annual processes—from major conferences to technical demonstrations to strategic reviews—may be in place to support reviews and decisions by senior leadership. A portfolio can also have targets beyond ones that are regimented or recurring, such those associated with acquisition or requirements milestones. Understanding the macro schedule will allow you to develop a calendar as part of your preparations that will support your entire tour.

Additionally, identify and meet with other stakeholders in order to gain diverse perspectives and develop broad expertise. Action officers

WORKING WITH CIVILIAN TEAMMATES

If you work alongside government civilians or contractors on your program, make an effort to understand their scope of responsibility and areas of expertise. They are often a valuable resource to help you identify key documentation while also providing important continuity on your program and in the organization. Because many uniformed AOs report directly from leadership positions in the fleet in which they were overseeing large groups of sailors, some officers are slow to realize that an AO on the OPNAV staff must be an expert on their assigned program—not just a manager of a few government civilians and/or contractors. If you have the opportunity to work with government civilians or contractors, tap into their expertise but do not let that prevent you from taking an active role in understanding your portfolio.

assigned a specific program—for example, a platform, weapon system, network, or sensor—should meet with their program managers (PM) and supporting staffs for detailed program review; program managers work within the acquisition community—normally under a systems command (SYSCOM), such as the Naval Sea or Air Systems Command (NAVSEA/NAVAIR), or the Space and Naval Warfare Systems Command (SPAWAR). You should also contact other key influencers on the OPNAV staff, Navy Secretariat, Joint Staff, Office of Secretary of Defense, and on fleet and other lower echelon staffs to build relationships, understand needs, and share relevant information.

Finally, spend time early and throughout your tour carefully considering the end state or objectives that you are trying to accomplish within your portfolio. Understanding these objectives will become essential as you transition from building your expertise to driving action within your portfolio.

DRIVE ACTION IN YOUR PORTFOLIO

While developing expertise within a portfolio should be your first area of focus when reporting for your assignment, driving action within that portfolio is your primary role and responsibility. This section will describe how you can be effective in driving action as part of your routine staff activity, during annual portfolio or program reviews, and when supporting major decisions. Your calendar of upcoming milestones, which provides a clear programmatic roadmap, will assist you in identifying and framing the objectives and decisions for which you are responsible.

RESULTS-FOCUSED ROUTINE

You will quickly find your calendar filling with meetings, phone calls, briefs, and other staff events. Many of these events will be outside your control—these you must support as best as possible. For those events over which you have more influence, you should ensure that each meeting has a clear purpose and defined outcome. Also, carefully evaluate the participants you invite to meetings. You need the right stakeholders with sufficient expertise and knowledge to support an effective meeting while being mindful that sessions with a large number of participants also can quickly become unwieldy and disorganized. Always insist that participants arrive for the meeting prepared; accordingly, preparation material must be disseminated well enough in advance to provide participants sufficient time to review.

You should routinely assess all meetings and events on your schedule to ensure your time is being spent effectively. For recurring meetings, evaluate the periodicity so as to avoid too few or too many meetings. You should also ensure that meetings are sequenced properly to support major milestones or critical events that you have identified on your macro schedule. Just as with an operational tour, you can apply a plan of action and milestones (POAM) approach to evaluate your meeting schedule and action plan as a staff officer. When using this approach, ensure you plan ahead to complete intermediate steps/tasks early while avoiding the tendency to jam the schedule with concurrent or overlapping events. Just as operational plans change so, too, will staff plans. Build flexibility into the schedule to accommodate staff friction and unaccounted delays.

Finally, include sufficient breaks in your schedule from routine meetings and use those breaks effectively. Continue to study and build expertise in your portfolio; learning should never stop! You also will need time to prepare for meetings, write papers and briefs, and seek input from trusted agents on the products you develop. It is also important to provide time to support your personal and professional development, which may mean saying "no" to some events or meetings that are not essential. Be thoughtful and strategic as you evaluate your calendar. Always consider informing your supervisor in advance when you are declining a meeting to ensure you have support from your leadership or alternate representation from your office, if required.

PORTFOLIO REVIEWS

AOs will normally conduct a portfolio or program review on an annual basis, often as part of the budget or POM process within PPBE. This will normally entail a PM providing a formal brief to the AO, who will then develop an OPNAV-specific assessment used by the Pentagon staff to make funding decisions in the annual POM process. These reviews are major events and offer an important opportunity for an AO.

When accomplishing these reviews, you must understand all guidance associated with the review and communicate that guidance as early as possible to a PM. Timelines and evaluation criteria are critical elements of this review process and should be discussed with the PM in advance to address any questions and to verify that you and PM understand and share expectations. Guidance often changes in the Pentagon; ensure you relay any changes to the PM quickly as they are physically located outside the Pentagon and may not have access to the same timely updates that you receive.

A program review should assess all elements of the program. Acquisition programs are normally evaluated by cost, schedule, and performance as measured against an acquisition baseline. During the program review, you must understand the current status of a program and how that status has changed since the last review, which helps to establish the trend of a program. You should also understand why the program has changed. If a negative change is observed, it will be necessary to explain why the change occurred—was the change due to a problem within the program or because of an external factor? Leadership will also want to know what has been changed within a program to correct the negative trends, along with your evaluation of the effect of that change.

When conducting program reviews, view the program through a war-fighting lens to evaluate the program's operational utility. Aim to review all analyses being conducted across the DOD that include your specific program (this spans from the "campaign level," which features large force-on-force models, to the "engagement level," which pairs individual

---

UNANTICIPATED FUNDING REQUESTS

The most common challenge an AO faces is overseeing a program
that is requesting additional funding due to some challenge experienced by that program. An AO must understand the reasons
for a funding shortfall, assess all other options to mitigate the
funding gap, and be able to provide—and explain—funding options
aligned with war fighting impacts. Given budget constraints across
DOD, senior leadership will demand this level of scrutiny by the
Pentagon staff.

---

weapons systems against another to gauge their efficacy). Much like the
cost, schedule, and performance assessment mentioned above, you should
understand the overall warfighting performance of your program along
with any changes in warfighting performance as compared with previous
analysis.

Armed with this information, you should develop a narrative for your
program that justifies the details for senior leadership. If programmatic
funding or strategy changes are needed, you must be able to clearly
articulate what the changes will accomplish along with the tactical and
operational warfighting impact if the program is not sufficiently funded.

MAJOR PORTFOLIO DECISIONS

Effective AOs drive specific action associated with their portfolio through
decisions that are normally made by one of two ways: through a written
decision memorandum that is routed and signed by a senior leader, or
following a meeting or in-person briefing in which key senior stakeholders
assemble to review and approve a recommendation.

Significant groundwork goes into assisting and preparing senior leadership to make often difficult and consequential decisions. You should first
coordinate with process gatekeepers to ensure right briefing formats are
used, and then you will prepare required briefing materials and background papers. Beyond the mere format, though, you must influence the
content, craft the narrative, and verify the accuracy and relevance of the

information included. This requires you to conduct the necessary research and synchronize with other organizations to ensure your program is ready for its upcoming review or milestone.

To support major leadership decisions, you must understand and explain the costs, benefits, and risks associated with the options being considered—information that is collected through open and transparent collaboration. By working with other stakeholders, a shrewd AO can identify unintended consequences along with positive and negative impacts that provide nuanced background for senior leaders. Effective coordination not only generates better information but also often reduces potential inter- and intra-organizational friction that could result from official decisions.

EDUCATE AND COLLABORATE

Effective AOs play a critical role beyond driving action in their portfolio. They are advocates for their program, but as "the expert," they also have a responsibility to educate others on their portfolio. This is done by authoring briefs or papers on a specific program or area, providing input to other AOs working on projects, writing or reviewing emails, and creating talking points for leadership.

UPDATING YOUR LEADERSHIP

Based on upcoming events or projected senior leader commitments, you should identify opportunities to provide information regarding your portfolio up and across the chain of command. Important developments in the program—both positive and negative—should be communicated, especially if that the information will be reported in the media or shared with congressional members or their staff. You should always aim to prevent important or emerging developments in your portfolio from surprising your leadership.

Additionally, monitor scheduled meetings in which your leadership may be required to participate. If the subject is associated with your program, either directly or indirectly, then you should provide read-ahead information or preparation material. To prepare your leadership for a major meeting, it can be helpful to meet with your leadership in advance to "pre-brief" them, offering them an opportunity to ask questions and better understand certain details—this can also guide the type and specificity of the advance material you provide. Whether you meet for a pre-brief or not, a one-page memo summarizing key portfolio highlights will normally be useful to a front office that is preparing their principal for an upcoming meeting and they will appreciate your initiative and attention to detail.

You should look for opportunities to share relevant information on your portfolio with others in the organization. Most staffs provide weekly or monthly updates to leadership via email or other formats. Make a note of when these submissions are due and then craft and provide timely updates on your program when appropriate. Keep your updates short, specific, and include a "so what" assessment that will help leadership to understand the point you are trying to express.

SHORT NOTICE TASKING

Even the most proactive and forward-thinking AO will be asked to develop short notice briefs, papers, or program updates—it is inescapable in the Pentagon. In large and dynamic staffs, these requests for information (RFI) can occur frequently and you will be expected to offer your support and to prioritize this work. When fielding a response to a short notice data call, it helps if you first understand *why* leadership is asking the question. Is it to prepare for a meeting (if so, where, when, and with whom)? Is it in response to some event (if so, what or why)? Having this context will enable you to provide the right level of detail at an appropriate level of classification. This will also help you to support your leadership to prevent the release of pre-decisional information.

INTERNAL, PRE-DECISIONAL, OR SENSITIVE INFORMATION

One common area of concern for release of pre-decisional information is associated with the President's budget. Until a presidential budget is released to Congress, specific funding levels within that budget should not be shared with Congress, industry partners, or the public. As such, when asked to provide funding information for meetings with Congress, industry, or the media, always provide funding associated with the most currently released budget. However, at internal meetings within Department of Defense it may be appropriate and even necessary to provide pre-decisional funding information (typically associated with POM) to support a meaningful discussion. This guidance also applies to classified information and for unclassified materials that contain the marking "For Official Use Only" (FOUO).

SUPPORTING YOUR COUNTERPARTS

Be open and creative in looking for opportunities to update other stakeholders on your portfolio. Keep a close eye on briefs and papers that are developed by other stakeholders that may include, be associated with, or be affected by your portfolio. Email, meet, or call your counterparts to understand what they are trying to accomplish and determine what information you can provide to support their project. This effort will help you to naturally build your professional network while ensuring other staff officers understand your portfolio and that your issues are accurately characterized in their work.

EMPLOY THE "TOOLS OF THE TRADE"

Just as an AO must learn their portfolio, they must also learn the tools used by the Pentagon staffs. This section will explore some of the common tools AOs are expected to use and explain how leveraging them effectively can enhance an AO's productivity and success.

COMPUTER SOFTWARE

The Microsoft Office software suite exists on most, if not all, government computers (at the time of publishing). You must be able to use Office programs—Outlook for email and calendar management, Word for document processing, PowerPoint for building and sharing briefs, and Excel for spreadsheets. If you are unfamiliar with them, spend some time early in your assignment learning the basic operations of these programs through online tutorials or by using the "Help" function within the programs themselves.

CALENDAR

As described earlier in this chapter, you must develop a calendar of upcoming milestones for your portfolio so you have a yardstick by which to measure required action. Writing down these milestones—whether in a notepad, a Word document, or PowerPoint slide—helps. You also need a way to manage your personal calendar to ensure you do not miss important meetings and deadlines. Most Pentagon offices use the calendar function within Microsoft Outlook to track meetings and senior leaders' schedules. Normally the staff of the senior most ranking officer planning to be in attendance will send out an invite from that leader's calendar to all prospective attendees. Whether planning a formal meeting or scheduling an informal coffee gathering, it is common to hear the refrain, "I'll send you an invite!"

One technological benefit of Outlook that facilitates coordination is the ability to share your calendar with other staff members so they can view your schedule. This function is particularly helpful when scheduling upcoming meetings because it allows a staff officer to view multiple calendars and find available time slots. As mentioned earlier, keep a close eye on your leadership's calendars so you are aware of upcoming meetings or engagements associated with your portfolio.

EMAIL
Email is the most common method used to communicate across the staff. While you likely have experience working with email, a few important practices are worth highlighting. Read your email several times a day so you can identify and act on urgent matters. Respond to emails addressed to you in a timely fashion (or as promptly as practicable)—doing so will not only assist the person reaching out to you but will also reflect positively on your office and organization. Develop a system to file and track important emails so you can track and follow up on required action. When sending or responding to emails, choose the addressee(s) carefully to avoid "spamming" inboxes of colleagues who may not benefit from the contents. Choose your recipient(s) deliberately and exercise care in those who are being "copied," or "cc'd"; it is generally assumed that the primary recipient will reply.

Additionally, keep your emails short, specific, and professional (obviously, email is not an appropriate forum for venting in public). If you do need to send a lengthy email, make sure you lead with a "BLUF" (bottom line up front) statement or a short summary to help readers quickly understand the purpose of your email. If you are requesting or directing the addressees to take act in some manner, clearly state what you need to the reader to do. Finally, email tends to be more formal than texting or using social posting apps. When using email—especially with more senior officers—avoid abbreviations associated with text messaging or informal communications (i.e., LOL or OMG). Leave time to proofread your emails before sending, and as a general rule to help gauge your tone, always assume that they will be forwarded.

PAPERS
One of the most common and influential activities AOs will be tasked to complete involves writing papers. When embarking on such a project, always verify the type of paper being requested and the correct

format—they can vary from short "point paper" formats to lengthier and more detailed "white papers." They are also delineated by their purpose of providing background (information papers) or requesting senior leaders take action (decision papers).

You may develop several products that will be included in a package for review by senior leadership. Often the first portion of a package will be a one-page memo that states what or why the information is being provided, or an action memo that states the specific decision or action being requested. The second portion of a package is normally the primary document being reviewed by leadership: namely an information paper or a document in which action is being requested. Other supporting background papers or briefs may be included. A coordination page is normally included, which details the other organizations that have reviewed and concurred with the package's contents.

As with email, you should strive to write clearly, accurately, and succinctly. Including the appropriate amount of background information will allow the package to stand on its own and provide all the information necessary for a senior leader. The goal is to avoid having the senior leader respond with follow-up questions that require additional time and staffing to provide a response. Anticipating questions that the principal may have will ensure the background information contains sufficient details to answer them. If you must include a primary document for background that is lengthy, consider developing a short summary and/or tabbing and highlighting the document so a senior leader can quickly find and discern the relevant information.

BRIEFS

As mentioned earlier, AOs are commonly tasked with developing Power-Point briefs. When assigned to make a brief, you must understand to whom and when the brief will be given, why it has been requested, what format (if any) is needed, and how the brief will be used. The same guidance for writing emails and papers applies: be clear, accurate, and succinct. Well-placed illustrations can also reinforce content or augment specific points.

Often briefs are sent out in advance of meetings—well-structured and developed explanatory information is very useful for senior leaders reviewing a brief prior to a meeting and can make the meeting itself more productive. PowerPoint slides can also be used to convey a position or provide information for senior leaders who may not have a face-to-face briefing scheduled. Consequently, because slides are often reviewed without the briefer present, you should ensure that the brief can stand on its own. Important points should be explained using a callout box on the slide itself or in the "notes" section below the slide.

For formal presentations, you may be asked to develop specific talking points or an actual speech that will be delivered with the slides. "Facer slides" provide the text of a speech or the talking points that accompany each of the background slides. When tasked with developing this type of presentation, attempt to meet with the designated speaker early to discuss the goal and/or desired outcome for the brief, along with any predetermined themes and messages. This will help you organize and develop the presentation more coherently.

BEST PRACTICES AND KEY TAKEAWAYS

Action officers serve on the "front line" of Pentagon staffs. By virtue of their position and knowledge, they have both the responsibility and opportunity to influence important military decisions. These key best practices will maximize your chances for success during an AO tour:

- Keep your writing short, accurate, and clear—don't assume others have in-depth knowledge of your portfolio.
- Drive action to achieve specific objectives or an end state within your portfolio; don't confuse activity with accomplishment.
- Be an advocate for your portfolio but don't be a zealot!
- Maintain professional relationships; don't allow organization friction to create personal conflicts.

CAPT Grady Musser is a career surface warfare officer and 1996 graduate of the U.S. Naval Academy who commanded USS *Farragut* (DDG 99) and currently commands USS *Leyte Gulf* (CG 55). Ashore, he served multiple tours in Washington, DC, including service on the personal staff of the Chief of Naval Operations in the Strategic Action Group (NooZ) and two tours in the Surface Warfare Division, most recently as the executive assistant. He also served as an action officer at the U.S. Pacific Command and at the Naval Aviation Warfighting Development Center.

9

FRONT OFFICE AND PERSONAL STAFF

CAPT MATTHEW DUFFY, USN

S erving on a flag officer's personal staff in the Pentagon can be one of the most challenging yet professionally rewarding chapters of your Navy career. Personal staff assignments (those who work directly for the principal and are described in detail later in this chapter) can offer a rewarding opportunity to witness firsthand how the business of our Navy is conducted. They also enable officers to observe up close how our senior leaders—arguably the most successful officers in the Navy who have succeeded both at sea and ashore—think, decide, act, mentor, and operate.

Practically speaking, the Pentagon is viewed by many as the "corporate headquarters" for the company to which we all belong. As discussed in previous chapters, officers seek assignments in Washington for a variety of reasons but for many, learning how the Pentagon operates and the manner in which the organization functions provides a critical career building block. You have likely heard the common Navy phrase "being close to the flagpole"—Pentagon service affords you the opportunity to work in close proximity to the biggest collection of flagpoles in a single location, but also to be near the tallest flagpole of them all.

Besides the professional development that comes from a tour on a flag officer's personal staff, you will also have the opportunity to significantly cultivate your own network. The close proximity to multiple flag officers and their staffs, coupled with the concentration of senior Navy officers in the Pentagon, will enable you to expand your existing cadre of seniors, peers, and subordinates—both inside and outside your warfare or community area. Your interaction with these folks will also affect your reputation—hopefully in a positive way. Service on a flag officer's personal staff will expose you to the best examples of leadership, the highest levels of decision-making, and provide a graduate education—indeed a "masters in the corporate Navy."

THE FRONT OFFICE

ROLES AND RESPONSIBILITIES

An admiral's front office is one of the most unique organizations in the Navy. In some respects, it is a command within a command. The composition of the front office varies based on the admiral's rank, which will be covered later in this chapter. Nevertheless, there are some common characteristics that span all Navy front offices in the Pentagon.

Like a squadron or ship, which is often a reflection of the leader who commands it, the front office typically adopts the persona of the flag officer. As a result, the personal staff's priorities, focus, professionalism, and culture inherently reflect those of the principal. However, one of the most important lessons for any front office employee is to ensure that you *never* assume the rank of your principal when interacting with others. Every front office veteran has heard stories of officers who have made this mistake. In the process, they likely tarnished their individual reputation—or worse—that of their boss or of the office itself.

In the Pentagon, the front office serves as a type of "command quarterdeck." All entrants should be welcomed with the utmost respect and professionalism. Front office personnel are in the customer service business—and are a direct reflection of the principal they serve. The best front office teams remain courteous, receptive, organized, responsive, and positive regardless of the circumstances or events of the day.

The personnel of the front office exist to ensure the flag officer is prepared to properly execute a range of events each day. Front office personnel solicit read-ahead (RAH) materials—briefing binders, presentations, memos, etc.—in advance and provide them to the admiral prior to a meeting. This early review prepares the principal for the event and informs his or her thinking—the intricacies of the issues discussed, the outstanding questions that must be answered, the options to be considered, and the timeline to make a decision. In short, the front office staff exists to ensure the flag officer functions in the most efficient and effective manner possible. *Time* is a flag officer's capital.

The best front offices also work proactively to coordinate activities up, down, and across the various chains of command that exist in the Pentagon. For example, the Deputy Chief of Naval Operations for Integration of Capabilities and Resources (N8; discussed in chapter 3) has near identical counterparts on the Joint Staff (J-8), Navy Secretariat (AS[FM&C]), Office

Wearing "the loop" and working directly for a flag officer is a unique, rewarding, and challenging opportunity. *U.S. Navy photo by MCC Specialist Elliott Fabrizio/Released*

of the Secretary of Defense (OSD[Comptroller])—not to mention the finance leads for the U.S. Marine Corps, Army, Air Force, Coast Guard, and National Guard Bureau. In other words, beyond simply working with the front offices above and below a particular branch in the OPNAV chain of command, front office personnel will interact regularly with colleagues outside the Navy both within the Pentagon and throughout the National Capital Region. This facet of the job is a key component that contributes to learning, professional development, and networking.

FRONT OFFICE COMPOSITION

Each front office's makeup—the number and type of staff, and their seniority—varies significantly based on the rank of the principal. Additionally, OPNAV front offices can often be organized differently from those on the Joint Staff or OSD. OPNAV front offices comprise sailors, government civilians, and contractor support. As one would expect, front offices in joint commands reflect the services they serve and are made up of personnel from across the Department of Defense. While the nominal front office makeup described below applies primarily to those found in OPNAV, this section will also acknowledge a few of the "joint world" nuances that deviate from the Navy's standard.

FOUR-STAR FRONT OFFICE

There are two four-star admirals stationed in the Pentagon: the Chief of Naval Operations and Vice Chief of Naval Operations. Additionally, a Navy four-star may also serve rotationally as the Chairman or Vice Chairman of the Joint Chiefs of Staff. (The Director, Naval Nuclear Propulsion Program [colloquially, "Naval Reactors,"] also led by an admiral, is located on the Washington Navy Yard.) Despite their similar rank, these flag officers' personal staffs differ in terms of size and composition. Moreover, it is common for the principal to adjust his or her staff structure upon assuming the office (reflecting his or her personality and other hiring mandates, such as department-wide manning initiatives or directed headquarters staffing reductions). After first summarizing the office constructs, later sections in this chapter will define job descriptions and functions of each staff position in greater detail.

Within his or her immediate circle, the Chief of Naval Operations is supported by an executive assistant (post-major command O-6), deputy executive assistant (pre-major command O-5 or O-6), flag secretary (administrative limited duty officer [LDO] O-4 or O-5), two aides (one Navy O-4, one Marine O-4), legal advisor (JAG Corps O-6), public affairs officer (O-5), protocol officer (O-3 or O-4), speechwriter(s) (O-3 to O-5), scheduler (civilian), flag writer (E-7 to E-9 yeoman), foreign policy or political advisor (state department foreign service officer or senior defense department government civilian), and security detail lead (civilian NCIS agent). The CNO also relies on another layer of supporting staff outside the front office: think tank–like advisors, special assistants, administrative staff, personal housing/quarters attendants, communications specialists, and additional members of the security detail.

The Vice Chief of Naval Operations, on the other hand, maintains a smaller staff. The VCNO typically has a single aide, a small cadre of inner-circle advisors, and fewer administrative personnel. Additionally, the ranks of these officers will be the same or, in some cases, one pay grade below their counterpart on the CNO's personal staff.

THREE-STAR FRONT OFFICE

The "N-code" deputy chiefs of naval operations, or DCNOs, make up the largest bloc of three-star flag officers in the Pentagon. These three-stars' personal staffs usually consist of an executive assistant (post-major command O-6), deputy executive assistant (usually a pre-command O-4 or O-5, or possibly a post-command O-5), flag secretary (administrative LDO O-3 or O-4), aide (O-3 or O-4), and a flag writer (E-7 to E-9 yeoman). There are numerous other vice admirals working in the National Capital Region and their personal staff compositions vary.

TWO-STAR FRONT OFFICE

Using OPNAV two-star flag officer division directors as a model, these Pentagon front offices tend to be slightly smaller than (and slightly junior) to those of the three-stars. A two-star front office will typically consist of an executive assistant (pre- or post-major command O-5 or O-6), deputy executive assistant (pre-command O-4 or O-5), aide (O-3), and flag writer (E-5 to E-8 yeoman).

ONE-STAR FRONT OFFICE

One-star front offices in the Pentagon normally consist of an executive assistant and/or aide (O-3 or O-4) and a flag writer (E-5 to E-8 yeoman). As a junior officer, you may feel that serving on a very senior staff is more prestigious; however, serving a one-star as the sole personal staff officer has tremendous benefits. First, you are responsible for a broad array of tasks and functions. Though demanding, you will be exposed to all facets of flag support service. Second, you will likely develop a more professionally intimate relationship with your boss compared to those serving on a more senior (and larger) personal staff. Finally, serving directly for a one-star flag officer may afford you many years of mentorship and a trusted resource as both you and your principal continue on in your Navy careers.

PERSONAL STAFF POSITIONS

While no single chapter or guide can serve as a single definitive source, this section outlines some of the typical functions and responsibilities of personal staff positions to which you may be assigned at various points in your career. (Even within this book, some job descriptions may vary based on the authors' respective experiences, the offices in which they served, or the manner in which a particular flag officer leveraged his or her staff.)

AIDE

Serving as an aide to a flag officer can be one of the most rewarding opportunities available ashore in the entire U.S. Navy. The aide is responsible for the immediate, real-time support of the principal. Aides are often intimately involved in long-range planning and are responsible for near-term execution of the principal's schedule. They are typically the first to greet the admiral in the morning and the last to leave. More than any other officer on staff, the aide is attached to the admiral constantly—thus becoming a de facto extension of the principal.

Practically speaking, the aide is charged with ensuring the admiral maintains his or her tightly planned schedule—a series of events that the aide, together with the flag writer (and, if applicable, a scheduler), was instrumental in crafting. You are likely to be required to collate RAH materials a day or two prior to every scheduled event so your boss may prepare in advance. If walking to a meeting within the Pentagon or driving to an engagement out in town, the aide should have already traced the route.

Once the engagement begins, the aide takes notes to share with the staff and to provide the principal a reference for future use. As the engagement nears its scheduled conclusion, the aide may flash a prearranged sign to discreetly signal to the boss that time is running short (aides are also empowered to voice a succinct time concern should an engagement run long—again, time is the admiral's capital!). Visitors, whose time may be less constrained than your principal's, may be inclined to let a meeting extend beyond its scheduled end and the admiral may often graciously comply. To that end, you may have to be the one to politely bring the meeting to a close (or remind your boss that it is time do so) in order to keep your principal on time for his or her next commitment. Finally, aides traditionally carry a small gift or coins for authorized exchanges at the conclusion of a meeting or event. (Note: As a new aide, it is very important to take the time to meet with your staff judge advocate to understand the "rules of the road" on giving, receiving, and documenting gifts for your principal, as well as what general support you can—or cannot—offer your principal legally and ethically.)

Though there are exceptions, aides often travel with their flag officer—typically a highlight of the job. Traveling affords you the protracted time to interact, listen, and learn from the admiral; forge a strong personal and professional relationship; and witness and participate in meaningful events away from the office.

EXECUTIVE ASSISTANT

The executive assistant (EA for short), is the senior officer on an admiral's personal staff (the Secretary of Defense and the Secretary of the Navy call their EA-equivalents a military assistant, or MA). The front office is very much a command within a command. As "captain" of the front office "ship," the EA is ultimately responsible for ensuring the admiral is supported to execute his or her responsibilities efficiently and meaningfully. The admiral often depends on the EA's recent operational and command experience, and relies on the EA as a sounding board for honest assessments and recommendations. Executive assistants in the E-ring have enjoyed significant professional achievement to earn these coveted assignments, and many four-star flag officer EAs (as well as some three-star EAs) are routinely selected into the flag ranks themselves following a successful front office tour.

DEPUTY EXECUTIVE ASSISTANT

Working in concert with the EA, the deputy executive assistant (also called the DEA, or deputy EA) is typically charged with managing the flow of all information to (and in some cases, from) the admiral. The deputy EA monitors, takes action, and follows up on both unclassified and classified email communication to and from the principal's account. He or she reviews and edits correspondence packages going to the admiral to ensure they are prepared according to the principal's standards and expectations. Additionally, the deputy EA receives, reviews, and processes the content coming from the admiral's office requiring further staff attention. In some instances, the admiral may have additional questions that should be addressed promptly—these tasks are then distributed to the appropriate Pentagon office via the official electronic "tasker" system for action.

Unlike the EA and aides, who often accompany the admiral out of the office (within the Pentagon or on travel across the globe), the deputy EA is anchored to the office to provide the "office manager" continuity to keep the remaining staff focused. Part of this responsibility may include managing the staff "battle rhythm"—morning stand-ups or end-of-day wrap-ups with the admiral, daily staff huddles, weekly staff meetings, etc. If the EA could be considered the figurative captain of the ship, the deputy EA usually handles executive officer–like functions. Finally, the EA-DEA relationship is critical. Although the EA is senior in both rank and authority, well-oiled front offices have EA-DEA teams who support each other, communicate honestly and continuously, and genuinely mesh both personally and professionally.

FLAG SECRETARY

The flag secretary, or "flag sec," is a cornerstone for any large front office staff's success. Pentagon flag secretaries are mostly administrative limited duty officers (LDOs) and act as the admiral's administrative lead. Anecdotally, the Pentagon's flag secretary professional network is one of the most effective in the entire Navy—they share information, field questions, and act on unique requests. Additionally, the flag secretary manages the enlisted administrative personnel and oversees the staff budget. As the deputy EA manages the information and packages flowing into and out of the admiral's immediate office, the flag secretary manages the flow of product into and out of the broader front office itself.

LEGAL ADVISOR

The legal advisor, a uniformed judge advocate general, has a diverse portfolio. A flag officer's legal advisor reviews and summarizes legal packages requiring action by the principal. In the senior-most offices in the Pentagon E-ring, these may include selection board results; complex travel plans for the admiral, spouse, and his or her team; and unique ethics perspectives on various activities (many JAGs on senior staffs also serve as the staff ethics advisor). Additionally, because interactions with industry and the private sector are routine in the Pentagon, the legal advisor ensures all statutory rules and guidelines about fair access and proper disclosure are followed.

PUBLIC AFFAIRS OFFICER

The public affairs officer, or PAO, leads the office's vital strategic communications efforts—a critical component for any senior leader seeking to advance ideas or influence deliberations in the modern world. Unlike their peers a generation, decade, or even a few years ago, PAOs now face a host of new challenges and must contend with around-the-clock news coverage, social media, instant feedback, the reality of political divides within Washington, and a complex national security landscape. The PAO is usually up early to review "CHINFO Clips" (an internal Navy product that compiles key articles of interest from the day's coverage), news wires, and mainstream media coverage. The PAO provides relevant news summaries to the admiral and staff, observes trends and key news topics of the day, and informs any public engagements on the admiral's calendar. More senior public affairs officers may lead a strategic communications team consisting of a speechwriter and/or enlisted mass communications specialist(s) (MCs). The PAO synchronizes the office's communications efforts, guides the development of articles or remarks, drafts press releases, serves as a conduit between the principal and media outlets, maintains the office's social media accounts, and facilitates "off the record" engagements with reporters—all in an effort to align messaging across the staff and with the department as a whole.

PROTOCOL OFFICER

Flag officers—particularly at the three- and four-star levels—regularly host events for key figures and senior leaders in government, industry, entertainment, and the arts. These events occur in their Pentagon office, personal quarters, at venues inside the Beltway, or in places beyond Washington. Protocol officers lead the preparation and manage the execution of these engagements, which are critical to exchanging ideas, informing decisions, building relationships to advance the department's objectives, and promoting the Navy's image and message with stakeholders and influencers. Additionally, protocol officers often serve as the direct liaison with the admiral's spouse (who may participate in social events in an official capacity) in order to plan, coordinate, and deconflict official functions as well as planned personal and family activities.

SPEECHWRITER

As will be described in greater detail in chapter 10, the speechwriter's assignment is complex and many functions overlap those of the scheduler, aide, and PAO. The speechwriter's involvement begins well in advance of the principal's scheduled visit: he or she will contact the event representative to glean key details of the engagement—such as the audience size, venue, audio-visual equipment arrangement, event background or context, desired themes and messages—and research detailed historical or unique facts to personalize the admiral's remarks. Depending on the principal's preferences, the speechwriter will normally meet with the admiral in advance to review the event, propose an outline or rough draft of remarks, and capture the principal's voice, priorities, and strategic messages. Each flag officer has specific preferences for delivery—font size, page layout, microphone placement, podiums; some prefer delivering remarks from spiral binders, notecards, loose-leaf pages, or from prepared PowerPoint slides. Though speechwriters may not be regular members of the admiral's travel party, there are often numerous opportunities within DC to attend speaking engagements, which will aid in the preparation of subsequent products.

SCHEDULER

Time is the admiral's most precious resource. Working with the EA and DEA, the scheduler manages the admiral's calendar. Informed by the admiral's guidance, priorities, and personal proclivities, the scheduler may accept or decline external requests to meet with the admiral or for the admiral to appear or speak at an event. The scheduler will also work with other front offices to coordinate engagements in which multiple flag officers will attend. An effective scheduler is able to politely decline, table, or reassign requests (to another office or lower echelon) that the principal is unable or unwilling to support. Schedulers are also masters at planning things in an organized fashion to minimize the principal's transition time and maximize productivity. On smaller flag staffs, the aide or flag writer may serve in this capacity in addition to their core duties.

FLAG WRITER

The enlisted flag writer works closely with the deputy EA, flag secretary, and scheduler to support the admiral's personal requests, correspondence, and material needs in the Pentagon and home offices. The flag writer maintains a unique and personal relationship with the admiral and many flag writers often follow a particular admiral through the course of several tours.

POLITICAL ADVISOR

On fleet, service chief, and combatant command staffs, the political advisor (POLAD) advises the admiral in matters relating to foreign affairs, domestic politics, and naval strategy—unique perspectives informed by his or her extensive background and civilian career in government, diplomacy, or academia. The POLAD interfaces with the State Department, country teams, and the service's international engagements division (OPNAV N5I). The POLAD helps develop naval strategy, plan international travel engagements, and execute foreign head of Navy (HON) counterpart visits.

SECURITY DETAIL LEAD

Service chiefs and some other senior officers are entitled to a protective service detail (PSD) while performing official duties. One or two civilian NCIS special agents typically lead these security details and are supported by a team of enlisted Navy and Marine masters-at-arms (MA) specialists. The MAs wear civilian clothes and many have attended special small arms training and/or defensive driving schools. The PSD or security representative travels in advance of a trip to familiarize themselves with the various locations the principal will visit, liaise with the local law enforcement authorities, and obtain vehicles to transport the admiral and staff.

As a general rule, the security detail can support the admiral for official business only. Thus, the CNO does not warrant a security detail when running personal errands or attending sporting events in a personal capacity. The security detail provides both a measure of security and a means for efficient movement and travel for the principal, maximizing his or her productivity. As a practical matter, many security detail leads have years of experience supporting flag officers or other senior officials, making them an important resource to, or sounding board for, the EA, deputy EA, and scheduler.

SECURING THE ASSIGNMENT

Many flag officer assignments handle specific subject areas—legislative affairs, budgeting, acquisition, strategy, and manpower, just to name a few. Your background and interests may help you gravitate toward a particular flag officer and his or her specialty. Securing one of these coveted assignments will provide a thorough education on that particular portfolio—and it may very well guide what future tours ashore you execute.

Due to their high visibility, most front office or personal staff positions require some sort of screening or nomination process. Though this procedure can differ depending on the job or office to which you are applying, each record is carefully vetted before it is cleared to proceed to a possible interview. In advance of an interview, BUPERS (or the incumbent office) will compile a package containing fitness reports, biography, recommendations, and any other pertinent information (in some instances, you may be asked to provide some of this material yourself). Before meeting the principal, it is generally a good idea to read his or her biography, perform an internet search for additional background, and to review any key documents or initiatives for which the office is responsible. You should contact the incumbent and request a phone or in-person conversation to become acquainted with the job duties and challenges. In so doing, you will be better prepared for the interview and demonstrate your interest in the position.

The interview itself may be in person, over the phone, or via a video teleconference (VTC). It is important to be on time (early); appear well groomed with a sharp uniform; and maintain a firm handshake, positive posture, and appropriate eye contact with those you meet. Everything—including your appearance, demeanor, and interactions with other staff members in the office leading up to your interview—is part of the evaluation. Interviews themselves tend to be cordial because by that stage, the candidate has generally been deemed qualified. The principal will likely use the interview to try to get a sense of whether or not the two of you will get along and to learn about your personal background, interests, and reflections on your own strengths and weaknesses. It is important not to sound over-rehearsed or too enthusiastic about the opportunity as this may question your purpose or reason for applying. At the scheduled conclusion, it is courteous to thank the admiral for his or her time and mention that you would welcome the opportunity to be part of their team. Finally, a day or two after the interview, it is encouraged to write a note or send a formal email thanking the admiral for his or her time and consideration—even if you are not ultimately selected.

PERSONAL STAFF "DOS AND DON'TS"

Though you will gather more advice in chapter 11, the list below is a short "Top Ten" summary of tips that you can keep discreetly at your desk to enhance your success in a front office personal staff position:

- Never assume the rank of the admiral.
- Your professionalism is a direct reflection on the admiral and the front office.
- Time is the admiral's capital—protect it and employ it efficiently.
- Use the experience to expand your personal and professional network.
- Attend as many engagements as allowed to maximize your learning.
- You are observed always—your spaces are, too (keep them both sharp!).
- Write emails as if you are standing face-to-face with the recipient.
- Do not overanticipate what your boss or others are thinking—you are not expected to be a mind reader.
- As it is in the fleet, front office service is a team sport.
- Never lose sight of what (or who) is important—despite the time "managing up" the chain of command, find time to mentor those junior to you.

CAPT Matthew Duffy has served three tours in Washington, DC, including service as the Deputy EA to the thirty-first CNO. A 1996 graduate of the U.S. Naval Academy, Captain Duffy is a career E-2C Hawkeye naval flight officer, having commanded at the O-5 (squadron) and O-6 (wing) levels. He is a recipient of the 2015 Vice Admiral James Stockdale Leadership Award.

10

SPEECHWRITER: THE PRINCIPAL'S VOICE

CDR GUY SNODGRASS, USN (RET.)

S erving as a speechwriter in the Pentagon is likely to be one of the most professionally rewarding tours of your naval career. While the personal aide or military assistant must execute the schedule and anticipate their boss' needs, you alone are expected to think and write like the principal. The words and products you craft will serve to convey their intent and, in many cases, set policy for the organization. No other role requires you to adopt the knowledge, understanding, and lexicon of your principal than that of speechwriter, and you will return back to a subsequent operational tour with a broad understanding of the topics and relationships that drive success in Washington, DC.

The speechwriter position is demanding. You are expected to be a well-informed generalist, able to write intelligently on a wide variety of topics ranging from manpower to force structure and everywhere in between. Accepting a position as speechwriter—regardless of your principal's rank or position—will empower you to work directly with relevant organizations and agencies to produce speeches, congressional testimony, articles, letters to constituents, and other products as the situation and your principal require.

SPEECHWRITING 101

While speechwriting provides an opportunity to make a real and tangible impact for your organization, you must never forget the paramount rule of speechwriting: it is never about you. You are unlikely to ever be publicly credited or acknowledged for the work you perform. You are expected to serve selflessly, advancing your principal's message and agenda.

This leads to one of the most interesting aspects of the job: the intimate study of your principal and his or her agenda, which primarily consists of the following main elements:

- Develop a solid working knowledge of, and rapport with, your boss.
- Understand your principal's primary themes, messages, and lines of effort.
- Conduct in-depth research to support upcoming speaking events.
- Coordinate with event organizers to tailor the event and shape the message.
- Bridge the divide between the audience and your boss to achieve the desired outcome.

KNOW YOUR BOSS

Developing an intimate understanding of your boss is the most critical aspect of speechwriting. There are two levels to this statement: who your boss is and what he or she stands for, and the more tactical realities of how he or she operates as a leader and public speaker.

PERSONA

To understand how your boss thinks, acts, and speaks, use all the tools at your disposal to gain a deep appreciation of who they are and what they are working to achieve. Research is your friend here: conduct an extensive study to determine what they have said since they first started speaking publicly. Seek out people they have led or worked with previously. Read everything you can get your hands on.

Some immediate questions that come to mind: Where did they go to school? Do they have a family about whom they like to speak? Are they actively involved in sports or do they follow any major sports teams? What do they like and dislike? What books have they read or are reading that may shape their thinking? Have any life or career experiences made a particularly powerful impact on them? What do they stand for and, perhaps just as importantly, what *won't* they stand for? Are they avuncular and jovial, or more cerebral and facts-based? Are they a good public speaker? Knowing your boss is critical to helping him or her connect with an audience.

If your principal is relatively junior, what you can find might be fairly limited; start with remarks they have presented in front of an audience. Your boss will likely have held onto notes or can provide their favorite quotes, turns of phrase, and resource materials to assist you as you get started.

On the other hand, working for a senior leader like the Chief of Naval Operations or a service secretary usually means that they have spent years in the spotlight, thus providing you with access to a treasure trove of publicly available materials and private notes or correspondence. Don't cut corners. Take the time to study everything you can find, as you'll usually be able to identify the "golden thread" that runs throughout their work. Additionally, as a member of the personal staff, request access to your boss' calendar (to see how they are spending their time) and email "Sent Items" (to see what they are saying about issues of importance and to whom). Monitoring the schedule and correspondence also enables you to track events at which your principal may have agreed to speak and for which you may be responsible, as well as infer potential forthcoming tasking that may be assigned to you.

Regardless of how long they have been in the public arena, at some point every leader begins to develop a well-defined public persona. Part of your job is to help your boss remain consistent. No one wants to take the stage only to directly—and accidentally—refute something they said a few months earlier. Consistency lends to their credibility. An in-depth knowledge of your principal ensures that they are up-to-date on the latest developments regarding the subject material while remaining consistent with what they have said in previous public forums.

PREFERENCES

It's also your job to tackle the more tactical realities of preparing your boss' remarks, to include aligning with how they like to deliver their remarks. No detail is too small, and you will be in a great position to assist the other members of your front office team. Do they prefer to read from a fully prepared script, or do they use talking points (hint: it probably depends on the venue). Does your boss prefer to stand behind a podium to deliver, or speak extemporaneously as they work the stage? Hold a handheld microphone or wear a lapel mic? Speak from remarks on loose pages or inserted into a binder? Do they prefer to work in some humor, or is it a "just the facts, Sam" approach? You get the idea.

Make yourself the expert on your boss' speaking preferences. Doing so will set each event up for success while also reducing pressure on the principal's aide-de-camp or military assistant, making you an invaluable part of the team.

At this point it is important to reiterate that *every principal is different*. Regardless of their preferences, your job is to understand them fully, anticipate and expect their needs, and then deliver. This will require a significant investment of time early on, but it'll be smooth sailing once you're dialed in.

Speechwriters must understand their principal's persona and speaking preferences. *U.S. Navy photo*

KNOW YOUR OUTCOME

When first starting out as a speechwriter it is tempting to simply dive in. You're excited: you have received your first assignment, some quick guidance from your principal, a few points of contact, then head back to your desk or over to the library to start digging in.

Stop. Your principal's time is precious. When they accept a request to speak—whether before Congress, as a guest at the Rotary Club, or to their own organization—it is backed by a motive. Your first task is to get to the heart of the purpose for speaking at the event. Depending on your boss' seniority, you might have an opportunity early on to sit down and discuss the event. This is typically the best course of action, as you get to hear directly from them why they accepted the event and what they hope to accomplish.

The reality is that the more senior your principal is, the less likely you are to have an opportunity to sit down with them to discuss every event. Accept the challenge of operating in an information-denied environment and turn yourself into an investigative journalist.

Your first stop should be your boss' scheduler. They will likely have the "five Ws"—who, what, why, when, and where—for the event, as well as the original invitation. Gather as much information as you can about the event, to include the organizer's name and contact information. Do not wait to make contact even if the event is months away. As discussed in chapter 9, you are a representative of your office: reaching out early makes you the first substantive emissary from your office. You can set the event up for success early on by collaborating with the event organizer.

One lesson here: everything is negotiable. Understanding your boss' intent—whether specific to this event or to their strategy as a whole— enables you to work with the event organizer for success. You do not have to accept what they offer as the last word. Part of your job is to work well in advance to design success for the team. Perhaps the organizer does not want to handle a Q&A session but you know your boss is best served by interacting with the audience following their prepared remarks. That's simple to arrange and becomes more achievable the earlier in the process that you start coordinating.

Another key point: though every speech may vary in terms of length or difficulty in preparation, every speaking event has a purpose—even if your principal is speaking to a local club in their hometown. It could be the chance to convey a new strategy to the American public, to extoll the virtue of the All-Volunteer Force, or to thank the audience for their support. Rest assured, your principal is not attending simply because it is a great way to pass a few hours. Determine the purpose of the event and all else will follow—this underpins your strategy.

Finally, understand who will introduce your boss and who (if anyone) will be speaking with them. In many cases, your principal will be the only one up on the platform and will own the event. If speaking with other leaders, determine the relative seniority of those speaking. If your boss is the most senior, you are responsible for driving message alignment. If not, work to ensure your boss is aligned with each speaker so that the overall flow of the event remains consistent.

KNOW YOUR AUDIENCE

Now that you've defined the specific outcome for the event to in a satisfactory level of detail, it's time to turn your attention to the audience. Knowing your audience is paramount to ensure your principal provides remarks that resonate. How many times have you been sitting in the audience listening to a speaker and thought, "Does this person not realize who they're talking to?"

This usually manifests because the speaker didn't fully appreciate their audience. Perhaps they are speaking at a war college but the remarks sound more like they were intended for junior personnel on board a ship or at the flight line. It is also common for senior leaders to mistakenly speak well above the level of their audience, conveying high-level strategic terms and concepts for which the audience lacks sufficient understanding. Regardless of the specific situation, it is painful to watch when a speaker's remarks fail to land with the audience.

Setting your principal up for success requires a good understanding of who the audience is, what message they want or expect to hear, and a bit about their background. First, identify the audience. Is it a family advocacy group? Chamber of Commerce? Congress? Will the remarks be closed to the press, open to the press, or televised? The tone, tenor, and language you write should be markedly different based on the group and whether the remarks are public or off-the-record.

Second, determine what the audience is expecting to hear. What is their overall level of knowledge on the general topic? You've determined *what* they want to hear, but what does the audience *need* to hear? As noted, you can shape this expectation by working early in the process with event organizers. Perhaps the original request for a speech mentioned that the audience wanted to hear "the latest updates from the Pentagon" but you know it is more important to focus on a specific policy initiative. You can easily make this change by working side by side with the event organizers to help shape expectations.

Third, knowing the background of the audience will also enable you to conduct in-depth research to support your boss. Maybe the group just passed a significant historical milestone or has a unique background story that you can work into the remarks. Identifying and incorporating these anecdotes helps to ensure that your principal sounds knowledgeable about the group they're with. It also lends credibility to your boss while reinforcing that he or she is excited to be with the group, rather than the event feeling like a forced march.

To recap: get to know the group your principal will be interacting with. Coordinate early and often. Your boss will be well represented and you'll develop a good working relationship with the group—a win across the board.

One last note: pass along pertinent details to other members of your team. Ask yourself: what do I know, who needs to know, and have I told them? Early on, you are likely to be the primary conduit for information flow between the group hosting the event and your principal's staff. Sharing what you know is critical for team success.

KNOW YOUR MESSAGE

So, you've developed a relationship with your boss, you have your marching orders, and you have worked with the event organizers to tailor the event to meet both their needs as well as your principal's needs. Now it is time to draft the remarks.

The remarks represent the vehicle by which your principal will connect the outcome to the audience. In many respects you are constructing a strategy linking the audience (*ways*) and the message (*means*) to achieve the desired outcome (*end state*). You will want to know the specifics of the event to tailor the message: how long is your principal expected to speak? What is the tone of the event? Is a Q&A session appropriate? Remember: your boss gets a vote. Shape the event early in the process as you begin to simultaneously pull your resources together.

The message is the connective tissue that ties your principal to the audience to achieve the desired outcome. Speechwriting is unique in that you are not writing a research paper—you are writing to compel. Be factually accurate, but do not feel bound to provide counterarguments or long-winded justification for a statement. Your boss is there as the expert, and the audience wants to hear a persuasive speech. In an academic setting, one crafts an argument to support a thesis ultimately building to a conclusion. In speechwriting, you typically tell the audience what you want them to know closer to the beginning, then follow with each major section of the speech supporting the main point.

A good rule of thumb is, "Tell the audience what you are going to tell them; tell them; and then tell them what you told them." Colorful stories, anecdotes, and facts are all great ways to support the speech, but the reason why your boss is there should ring through loud and clear.

One of the best aspects of speechwriting is the opportunity to work with a diverse set of experts while drafting remarks. This can include other principals, their immediate staff, or SMEs. Again, cast a wide net. For example, if speaking to a technical audience about a highly complex system or capability, don't just talk to the staff's resident expert. Reach out to laboratories, congressional staffs, and think tanks. You will build a mosaic of knowledge that will ensure your principal is well versed on the subject, and you will introduce yourself to a wide variety of experts in the process. The relationships you build now will continue to bear fruit for years to come. Compile as much research and information as time allows. Rapidly digest everything you come across, retaining valuable nuggets while quickly shedding extraneous material.

One quick word of caution: keep your eyes and ears tuned for the "third rails" of the topic your boss is speaking on. The best speech can be easily derailed by a statement that demonstrates that your principal is out of touch. Be aware of these issues and share them with your boss so that they have the full context if answering questions during a Q&A session.

BE TRUSTWORTHY, BE FLEXIBLE— AND NEVER TAKE YOURSELF TOO SERIOUSLY

Depending on your principal's seniority, you might find that you are operating with a great deal of autonomy. Trust is always key to success and even more so in this circumstance, as you may find yourself in a position of incredible latitude. Your boss sets policy when speaking, so the words you write will carry great weight. Keep this fact in mind and work to reinforce the trust on a daily basis between you and your principal. Be an honest broker. You are writing for your boss—not for yourself—and many times you will need to carry the water for other senior leaders to ensure the boss has all the facts.

Developing a trusted relationship as a speechwriter is a unique proposition. Because of the demands on your boss' time, trust must be cultivated from afar. Perhaps counterintuitively, if done well, it is likely to result in less, not more, face time with your boss. You know you have hit your stride when the boss trusts you to get the job done with only their "commander's intent," minimal interaction, and minor reworks to the draft you produce. This is the acme of speechwriting skill—taking as little of the boss' time to help them deliver the best possible result.

Flexibility is also key to a speechwriting job and most positions on the front office staff. For starters, because of their busy schedule, your principal may be comfortable waiting until only a day or two before an event to review your draft—a fact that can compress your turnaround time and potentially inject a level of stress into your work. Additionally, you might spend months crafting the best speech of your career only to have the event canceled, or maybe the boss walks out on stage with the speech in hand only to set your work aside and not refer to it at all.

Another quick lesson: perfect is the enemy of good enough. Many a new speechwriter will spend more time than required conducting research in order to produce a transcendent set of remarks for their principal. This becomes a self-defeating endeavor, as the principal benefits by seeing an 80 percent solution earlier in the process rather a 100 percent solution the day prior to the event. Remember: your boss—not you—will be required to present the remarks. They will want plenty of time to review and edit the first draft. In addition, you are also likely to be working on multiple speeches simultaneously. Be judicious with your time and invest it wisely. Prioritize getting a draft to your boss early so that you can receive feedback and adjust accordingly. Never paint yourself (or your boss) into a corner by turning in your remarks too close to the actual speaking event.

Again, your job and sole purpose is to empower your boss. Most principals are iterative, meaning they think through the event and refine their own thoughts in the weeks (or days) leading up to the event. They are likely to try out language and messages in closed-door settings as practice for the main event. If done well and with enough opportunity, they may not need to read directly from their speech because they have already internalized it.

In short, never take yourself too seriously. Take pride in a job well done. Remember that you are the speechwriter, not the speaker. If your boss does not read directly from your text, it is likely because your hard work and dedication early in the process enabled him or her to practice more, making them less—not more—reliant on their prepared remarks on game day. The entire team succeeds when your boss succeeds. Your work ethic and dedication will speak for itself, and you will find your stock rising throughout the organization.

As speechwriter you are merely a supporting actor in a grand play but you never know—perhaps one day you will be that person up on stage delivering the message for an organization you lead. Be purposeful and use this opportunity wisely. Your ability to read widely, think deeply, and learn how to position for success as a senior leader might never be greater.

KEYS TO SUCCESS

- Earn your boss' trust—then work relentlessly to keep it.
- Time is your principal's most precious resource. Learn to accept minimal (and sometimes no) guidance and still produce excellent results,

understanding that less interaction—not more—enables your principal to use their time wisely.

- Stay organized—you will likely be working multiple events simultaneously.
- Do not wait to make a difference—*make* things happen, do not *let* them happen.
- Anticipate and expect problems. Play "what if" regarding your boss' speech.
- Attention to detail rules the day. You owe it to your boss to ensure that what you hand them is ready to go the minute you hand it over.
- Approach every speech as if *you* were ultimately going to be the one giving it.
- Attend every speaking engagement you can to observe your principal in action and inform future remarks.
- Develop relationships with your fellow speechwriters who can provide research, serve as sounding boards, and offer similar (yet different) perspectives.
- Have fun! Use this tour as an opportunity to read widely, think deeply, and introduce yourself to a wide variety of talented people.

CDR Guy Snodgrass, USN (Ret.), served two tours in Washington, DC, including service as speechwriter for the Chief of Naval Operations and as Director of Communications and chief speechwriter to Secretary of Defense James Mattis. A 1998 graduate of the U.S. Naval Academy and 2000 graduate of the Massachusetts Institute of Technology, Commander Snodgrass is a career F/A-18 naval aviator, having commanded VFA-195, forward-deployed in Atsugi, Japan. He was valedictorian of his U.S. Naval War College class and a recipient of the 2010 Michael Hoff Attack Aviator of the Year and 2010 Navy and Marine Corps Leadership awards.

11

PENTAGON SAFETY TIPS

RDML FRED W. KACHER, USN

E very year, leaders from the fleet head to the Pentagon for the first time. Though most opportunities in Washington are fast-paced and stimulating, front office and staff jobs that directly support the leadership of our Navy and the DOD are among those most challenging. For those entering these high-tempo, high-visibility jobs—such as an aide, special assistant, or executive assistant—keeping a few things in mind can make the transition from the fleet more successful. More broadly, these tips will help make any newcomer to the Pentagon more equipped for their upcoming tour there.

GET YOUR LIFE TOGETHER BEFORE YOU REPORT

Although your peers may be heading to shore jobs with a more generous pace, the persistent rhythm of front office jobs (or even tough portfolios as a member of a directorate staff) can make them less forgiving in offices where every member is essential. If you are coming off sea duty, take leave, recharge, and make sure you and your family are well situated prior to starting the job. Think carefully about where you will live—living as close as possible to the office or to mass transit translates to less commute time and that directly translates to more time with your family.

LISTEN CLOSELY TO YOUR RELIEF

Do everything you can to get a face-to-face turnover. Just like a ship or squadron, the information you glean during turnover is often the last "free" knowledge you will get. The job you are entering will likely be vastly different than the one you left, so listen carefully and reserve your opinions until you have lived in your predecessor's shoes for a while.

BE YOUR "BEST SELF" AT ALL TIMES

As a member of your principal's personal staff your behavior will be intrinsically linked to your boss. In some ways, until you are in command, your actions will never be more scrutinized, particularly if you are wearing a loop on your shoulder. Your uniform, fitness, and attitude are all fair game. And remember: others will judge you not by your intentions but by your actions. Be positive and, no matter what, keep your composure.

IT IS NOT ABOUT YOU, IT IS ABOUT THE INSTITUTION

The vast majority of senior leaders for whom you will work will be extraordinarily dedicated human beings who are trying to do the right thing now and for our future. Accordingly, a strong ethos of selflessness runs through the best front offices and there is not a lot of room for self-interest. Senior leaders don't want "strivers" with their own agendas; instead, they are looking for those willing to put the broader organization's needs before their own.

LONG HOURS ARE LIKELY

Yes, these are usually part of the job. We are not living in a nine-to-five world in the operational Navy and our leaders do not live that way either. Early mornings to prepare for the day ahead, later hours to secure the office for the day, and supporting the boss for evening events may very well be part of the job. Over time, you will likely discover just enough flexibility and slack in the tempo to grab a quick workout or take a little leave but do not count on either during the early stages of the job as you work to catch your stride.

HIGH PERFORMANCE, LOW DRAMA

Front office teams often work in close quarters with no privacy in the most visible part of the organization they represent. The best teams and teammates embody confidence without ego. Integrity and discretion are also essential. Most principals will tolerate an occasional mistake—so long as they are not repeated or catastrophic—but none I have worked for stood for a failure of integrity or discretion. The advice we learned as children to always tell the truth and never gossip still pertains.

ALL-STARS ABOUND

While we have all met exceptional people throughout the Navy, the concentration of excellence that surrounds our leadership can be pretty extraordinary. In addition to strong line officers, you will interact more frequently with staff corps and restricted line officers—JAGs, PAOs, and other specialists—who we do not encounter as often in the fleet as junior officers. Many, by nature of their career fields, will have far more experience working on senior staffs (and advising senior leaders) so they can be good sounding boards on staff dynamics and history.

EXPECT TO ENCOUNTER A DIFFICULT PERSONALITY EVERY ONCE IN A WHILE

Senior staffs often attract folks with a healthy ego to match their strong abilities. You will encounter strong, able leaders who will fight very hard for their organizations and their beliefs. Some may be abrasive or, more rarely, toxic. Work hard to stay above the fray, be respectful to your seniors, but do not be a doormat either.

DON'T FORGET WHERE YOU COME FROM— AND WHERE YOU ARE GOING BACK TO

As important as the work you may be doing in a front office is, our profession's foundation remains leadership at sea. Those who keep their perspective do not get intoxicated by "palace intrigue" or creature comforts; even in an office, the warfighter at sea or in the field should come first.

ENGAGE YOUR CIVILIAN TEAMMATES

If you come from the fleet, your contact with Navy or DOD civilians may have heretofore been limited. At the Pentagon, you will work alongside civilians every day. Many civilian professionals serve in a single office longer than a naval officer's rotation, which makes them important sources of institutional and programmatic knowledge. Many of these individuals are exceptional but the expectations and conditions under which they serve are different than those in uniform. Nevertheless, the vast majority of our civilian professionals will be valuable resources if you engage them as partners.

BE NICE TO GATE GUARDS AND ADMINISTRATIVE ASSISTANTS

This old adage will save you quite a bit of trouble—and I have been saved countless times by both. Confidential assistants who are assigned to some of our most senior civilian and military leaders are among the most talented and knowledgeable professionals in the Pentagon. Ignore them or treat them offhandedly at your own peril.

GO ON TRIPS AND ATTEND MEETINGS

Depending on your position, you may be required to go on trips and attend meetings. Even if you are not typically included, do your best to seek out these opportunities when appropriate to do so. While we always want to be good stewards of the taxpayer by not unnecessarily padding the numbers of a travel party, trips often represent the fastest way to build camaraderie and accelerate your assimilation on the team—whether you serve in a front office or part of a broader branch or division in an OPNAV or Joint Staff directorate. More importantly, these opportunities will accelerate your understanding of your boss as you watch him or her deliberate, challenge the staff, and ultimately make decisions that impact our future.

BE CAREFUL ABOUT SPEAKING FOR YOUR BOSS

If you are an executive assistant, an aide, or an influential action officer, you will often be telegraphing your admiral's desires or standards to others, but remember that only one person has earned the stars on your boss' collar—and that isn't you. You need to be diplomatic but forthright and whenever you hear yourself saying, "The admiral wants . . . ," be very, very careful.

RELATIONSHIPS MATTER

On the waterfront, having friends in different departments and in other commands helps. Front offices and staffs work the same way. Tough issues often cross "organizational seams" so teamwork and coordination are important. Do not be so "busy" that you crowd out time for building relationships that you may come to rely on when the going gets tough.

WHO OWNS THE SCHEDULE?

As Secretary of the Navy Gordon England observed, time once spent is gone forever. Across the Pentagon, people will be pushing for more time, looking to save time, and fighting for your boss's time. Managing your boss' "most precious resource" may well be the most difficult and emotional process in the office. Understand who can say "yes" to scheduling requests, who can say "no" (sometimes this is not the same person), and how the office collectively manages this process.

HAVE YOU THANKED AN ACTION OFFICER TODAY?

If time is the coin of the realm on the E-ring, action officers are the life-blood. To make meetings count and more complex issues manageable, AOs prepare read ahead materials that enable a principal to read, review, and seek follow-up prior to the meeting. More significantly, they are often managing million-dollar programs or high-stakes relationships with another nation's Navy—often with very little fanfare and visibility. If you serve on an admiral's or senior civilian's personal staff, treat action officers like gold when they visit the front office—you could not do your job without them. For those reading this book who will serve as action officers, return the favor and build a good relationship with your peers in the front office. In no time you might be selected for a similar front office position (in fact, good action officers are often drafted into these high-visibility options after a year or two in the job).

STRIVE FOR BALANCE ANY WAY YOU CAN

Serving on the E-ring is both a marathon and a sprint. I did not always get it right. You won't have endless time and it is probably not the time to pick up a new, time-consuming hobby. Make every minute out of the office count by focusing on your family and maintaining your health and fitness. The nature of the work can be intellectually taxing as well, so make time for outside reading, even if it is just a few pages before bedtime.

Although these jobs—whether in the E-ring or another bustling part of the Pentagon—can be both hard and humbling, you will learn from some of the masters of our profession. You will also see, hear, and learn things that most of your peers won't experience for years. In some cases, the men and women you work for will become lifelong mentors. Through it all, you will work in a world with constrained resources, no perfect solutions, and good but imperfect people trying to do the best they can. Work hard, be flexible, and most of all, remember that important work awaits you back in the fleet.

RDML Fred W. Kacher is a surface warfare officer who has served three tours in the Pentagon and one in the White House.

12

REFLECTIONS ON SERVICE AT THE PENTAGON

VADM DOUG CROWDER, USN (RET.)

A s an unmarried ensign in my first ship home-ported in San Diego, I would from time to time get together with my favorite uncle who lived up the coast in Orange County. Bill was no more than twenty years older than me but seemed to live a wonderful life in Southern California. He was vice president, West Coast sales for a major computer company—back when you needed a large, separate room for your computer. I marveled at how an early forty-year-old could attain such a position so early in his career.

Over dinner one night, I opined that he would probably be the CEO of the company by the time he was fifty years old. His answer was no, because he told the current CEO that he wouldn't come back to the home office and that all he wanted to do was to stay in Southern California and sell computers. He told me that, therefore, he would never move up the chain at his company—nor should he.

Then he turned to Ensign Crowder and said that it is the same in any large organization: if you are not willing to serve at headquarters and really learn the ropes of the organization, then you probably start to top out as some juncture. He said he never really understood the policies, finances, and strategic direction of his large company—but boy, could he sell computers. So, Ensign Crowder, you'll need to make the same decision someday. Fast forward thirty-five years, I retired as the Deputy Chief of Naval Operations (Operations, Plans, and Strategy), my tenth Pentagon assignment, combined with nine sea duty tours. I don't really know if it was me who pushed "the system" for all of those assignments or the system that pushed me. But it is clear to me that my Pentagon duties over the years gave me a very broad understanding of the Navy and national security affairs. It was also rewarding in the sense that most of Navy's key

175

VADM Doug Crowder addressing sailors in Yokosuka, Japan, on July 11, 2008. *U.S. Navy photo by MC2 Matthew Schwarz/Released*

policy decisions were made in the Pentagon and I had an opportunity to help shape them. I am also convinced that my Pentagon experience greatly shaped my effectiveness during my nine tours at sea, including five in command. So if you are heading to the Pentagon, here are a few words of wisdom for you.

HIT THE DECK RUNNING

FOR JUNIOR OFFICERS (NON-FLAG OFFICERS)

When reporting to your Pentagon staff, have your personal life settled if at all possible—move completed, kids in school, leave taken, etc. Why? Because the staff position you fill now makes you the "expert" on those issues/programs. You are probably coming from sea duty and have little understanding of the issues you have inherited or, at best, not familiar with their current state of play. To make matters worse, you often inherit an "empty chair"; that is, your predecessor has already detached to make their en route training pipeline as they head back to the fleet. And "Murphy" will tell you that your issue/program will be the "flap de jour" soon after you arrive. Your flag officer really does not care that you are newly reported. So, go into overdrive the minute you report. Quickly get up to speed, meet with other officers who also track the issue/program. And if you are lucky, you won't be called up to the E-ring the first week you are in town—but don't bet on it.

FOR FLAG OFFICERS
Your task is more about getting out and establishing contacts, first within your staff and, if applicable, on the other service, secretariat, Joint Staff and OSD staffs. Have each section of your staff in for an intensive update on the issues they are working. Two benefits of these meetings: first, you get a quick booster shot of knowledge, and second, you meet those action officers critical to your organization.

DON'T JOIN THE "BITCHING CLASS"

FOR JUNIOR OFFICERS
One of the first things I noticed during my first tour on the Chief of Naval Operations (OPNAV) staff was an almost incessant amount of complaining about being in the Pentagon instead of at sea. It almost reaches bravado level when two or more naval officers meet, a proverbial badge of honor. My advice: don't join that club. Be positive and appreciative of the opportunity to help shape key decisions that will affect the entire Navy. Also, you will stand out as one who understands the importance of the decision process. Learning the ropes is a real education and puts you in a better professional position when you do return to the fleet.

FOR FLAG OFFICERS
The same advice applies to you. Additionally, positive and upbeat leadership of the officers working for you in the Pentagon is too often overlooked. Make sure you are sending the right signal to your troops—what we do here is important. Take that staff officer with you to brief Navy's top leadership whenever you can—and let him or her brief the issue. I still remember the first time I briefed the Secretary of the Navy. My three-star boss introduced me and allowed Lieutenant Crowder to present the brief—and that was almost forty years ago. I went home that night feeling like a million bucks.

LEARNING THE ROPES

FOR JUNIOR OFFICERS
A first tour of duty in Washington is a steep learning curve for most. It is steeper if you avoid or are reluctant to get out and about and learn. Find a mentor, attend some meetings chaired by others in your division, pick everyone's brain, etc. The more you know the lay of the land, the players and the issues—and the sooner you do—the more effective and valuable you are to your organization. Keeping a low profile because you are not very experienced is counterproductive to your growth as an action officer.

You should not be afraid to say you do not know something or even how the staffing process works. Sign up for the action officer course as soon as you arrive. Asking more experienced officers to explain key issues is a good thing, but then put that knowledge to work. Someone always has the answer—do not be reluctant to seek them out. And be honest and earnest—you are on a mission to become an important asset to the team.

FOR FLAG OFFICERS

You too must quickly learn the ropes. Cultivate fellow flag officers on your staff. The mutual protective society is alive and well and you need to be a prime member. Sit down with small groups of your staff officers early on. Have them tell you what they think is important, the state of play, and potential shoals to avoid. A good way to do this is to schedule monthly "hours of power" with each of your shops. Let them tell you what they are working on and its state of play. Most importantly, conduct a dialogue with your staff.

PERSONAL RELATIONSHIPS

FOR JUNIOR OFFICERS

As in most organizations, establishing personal relationships is important. Invest the time to do so early on. It is an investment that will pay off handsomely. Cold calling an action officer who also works your issue when the crunch is on is too late. Get out of your office and meet colleagues face to face. Meeting for breakfast or lunch is a good way to do so. Even a brown bag lunch in the office builds personal relations. I had a fellow OPNAV staff officer that I didn't know well invite me to lunch in his office for hot dogs and a general bull session on what was going on in the Pentagon. It was great, and we established a close working relationship. Later I found out that he had done the same thing with a different person every week. He was the best-connected and most knowledgeable officer in the building.

FOR FLAG OFFICERS

All of the above for junior officers applies to you. Additionally, you should be establishing personal relationships with your issues counterparts in the other services and, if applicable, the service secretary and OSD staffs. Follow up with phone calls when an issue crosses your desk that also affects one of your contacts. Share information with them and keep them from being surprised. In the end, they will reciprocate, making you even more effective. Develop a personal relationship with the key executive assistants (Navy captains) on the OPNAV and SECNAV staffs. They know more than most and can help you to hit the mark with your own staff work.

BRIEFINGS: LESS IS MORE

FOR BOTH JUNIOR OFFICERS AND FLAGS

Building PowerPoint briefs has become a way of life in the Pentagon. Do what you can not to add to it. Some PowerPoint briefs appear to be measured by throw-weight—not just the number of slides but also the amount of words that can be squeezed onto the page. These briefs often appear to be "cut and paste" drills from a previously well-written paper. As often as possible, try briefing without PowerPoint at all. Engage your interlocutor in a conversation and an actual dialogue on the issue at hand. If PowerPoint cannot be avoided, make simple slides with short word bullets that merely guide you through the points you want to make. In my experience, it is much more effective to oblige those you are briefing to *listen to you* and not just read your slides. If necessary, provide a point paper on the topic as a read ahead. PowerPoint slides packed with full paragraphs and megabytes of information can be briefed by anyone. Short bullets cause the recipients to focus on you and your knowledge and recommendations. Plus, it will be a wonderful break from the dreaded "death by PowerPoint."

CIVILIANS: THEY SERVE, TOO

FOR JUNIOR OFFICERS

Those coming to the Pentagon for their first tour too often see civilian members of staffs as second-class citizens. How many of these guys have ever deployed overseas or in combat? It is a big mistake to look at things that way. Although some civilian staff members have served on active duty, many have not. However, they too have chosen to serve their country in a civilian capacity. We should respect them for their service. Ignoring them—or worse, being condescending—is unprofessional and foolish. Many have served years in a specific segment of our business and are walking encyclopedias on the ways of the Pentagon. You ignore them at your own peril. Cultivate relationships with key civilian staff members. They will judge your sincerity and are eager to share their expertise when your interest in them is genuine.

FOR FLAG OFFICERS

Cultivating a personal relationship with key senior civilians is crucial. Respect their rank, especially Senate-confirmed folks such as service assistant secretaries and similar senior-level civilians in OSD. Avoid over familiarity until they initiate it. Make a point to call on those senior civilians in your sphere of interest. Invite them to service events or even trips to see our sailors and Marines at sea and in the field. Develop a personal relationship based on mutual interest and trust. Many civilians will be back in more senior positions in the future—and so will you. Offer your counsel but don't preach (or condescend). A good relationship will set conditions for them to seek your counsel often.

WHAT LANGUAGE ARE YOU SPEAKING?

FOR BOTH JUNIOR OFFICERS AND FLAGS

I would often attend briefings given by flag officers to senior civilians and watched the gap of understanding not close very much due to "language barriers." At one particular briefing a three-star officer said "Hooah"—used sequentially as a verb, noun, adjective, and question mark—at least thirty times during a twenty-minute brief on a very important subject. The senior civilians in the room were not impressed. Know your audience. When briefing senior civilians in OSD, you should not use the same vocabulary and tone as talking to your division on the ship or your company of Marines. And do not show up to the meeting with a vanguard of your staff officers in tow. Most senior civilians (for example, deputy assistant secretaries) do not have staff and wonder why your need an echelon of action officers to accompany you. It may leave the impression that you do not know the issues—or worse.

EXPAND YOUR HORIZONS

In conjunction with building relationships in the Pentagon is building contacts with national security professionals elsewhere in Washington.

FOR JUNIOR OFFICERS

Join discussion groups that get together evenings to look at current defense policy issues, often with significant guest speakers. One example is the Strategy Discussion Group (SDG). This community of like-minded professionals meets once a month or so and almost always with a speaker with real expertise on issues. Past speakers include service chiefs, senior DOD leaders, key congressional staff, etc. The Center for Naval Analyses also sponsors a similar sort of speakers series—and there are many more.

FOR FLAG OFFICERS

Have someone track the public discussions sponsored by the various think tanks in town, such as the Center for Strategic and International Studies (CSIS), Heritage Foundation, Brookings Institution, Center for a New American Security—and there are many, many others (as described in chapter 16). Better yet, get on the event announcement email list of a few of these organizations. More importantly, try to attend an event of interest each month or so. Doing so benefits you in two distinct ways: you will hear different perspectives on key issues *and* meet other national security professionals who you can add to your contact list.

IF YOU DON'T UNDERSTAND CONGRESS, YOU DON'T REALLY UNDERSTAND WASHINGTON

FOR JUNIOR OFFICERS

Work with your service's congressional liaison and legislative affairs (LA) folks to find opportunities to attend a few Senate Armed Services Committee (SASC) or House Armed Services Committee (HASC) hearings (or those of their subcommittees). Keep in contact with the officers in your LA office who are involved with programs you work on. Find a junior staffer on HASC or SASC staff and start a professional relationship.

FOR FLAG OFFICERS

So much of what you do connects directly to the various committees and subcommittees on the Hill. Get to know key senior staff members. Meet some for breakfast. Attend events on the Hill. Take the time to really learn how to operate and navigate Congress—and its many shoals. Your service LA chief should be your guide and mentor. Connect with him or her early in your tour and often throughout.

THE TANK

FOR JUNIOR OFFICERS

One of the key decision-making forums in the Department of Defense is the meeting of the Joint Chiefs. They meet, usually a couple of times each week, in a secure conference room nicknamed "the Tank." Their operations deputies (three-star general officers/flag officers) also meet there to consider issues and prepare for follow-on discussion by the chiefs.

For Navy, OPNAV N3/N5 staffs most issues. For the Marine Corps, the Deputy Commandant for Plans, Policies, and Operations (PP&O) staff is normally in the lead. It is always good to have a broad understanding of key issues. If nothing else, get a copy of the published (though not widely distributed) Tank schedule to see what the key, current issues top military leaders are dealing with. And figure out a way to visit the Tank when meetings are not ongoing.

FOR FLAG OFFICERS

It is important to be aware of the issues going to the Tank. In some cases, you may want to make an input to your service chief's staffing process. Usually you can best do this through the operations deputy (N3/N5, PP&O, etc.). I found this sort of flag officer input most helpful when I was the Navy's operations deputy.

THE POWER OF IDEAS

My own experience in the Pentagon showed me time and time again that the Building really runs on the power of ideas. The officer, junior or otherwise, who best articulates an argument, a proposed policy, or a new way ahead is extremely valuable, regardless of rank. Flag officers should establish a culture that ensures the best ideas and proposals get to them—no matter who conceived them. Rank is important, but the power of ideas trumps even that.

In many cases, some of our best ideas and concepts come from those working the issues every day. I remember struggling with the challenge of greatly increasing Navy's ability to forward deploy forces in the aftermath of the attacks of September 11, 2001. A young commander/O-5 on my staff was the prime mover in developing the Fleet Response Plan in 2002, a fundamental change in our ability to surge-deploy forces in time of crisis. As I write this paragraph, that young O-5 is an active-duty four-star admiral. For junior officers, critical thinking and the ability to articulate your ideas both verbally and in writing are key skills that will make you a most valuable member of the team. Don't hesitate to make your ideas known. After all, this is *your* Navy, too!

VADM Doug Crowder, USN (Ret.), is a career surface warfare officer who served in nine different assignments afloat and two additional fleet assignments, culminating in command of the U.S. Seventh Fleet (2006–8).

Ashore, he served in ten different jobs in the Pentagon, including four as a flag officer. His final assignment was as Deputy Chief of Naval Operations (Operations, Plans & Policy) N3/N5 (2008–10). He served as chairman of the Olmsted Foundation (2013–19). Admiral Crowder is an Olmsted Scholar having studied at the University of Lausanne, Switzerland, from 1980 to 1982.

PART IV
"ACROSS THE RIVER"

13

THE WHITE HOUSE

CAPT JOSEPH A. GAGLIANO, USN

T he White House is awe-inspiring. There is no comparable feeling to walking up West Executive Avenue—"West Exec"—and entering the West Wing for the first time. Attending a meeting between cabinet officials and the President in the Situation Room feels historic. You cannot help but feel that you are in a very special place during even the most routine daily events. This feeling emerges from one inescapable presence: the presidency.

To be sure, there is a marked difference between the President and the presidency. The former reflects the individual; the latter represents the institution. While the President is important, the tenure of the man who resides in the White House is fleeting compared to the enduring nature of the institution. The presidency has persisted—and will remain—throughout the history of this republic. Interestingly, our best presidents have understood this relationship, often making decisions that do not benefit themselves or their administration but rather serve to protect the institution for future presidents. The magnitude of this institution permeates everything that occurs at the White House.

While some may approach working for the President as tantamount to staffing any other principal, an assignment at the White House offers an opportunity to actively contribute at the highest levels of government. Serving the President becomes a daily affirmation of supporting the presidency and every day provides countless opportunities to do so. From conducting interagency meetings to further the President's agenda to transmitting cabinet direction to communicate presidential intentions, to writing memos to answer the chief executive's questions—every piece of business centers on the Oval Office.

This chapter is designed to help you, as a rising defense professional, understand how national defense policy is coordinated at the White House

The White House complex encompasses eighteen acres just north of the National Mall. *U.S. Marine Corps photo by LCpl Micha R. Pierce/Released*

and, when necessary, approved by the President. This discussion will center on the National Security Council staff, which acts as the President's personal staff for all national security affairs and is the organization within which most active-duty officers assigned to the White House are placed. This chapter also explains the NSC history, purpose, structure, and key players. Finally, it describes daily life on this special staff.

THE GROUNDS

To the casual observer, the White House may appear to be an iconic building that holds a small staff. In reality, the President and his staff encompass a large number of people and office space—often referred to as the "eighteen-acres of the White House." This term highlights that the White House is in reality a campus of government buildings and functions rather than a singular building. The White House campus is composed of numerous offices that span the responsibilities of national-level decision-making, from policy that is strictly domestic in nature to national security policy pursued far from American shores. This campus includes the Residence, West Wing, East Wing, Eisenhower Executive Office Building (EEOB), North Lawn, and South Lawn. The President's staff also extends to several buildings beyond the White House grounds, such as the New Executive Office Building (NEOB) across Pennsylvania Avenue and the Office of the U.S. Trade Representative across 17th Street.

THE PRESIDENT'S STAFF

The White House Chief of Staff oversees every employee who supports the President. This staff is composed of hundreds of individuals organized under the Executive Office of the President (EOP), an immense organization that includes:

- Office of the Vice President
- National Security Council
- Office of Management and Budget
- Council of Economic Advisers
- President's Intelligence Advisory Board
- Office of Science and Technology Policy
- Office of National Drug Control Policy
- Office of the United States Trade Representative
- Council on Environmental Quality

The DOD interacts with several of these offices. For example, DOD often answers questions from the OMB, the office charged with overseeing all budgeting and expenditures throughout government. The DOD also works with the Office of Science and Technology Policy in exploring cutting-edge research. Additionally, it is common for the DOD to receive questions from the Vice President, who customarily maintains a keen interest in troop issues. Nonetheless, the National Security Council is the center of foreign policy and defense issues, so the DOD spends more time interacting with the NSC staff than any other office at the White House.

THE NATIONAL SECURITY COUNCIL

BACKGROUND AND HISTORY

Following the conclusion of World War II, congressional leaders sought to reformulate the national security establishment to address several concerns. First, the federal government's wartime structure was characterized by a concentration of power under President Franklin Roosevelt and his handful of advisors. This arrangement left numerous departments and agencies shut out of the decision-making process, including those with key national security equities. Second, a central change to national defense was the creation of the Defense Department, and Congress believed vesting statutory powers within the fledgling department would be necessary to preventing the elder State Department from marginalizing this new-comer—particularly with respect to foreign affairs issues. Third, the United States invested heavily in postwar international organizations and legal institutions to prevent the recurrence of world war, and the government required an internal body to coordinate the instruments of national power to engage effectively in these emerging international mechanisms.

To this end, the National Security Council was created under the 1947 National Security Act. The bill stated, "The function of the Council shall be to advise the President with respect to the integration of domestic, foreign, and military policies relating to the national security so as to enable the military services and the other departments and agencies of the Government to cooperate more effectively in matters involving the national security." It also listed two duties: first, to "assess and appraise the objectives, commitments, and risks of the United States in relation to our actual and potential military power, in the interest of national security; for the purpose of making recommendations to the President"; and second, to "consider policies on matters of common interest to the departments and agencies of the Government concerned with the national security, and to make recommendations to the President." Although the council's composition and structure has evolved over the last several decades, its function and duties largely have adhered to the original intent.

EVOLUTION AND MAKEUP

The National Security Act also established the NSC's original member-ship, a roster that included the President, Secretary of State, Secretary of Defense (a position created under this legislation), Secretary of the Army, Secretary of the Navy, Secretary of the Air Force, Chairman of the National Security Resources Board (later disestablished), and secretaries and undersecretaries of other departments selected by the President. This membership was amended two years later with the 1949 National Security Act Amendment, which removed the cabinet-level status of the military departments by legislating their "unified direction under civilian control of the secretary of defense." This law also created the position of Chairman of the Joint Chiefs of Staff. In the end, the NSC evolved to include four statutory members—the President, Vice President, Secretary of State, and Secretary of Defense—but the President can add leaders from any other departments and agencies as desired.

The original council also did not include a figure known today as the National Security Advisor; instead, it was headed by a civilian executive secretary who acted more like an administrative coordinator than the President's closest representative for national security issues. This approach to institutional organization was not unique in this era. For example, the original Joint Chiefs of Staff did not include a chairman but rather, was headed by a director who was required to be junior to each service chief.

The newness of the council during the Truman, Eisenhower, and Kennedy administrations resulted in early swings in both character and function. The NSC staff initially was sourced from the armed services and largely performed a liaison role back to the Pentagon—particularly during the Eisenhower administration, as this arrangement suited the former army general's decision-making style. When President Kennedy entered office, however, he preferred more academically oriented national security decision-making, forcing the NSC to add more civilians to the staff.

The most significant event that shaped the long-term makeup of the NSC staff occurred in the first year of the Kennedy administration. Less than three months after the inauguration, 1,400 Cuban exiles launched a botched invasion on the southern coast of Cuba at the Bay of Pigs. The CIA trained the exiles, and the plan's success depended on U.S. bomber support (which was made covert under the story that the bombers were in fact Cuban aircraft flown by defectors). However, the cover story quickly unraveled and Kennedy was reticent to openly commit support for the invasion. Moreover, the landing site was changed at the last minute, and the President was not aware of the associated risks before he gave the order to proceed. The invading force came under immediate heavy fire, and over the next day, the Cuban military advanced on the beach with 20,000 troops to defeat the invasion.

This event irrevocably changed the evolution of the NSC staff as Kennedy gleaned two key lessons from the failed invasion. First, the President's decision-making space was constrained by the information provided by departments and agencies. He relied on the CIA and Defense Department to provide analysis and recommendations based on their own intelligence, and an enduring characteristic of governments is that recommendations often can be colored—intentionally or not—by the interests of the department or agency from which they were generated. Second, because all departments and agencies employ their own jargon, the predominantly civilian staff lacked an in-house "translator" who can make information clear for the President. Consequently, Kennedy was forced to make decisions without a clear understanding of the situation.

Following the Bay of Pigs incident, Kennedy initiated two significant changes that remain today. First, he commissioned a White House center where intelligence cables could be received and analyzed. Built in the former President Roosevelt's infamous "map room," it remains today as the White House Situation Room. Second, Kennedy moved the NSC staff leadership—the National Security Advisor, Deputy National Security Advisor, and NSC Executive Secretary—into the West Wing. These two changes offered the President on-call access to an independent flow of information and an advisory team right around the corner that could make recommendations based on the President's interests—rather than those of subordinate departments and agencies.

PURPOSE AND FUNCTIONS

From its origin, the NSC was centrally designed to serve presidential decision-making. The entirety of this organization is designated as the President's staff, meaning their primary organizational loyalty is to pursuing the President's agenda. Despite the legislative formality in establishing the National Security Council, the term "NSC" is often used in Washington with less precision. By the strictest definition, meetings of the National Security Council are those chaired by the President and attended by the statutory members outlined in the National Security Act and its associated Amendment. In fact, NSC meetings chaired by the President are rare compared to the numerous subordinate meetings that occur multiple times each week. A more common—and useful—definition typically used inside the Beltway is that NSC meetings are those coordinated and chaired by a member of the NSC staff.

Beyond simply facilitating senior-level meetings, the NSC staff also maintains the White House Situation Room, which is customarily referred to by the acronym WHSR (pronounced "WIZ-er"), "Situation Room," or simply the "Sit Room." As discussed above, WHSR resides in the West Wing and directly supports the White House leadership in remaining apprised of world events. It also serves as the President's communications center, connecting White House leadership with other U.S. government leaders, as well as facilitating diplomatic phone calls between the White House and foreign leaders. WHSR maintains a watch floor manned around-the-clock to perform these functions and, consequently, comprises a substantial portion of the NSC staff.

STRUCTURE AND COMPOSITION

Every administration outlines NSC business rules in a presidential directive that establishes membership and procedures for the next four years; other than the statutory members, the President can arrange the NSC and its functions however they desire. These presidential directives come by different names based on administration preferences—the Clinton, Bush, Obama, and Trump administrations referred to them as National Security Presidential Memorandums, Presidential Policy Decisions, National Security Presidential Decisions, and Presidential Decision Directives, respectively—but they all serve similar functions. In what is traditionally the first directive dispatched, the newly elected President identifies the members of the National Security Council and the committees that feed their decision-making. Despite differences from one administration to another, every organizing directive over the last three decades has featured largely similar structures.

At the top of this structure is the formal council, composed of the President and the principal NSC members. In addition to the statutory members, principal attendees customarily include the cabinet officials from national security–related departments and agencies, such as the Secretary of the Treasury, Attorney General, Secretary of Energy, Secretary of Homeland Security, and United Nations representative. The Chairman of the Joint Chiefs of Staff and Director of National Intelligence (who serve as statutory advisors to the NSC), as well as the Director of the CIA, usually join these principals. When economic issues play a particularly important role in a given discussion, this group can expand to include the Secretary of Commerce and U.S. trade representative. Not all formal NSC meetings aim to produce presidential decisions, as it is common to schedule "NSC time" to solicit the President's policy preferences and feedback in person.

The NSC staff is organized around geographical and functional directorates each led by a "senior director." Geographically, there are offices that focus on regional areas such as the Middle East, Europe, Far East, and Western Hemisphere, and each office has specialists appointed to oversee policymaking for countries within that region. For example, the directorate handling security affairs in East Asia will have directors assigned for each

The National Security Council exists to facilitate presidential decision making. *NARA*

country in the region, such as South Korea, Japan, and China. Functionally, there are offices that focus on global issue areas—including intelligence, economics, and defense policy—that extend beyond individual regions. This arrangement seeks to balance the staff between the requirement to hire area specialists and the desire to develop comprehensive foreign policies that are consistent globally. The former is a prerequisite for informed national security decision-making and the latter befits a superpower.

The vast majority of the staff—nearly 90 percent—is composed of nonpolitical, career service officers from organizations throughout the federal government. While the composition of NSC staffs varies from administration to administration, the leadership typically fills most positions in regional and functional directorates with specialists from the State Department, Defense Department, and intelligence community. The workhorses of the NSC staff are the "directors," who are typically brought onboard for appointments lasting one or two years, after which the director will return to their home department or agency to resume their career progression. These assignments are enhancing to rising individuals—regardless of their home department—because the experience allows them to better support their department's leadership when interacting with the White House. This experience becomes even more valuable if that individual is promoted to the senior executive service or general officer/flag officer ranks.

Those not drawn from subordinate departments and agencies are known as "direct hires." This small group principally is composed of special assistants focused on staff administration and individuals hired from outside government who hold special skills. Special assistants are the lifeblood of the NSC staff and their expertise in staffing the administrative work brings national security policy from ideas to fruition. Moreover, their detailed understanding of presidential records requirements ensures future historians and international relations scholars can explore how the President reached specific decisions.

Of note, the size of the NSC staff is a popular target among the political class. The staff has grown considerably since its inception, a trend that is not attributable to any particular political party or administration. One pattern that is similar between successive administrations, however, is an initial desire to reduce the staff size prior to taking office only to realize the overwhelming amounts of intelligence and pace of national security work necessitates a large staffing footprint. The NSC staff provides the President with independent information, analysis, and recommendations that become indispensable once they are responsible for national security decision-making.

LEADERSHIP

Three key individuals head the NSC staff. At the top of this organization is the Assistant to the President for National Security Affairs (APNSA), more commonly known as the "National Security Advisor." As discussed above, this position did not appear in the original NSC design, but over the decades, the National Security Advisor has achieved quasi-cabinet-level status. Unlike cabinet secretaries, the National Security Advisor does not require congressional confirmation. Additionally, the APNSA's status as the President's go-to person for day-to-day national security issues creates a tight-knit working relationship between the advisor and the President. This relationship carries an associated authority based on a presumption that they speak directly for the President. Cabinet secretaries may hold official relative seniority but if they wonder where the President stands on a particular issue, they will call the National Security Advisor and ask, "Where is the President's thinking on this?" As such, when the National Security Advisor chairs a meeting and states the President's policy preferences, they have outsized influence relative to their cabinet-level counterparts. This position achieved celebrity status first under Henry Kissinger during the Nixon administration and has since remained a high-visibility position.

The second key NSC leader, the Deputy Assistant to the President for National Security Affairs (DAPNSA), falls immediately under the National Security Advisor and is more commonly referred to as the "Deputy National Security Advisor." This official provides day-to-day guidance for the NSC staff and communicates with their counterparts throughout the inter-agency, namely the second in command for each department and agency.

Third, the Executive Secretary and the Chief of Staff coordinate admin-istrative efforts within the staff and communications external to the staff. Within the NSC staff, they ensure all material presented to the President and National Security Advisor have been coordinated properly between regional and functional directorates and is formatted uniformly. External to the staff, they transmit and receive formal communications between the White House and departments and agencies.

COMMITTEES

In preparation for meetings with the President, the Principals Committee (PC)—referred to colloquially as "the Principals"—meets beforehand in what comprises the second level of NSC decision-making. The PC receives recommendations from subordinate committees and nominally follows one of three decision-making paths. First, it could form consensus around a specific course of action and forward it to the President as the Principals' recommendation. Second, it could form consensus around a whole-of-government execution plan, given that it does not reach the threshold required for presidential review. Third, it could return an issue to subordinate committees for further refinement or to consider additional options. Principals Committee meetings are chaired by the National Security Advisor, contributing to quasi-cabinet-level status by empowering them with agenda-setting authority and placing them as a first among equals on the Principals Committee.

The next level down is the Deputies Committee (DC), which is composed of the second-in-command of each department and agency. Deputies Committee members typically include the Deputy Secretary of Defense, Deputy Secretary of State, Deputy Secretary of the Treasury, Vice Chairman of the Joint Chiefs of Staff, and so on. Similar to the Principals

Committee, the Deputies Committee receives recommendations from subordinate committees and nominally chooses one of three paths: form consensus around a specific course of action and forward it to the Principals Committee; form consensus around a whole-of-government execution plan, given that it does not reach the threshold required for PC review; or return an issue to subordinate committees to be developed further. The Deputy National Security Advisor chairs Deputies Committee meetings.

Subordinate to the DC reside a number of coordination committees. Although the PC and the DC retain their name between administrations, the naming convention for this level of coordination changes—such as Policy Coordination Committees or Interagency Policy Committees—but their function remains the same. Each committee is established to address a specific issue or issue area, and they can be created on an ad hoc basis or as standing committees that meet regularly. Attendees are normally at the assistant secretary level, to include assistant secretaries of state, assistant secretaries of defense, assistant secretaries of the treasury, and so on. Since departments and agencies employ many assistant secretaries to cover regions or functions, each department and agency will send the relevant individual to suit the meeting. These meetings usually form a starting point for formal interagency coordination and will carry the burden of developing options for national security decision-making.

It should be noted that not all NSC meetings are held as formal, in-person gatherings. When an issue requiring decision does not appear to be controversial or portend opposing positions between departments and agencies, the National Security Advisor or Deputy National Security Advisor may call for a "paper PC" or "paper DC." In these cases, the NSC staff develops policy papers and associated recommendations for review by the PC or DC. The NSC staff circulates these papers to attendees through formal channels, and each relevant department and agency is given a period of time to provide feedback. Once all replies are received, the NSC staff will consolidate and send a summary of conclusions to departments and agencies.

Given the relative seniority of coordination committee attendees, action officers accomplish the vast majority of supporting work. The NSC staff convenes lower-level synchronization meetings to solicit ideas, leverage expertise, or gauge interagency consensus prior to calling a coordination committee meeting. These working-level meetings also can be directed by coordination committees to develop options prior to forwarding to the

DC. Since these ad hoc gatherings do not have the same strict attendance restrictions placed on higher-level meetings, sub-coordination committee meetings are the best opportunity for action officers to participate in national security decision-making at the White House.

INTERAGENCY INTEGRATOR

The NSC staff's primary responsibility is to serve the President, but it provides a more important function for the rest of the executive branch of government. As Mike Wisecup describes in chapter 15, interagency coordination is critical to facilitating whole-of-government solutions in response to complex national challenges.

The term "interagency" is an adjective; there is no building or organization that houses "the interagency" where disputes are resolved. Instead, disagreements are addressed through an interagency process that aims to ensure all points of view are considered. The National Security Council is uniquely suited to bring together the numerous departments and agencies, particularly when competing bureaucratic interests could otherwise inhibit a consensus recommendation for the President. When the Principals Committee presents a recommendation to the President, not every department and agency will say their preferred option was selected; however, they should agree that their concerns were heard—whether by the principals, deputies, or coordinating committee.

As the National Security Council evolved over the years, one important change occurred during the George H. W. Bush administration that transformed interagency coordination. The DC became the key instrument of policy development. This arrangement has endured because the Deputies Committee strikes a balance between seniority and availability. Principals Committee meetings require aligning the principals' schedules, which often requires delaying meetings by weeks to ensure all interested principals are available to attend. Conversely, DC meetings can be scheduled weekly or even more frequently, because compared to their principal bosses, they have more flexible schedules. In the end, the deputies are senior enough to possess the authorities to commit support from their department or agency but flexible enough to attend regular interagency meetings. This development seems logical in retrospect but given the near political necessity to distinguish one administration from its predecessor, it took a good deal of foresight and flexibility for the Clinton administration to keep this Bush-era development. Maintaining this signature change by National Security Advisor Brent Scowcroft involved some political risk, but in the long run it helped institutionalize an enduring method of achieving efficient interagency consensus.

In addition to this formal interagency policy development, the NSC staff also facilitates immeasurable informal interagency communication. For example, directors convey the President's policy preferences to their interagency counterparts. While departments and agencies are free to develop independent options and recommendations for consideration, understanding the commander in chief's bounds of acceptable and unacceptable options will save countless staff hours ensuring they are not developing options that never stand a chance in the President's eyes. The NSC staff also helps interagency counterparts build effective interagency networks, whether through in-person meetings at the White House or wide-scale email communications. Staff directors are also responsive to queries between departments, such as a request from a DOD action officer seeking their counterpart at the State Department.

The NSC directors can also represent the policies of departments and agencies with the non-NSC White House staff. The President's staff performs a number of functions—speechwriting, advance travel planning, domestic policy—and these groups can have widespread impacts on national security policy. To ensure the President does not inadvertently contradict existing policies driven by subordinate departments and agencies, the NSC staff frequently coordinates on the language of an upcoming presidential speech or goals for a pending presidential visit, ensuring whole-of-government policy consistency. The NSC staff also can assist departments and agencies by finding opportunities for the President to support their goals. For example, if the NSC director knows something is a priority for one department, he or she can help shape the President's schedule and speeches to support it.

Despite the significant influence of the NSC staff on national security decision-making, care must be given to prevent this staff from becoming "operational." The staff is designed to support the commander in chief and facilitate interagency consensus building in developing recommended options for the President. The Reagan administration and its successors learned important lessons from the indictments and convictions that resulted when NSC staffers acted with what they wrongly perceived to be the authority to direct military of government operations. Simply put, they do not. No individual on the NSC staff can direct departments and agencies to commit resources toward one initiative or another. Instead, the staff's influence emerges from an ability to frame issues for the President and convey the President's desires to departments and agencies—but one should never forget that White House decision-making authority resides solely in the Oval Office.

WHITE HOUSE MILITARY OFFICE

While the National Security Council is responsible for all defense policy at the White House, it does not coordinate day-to-day military support for the President. The White House Military Office (WHMO, pronounced "WHAM-oh") is responsible for providing this support and, with the only military members routinely appearing in uniform, becomes the most visible military presence at the White House. Within the EOP organization listed at the beginning of this chapter, WHMO is considered a subunit under the White House Office.

WHMO oversees several individual military units, including:
- White House Communications Agency
- Presidential Airlift Group
- Naval Support Facility Thurmont (Camp David)
- Marine Helicopter Squadron One (HMX-1)
- White House Transportation Agency
- White House Medical Group
- Presidential Food Service

WHITE HOUSE SOCIAL AIDES

In addition to providing officers for the rotation of military aides who follow the President every day (those who carry the "nuclear codes" in a briefcase referred to as "the football"), WHMO's ceremonies coordinator oversees the White House social aide program. In contrast to the military aides, this program, established in 1902 during President Theodore Roosevelt's administration, supplies a collection of forty to fifty volunteers from around the National Capitol Region who are not permanently assigned to the White House. Distinguished by gold aiguillettes worn on the right shoulder (in contrast to flag officer aides, who wear blue and gold aiguillettes, or "loops," over the left shoulder), social aides assist with nearly every public White House event, including luncheons, receptions, briefings, parties, ceremonies, state dinners, formal balls, and the presidential inauguration. Among their duties, they are expected to interact with guests, escort dignitaries, and coordinate personnel movements. In exchange, social aides receive a "behind-the-scenes" view of White House operations and a front-row seat for some of Washington's highest-profile events, such as congressional balls, Kennedy Center Honors, Medal of Honor ceremonies, and White House holiday parties.

Social aides represent all five services, and while the program was restricted to male-only aides until 1969, it since has been opened to include both genders. To be accepted into the program, social aides must be officers in the grades of O-2 to O-4, unmarried, stationed in the area, and serve in day jobs with scheduling flexibility to support an average of two to four morning, afternoon, or evening events per month (more during the holidays). They must also feel comfortable interacting with the public and operating under pressure, maintain a professional appearance in uniform, project an air of poise and confidence, and possess a professional record of sustained superior performance. Additionally, social aides receive special clearances and must have at least eighteen to twenty-four months remaining in their current assignment. After endorsement by the applicant's military chain of command, candidates submit an application to their respective branch's program manager (whose information can be found at the Pentagon's White House Liaison Office) and undergo a rigorous interview process conducted by current aides, WHMO, and other clearance officers. Applicants selected can remain in the program until they transfer away from Washington, marry, or promote to O-5. Aides develop a strong sense of camaraderie and personal friendships, and program alumni—whose number approaches one thousand—remain connected long after their service through the Society of White House Military Aides.

LIFE ON THE WHITE HOUSE CAMPUS

The White House has a reputation of requiring staffers to work long hours, including frequent nights and weekends. This reputation is well deserved. The combination of working directly for the President, the professionally oriented people who volunteer for White House duty, and the nature of the work create a culture where the flow of work is continuous and relentless. To borrow from an enduring Navy sentiment: time, tide, and staffing the President wait for no one.

The hours aside, working for the President is unlike serving any other principal. Naval officers are accustomed to public affairs sensitivities, but no military officer is subject to the amount of public scrutiny applied to the President on a daily basis. The President's schedule is public knowledge, and members of the White House press corps unceasingly ask for the President's reaction or planned responses to national security events worldwide.

The NSC staff is responsible for ensuring the President and senior White House officials are never caught off guard when faced with these questions. The advent of cable news marked the birth of the twenty-four-hour news cycle, an evolution further accelerated by internet news and social media. When U.S. forces come under attack overnight in some remote location, the White House is expected to have a response by morning's opening of business.

In the immediate aftermath of an emergent event, the NSC staff will prepare the National Security Advisor to brief the President on the details of a specific event. Staffers also will prepare talking points for the White House press secretary to use during the daily press conference. These talking points may be used to preempt questions for a particularly high-visibility event; if the event is more obscure, they may be prepared under the "if asked" moniker. In effect, the press secretary will have these points at the podium for reference in case a reporter asks about the event. While nearly every task at the White House is colored by politics, this element of the job particularly strains the nonpolitical nature of military duty. NSC staffers are cognizant they work for political masters but this does not obviate a naval officer's responsibility to be truthful. Politicos who seek to spin events will push directors to adjust talking points for political reasons; this is the nature of politics. In this environment, military officers are required to provide accurate talking points, and when they are adjusted for political reasons, directors simply advise whether those adjustments remain within the bounds of truthfulness.

In the longer term, the staff will head interagency coordination toward a whole-of-government response, regardless of whether it requires a presidential decision. This effort could involve a deliberate approach that works its way through a Policy Coordination Committee, Deputies Committee, and Principals Committee. For urgent issues, the discussion could proceed immediately to a PC meeting, referred to as a "snap PC." No matter the time constraints, the NSC staff is responsible for communicating the agenda and providing issue papers to frame the discussion.

As mentioned above, the type of people who volunteer for White House duty contributes to the work culture. Applying for these positions often is competitive and involves multiple rounds of interviews. Combined with a clear expectation that the job involves long hours, the NSC staff naturally draws so-called type A personalities. The amalgamation of pressing work with personalities that favor urgency and embrace impatience is (at best) a match of personas to work requirements and (at worst) a mutually constitutive relationship where urgency accelerates into hyper-urgency. Regardless, anyone considering White House duty should fully appreciate the intensity of this environment.

There are plenty of staff privileges that accompany White House duty. For example:

- *White House Tours.* The White House conducts tours that include the East Wing lobby and lower levels of the Residence. While these tours are available to the public, regular visitors must secure tour spots through their congressman, senator, or administration official. NSC staff may reserve tour spots for anyone they desire—interagency colleagues, family, and friends—up to thirty days in advance.

- *West Wing Tours.* The tours described above are confined to the museum-maintained areas of the White House; the working nature of the West Wing, combined with the higher security requirements, make general tours untenable. NSC staff, however, can escort guests through the West Wing. This type of tour takes visitors past the White House Mess, Situation Room, Rose Garden, Cabinet Room, Oval Office, Roosevelt Room, White House Lobby, and Press Briefing Room. Since few people outside government can access these areas, sharing this experience with family and friends is a particularly noteworthy privilege.

- *White House Special Events.* The White House hosts several high-visibility events each week, and attendance is strictly limited. NSC staff frequently can attend these otherwise exclusive events. For example, the President routinely hosts ceremonies honoring championship teams from the NFL Super Bowl, MLB World Series, NBA Finals, NHL Stanley Cup, and NCAA. The White House also hosts holiday events throughout the year, such as the Easter Egg Roll, Fourth of July Fireworks viewing, Halloween trick-or-treating, and White House holiday decorations viewing that NSC staff can attend.

- *Kennedy Center Box Seats.* When the President is not using his box at the John F. Kennedy Center for the Performing Arts, these tickets are provided to the White House staff. Senior administration officials often claim these tickets, but given repeated performances during the season, it is common for NSC staff to enjoy this opportunity on occasion, as well.

CONCLUSION

For most, serving at the White House is a once-in-a-lifetime experience. It presents a unique combination of intensity, high visibility, and importance that is challenging for even our most capable officers. So long as you have the flexibility in your personal life to make such a professional commitment, this opportunity will provide experiences that will serve you throughout your career. Learning how the NSC directs interagency coordination, as well as watching how departments and agencies interact with the White House, is invaluable for anyone supporting DOD leadership. Simply put, seeing this system from the inside is the best preparation for excelling from the outside.

There are many benefits from White House duty but, to be sure, the true benefit is serving the country at the highest level of government. Strategic and operational decisions are made there on a daily basis, and naval officers on the staff are specially positioned to ensure the sailors and the Navy are served well.

CAPT Joseph A. Gagliano is a politico-military specialist, naval strategist, and surface warfare officer. He has served as the Director for Defense Policy and Strategy for the National Security Council at the White House, a strategist on the Joint Staff in the Asia Political-Military Affairs Directorate, the Strategic Planning Team Leader for OPNAV NooX, and the commanding officer of USS *Independence* (LCS 2). Captain Gagliano holds a PhD and a master's degree in international relations from the Fletcher School of Law and Diplomacy at Tufts University and a master's degree in national security and strategic studies from the U.S. Naval War College.

14

WORKING WITH CONGRESS

LCDR JAMES HAGERTY, USN

The Congress shall have Power . . . to provide and maintain a Navy.
—Article I, Section 8, United States Constitution

I n all likelihood, your career to date has been confined exclusively to the
executive branch of the United States government. As a commissioned
officer in the U.S. Navy, you ultimately work for the President—the head
of the executive branch. However, your job in the Pentagon—whether in
requirements, strategy, financial management, or any other DOD function—will undoubtedly require some level of interaction with Congress.
Congress is a much different organization than the military or even DOD's
civilian-staffed offices. The military is a hierarchical organization that
makes decisions through a clearly defined chain of command. Congress, on
the other hand, is a flatter organization that reaches decisions by achieving
consensus. Though military officers accustomed to rapid decision-making
from superiors may find congressional deliberations painstakingly slow,
Congress is simply operating inside a system that the framers of the Constitution developed more than two hundred years ago—a system that,
while imperfect, has served our republic well since its inception.

It is essential for the Navy to maintain a healthy relationship with Congress in order to ensure it is adequately resourced to accomplish its mission—defined in Title 10 U.S. Code as the ability to "conduct prompt and
sustained combat . . . operations at sea." In fact, the Constitution explicitly
grants the power to provide and maintain a Navy to Congress—not to the
President. The elements necessary to maintaining this relationship range
from annual testimony by the SECNAV and the CNO to action officer
briefings to congressional staff on specific programs. In short, all Navy
officers—especially those working in the Pentagon—have a role to play
in supporting the Navy's relationship with Congress. This chapter seeks

to increase your familiarity with how Congress functions as a lawmaking body, explain how Congress conducts oversight of the executive branch, outline the key ways that the Navy maintains its vital relationship with Congress, and offer advice for your interactions with members of Congress and congressional staff.

COEQUAL BRANCHES OF GOVERNMENT

As you may remember from your high school government class, the Founding Fathers created a system with three coequal branches of government: the executive, legislative, and judicial branches. The three branches share power through a system of checks and balances that guarantee no single branch obtains too much power or oversteps its constitutional authority. As a byproduct of military culture, officers adjudicating differences between two large organizations tend to ask, "Which one is senior?" However, when it comes to the working relationship between DOD and Congress, seniority is not a principal consideration. Congress makes laws, provides oversight, and appropriates funds, while the executive branch enforces those laws and executes missions using resources allocated by Congress.

ORGANIZATIONAL CONSTRUCT

The United States Congress is a bicameral legislature containing an upper chamber, the Senate, and a lower chamber, the House of Representatives. Both chambers have unique features that shape how they provide oversight of the executive branch.

U.S. House of Representatives:

- 435 members: one per congressional district, with the number of representatives per state determined by population; elected to two year terms
- Legislation passed via simple majority
- Retains exclusive authority to initiate legislation to raise revenue
- Debate for each bill is determined and structured by a rules committee and the rule is voted on by the full House before debate commences
U.S. Senate:
- 100 Senators: two per state, elected to six year terms
- Legislation passed via simple majority; however, debate is limited by cloture motions, which often require 60 votes to pass
- Maintains responsibility to provide advice and consent on executive nominations (including cabinet officials and commissioned military officers) and ratify treaties

Each chamber's unique features and authorities affect their operation and function. The Senate's longer terms and complex debate rules have earned it a reputation as the "world's greatest deliberative body." The House's larger size, higher turnover, and ability to move legislation swiftly have won it the nickname of the "People's House."

OVERSIGHT COMMITTEES: AUTHORIZERS VS. APPROPRIATORS

Both the House and the Senate are organized into committees that are arranged by subject matter in which the bulk of legislative work is accomplished. Each committee has oversight jurisdiction over specific executive branch agencies. The four congressional defense committees are the House Armed Services Committee (HASC), the Senate Armed Services Committee (SASC), the House Appropriations Subcommittee on Defense (HAC-D), and the Senate Appropriations Subcommittee on Defense (SAC-D). These four committees exercise oversight by holding hearings, drafting legislation, and then voting that legislation "out of committee" where it is then debated on the House and Senate floor.

The HASC and SASC (commonly referred to as the "authorizers") authorize funds to be appropriated and set policy for the armed forces. Their primary legislative vehicle is the annual National Defense Authorization Act (NDAA). Key items authorized in the NDAA include new program starts, multiyear procurement authority, personnel policy changes, end-strength authorization, operational authorities, pay raises, and military construction. Additionally, there are several subcommittees inside of the HASC and SASC. HASC and SASC Seapower subcommittees have jurisdiction over Navy procurement (including shipbuilding), and the Readiness subcommittees have jurisdiction over readiness activities in all services, including Navy maintenance.

The House and Senate appropriations committees (commonly referred to as the "appropriators") appropriate funds for the executive branch to expend. When funds are appropriated via an appropriations bill, they are set aside by the U.S. Treasury for a distinct purpose and set period of time. Executive branch agencies such as the DOD are then granted authority to withdraw these funds according to the parameters set forth in law. They each have twelve subcommittees that draft one of the twelve annual appropriations bills. Navy funding is primarily appropriated via the Defense Appropriations Bill with a smaller amount appropriated in the Military Construction/Veterans Affairs (MILCON/VA) Appropriations Bill.

Members of the Joint Chiefs of Staff appearing before the U.S. Senate. *U.S. Navy photo by MC2 Martin L. Carey/Released*

CONGRESSIONAL STAFF

Most of the Navy's interaction with Congress is accomplished with and through congressional staff. Action officers have the potential to interact with congressional staff through several means. Officers may be required to answer written congressional requests for information (RFI), prepare reports to Congress as directed in prior legislation, or be a part of a team that briefs staffers in person on a specific program or subject. In executing these activities, you will interact with two distinct types of congressional staff: personal staff and professional staff.

PERSONAL STAFF

Personal staffers work in the offices of the individual members of Congress. Though each office is organized slightly differently, the personal staffer handling defense-related matters is typically called the Military Legislative Assistant (MLA); most senators and representatives on defense committees have an MLA. These staffers work on a wide range of issues, including preparing members for meetings and hearings, liaising with committee staff, developing legislation, drafting hearing questions and official correspondence, tracking member interests, responding to military-related constituent questions or concerns, building relationships with constituent groups and advocacy organizations, and providing voting recommendations.

Issues handled by personal staff are often directly related to matters inside the elected member's state or district like key installations or defense contractors.

PROFESSIONAL STAFF

Professional staff members (PSM) work for a specific committee and are considered to be SMEs, with many having extensive military, industry, academic, or other relevant expertise. Due to the nature of their work, PSMs are granted a higher level of security clearance than personal staff and are also permitted to view business sensitive information (for example, proprietary information that, if shared, may give one defense contractor an advantage over another). Professional staff members are divided between the majority and minority staff. The *majority staff* works for the committee chairman (the senior member of the majority party), while the *minority staff* works for the ranking member (the senior member of the minority party). Key PSMs who work extensively with the Navy include the HASC and SASC Seapower subcommittee staff and the HAC-D and SAC-D subcommittee staff who handle Navy appropriation accounts.

In general, legislative engagement strategies focus heavily on PSMs because they have the most direct input on defense-related legislation and have access to, and the ear of, the powerful committee chairman or ranking member. This is not to say that the unique perspective provided by MLAs should be discounted. MLAs are often best positioned to provide direct feedback from individual members. They also draft many of the questions that members may ask in hearings and make voting recommendations on specific legislation based on their expertise and research.

CONGRESSIONAL LIAISONS

After identifying the key congressional staffs that shape the Navy's interaction with Congress, it is worth highlighting the important role of congressional liaisons. All interaction between the Navy and Congress is facilitated through either the Navy's Office of Legislative Affairs (OLA) or the Navy Appropriations Matters Office (which works within the Fiscal Management Division). The existence of two separate legislative affairs organizations inside the Navy—one for authorizers and one for appropriators—is mandated in legislation and mirrored by the other services and the OSD.

NAVY OLA

The Chief of Legislative Affairs (a two-star admiral) leads OLA and reports to both the SECNAV and CNO. OLA handles liaison duties for

the members and staff of all congressional committees *except* the appropriators, who are handled by FMBE. OLA is staffed to deal with a wide
range of congressional activity, including congressional operations and
budget, public affairs, Navy program support, legislative counsel, and
member and staff travel support. The OLA front office and the majority
of its directorates reside inside the Pentagon. There are also House and
Senate liaison offices located on Capitol Hill. OLA is organized as follows:

LA-0 (Front Office). Comprises the Chief of Legislative Affairs (CLA),
Deputy Chief of Legislative Affairs (typically an O-6), and front
office staff.

LA-1 (Travel/Budget). Government civilians who assist with congressional
travel planning and manage OLA's budget.

LA-2 (Public Affairs/Constituent Services). Active-duty and civilian
personnel who prepare public affairs talking points, coordinate
media engagements, and manage responses to constituent inquiries.

LA-3 (Senate Liaison). A team comprising an O-6 director, O-5 deputy, and
three or four junior officers (O-3) who serve as the "Face of the Navy"
in the Senate. LA-3 plans and executes congressional travel, serving
as military escorts for senators and Senate staff. They also serve as
a first point of contact for Navy inquiries in the Senate, directing
communication to the appropriate channels in the Pentagon. LA-3's
office is on Capitol Hill in the Russell Senate Office Building.

LA-4 (House Liaison). Structured to perform an identical function of LA-3
in the House of Representatives. LA-4's office is on Capitol Hill in
the Rayburn House Office Building.

LA-5 (Navy Programs). Led by a GS-15 government civilian, this team of
mostly O-4, O-5, and O-6s manages Navy programmatic portfolios.
They interface with the Navy Staff, lower echelon commands, and
Navy program executive offices (PEOs) to provide members and
staff from authorization committees with subject matter briefings
on key programs, issues, and capabilities.

LA-6 (Legislation). This team comprises Navy JAG, Civil Engineer Corps,
Human Resources, and Medical Service Corps officers who track,
advise, and report on pending or forthcoming legislation as it moves
through Congress. LA-6 also assists managing the Navy Legislative
Fellows Program (discussed later in this chapter).

FMBE

Though FMBE is a smaller organization than OLA, it performs the essential role of handling appropriations matters. It is typically led by a Navy captain who, while working closely with CLA, technically works within the Office of the Assistant Secretary of the Navy, Financial Management and Comptroller (ASN[FM&C]). Like CLA, the director of FMBE also has a significant amount of interaction with both the SECNAV and CNO due to the importance of the appropriations process.

Officers assigned in legislative affairs who work on Capitol Hill (LA-3 and LA-4) or spend a large amount of time on the Hill (LA-5 and FMBE) are typically authorized to wear civilian clothes when performing their official duties.

OTHER LEGISLATIVE LIAISONS

OSD has a large legislative affairs organization (OSD LA) that oversees the legislative engagement of the entire DOD. Additionally, the Joint Staff has a smaller legislative affairs organization (Joint Staff LA) that supports the legislative engagement of the Chairman of the Joint Chiefs of Staff and is responsible for liaison with Congress on joint force issues, including current operations and joint requirements. The COCOMs also have small congressional liaison offices in the Pentagon. Of note, the Army and Air Force refer to their congressional affairs teams as legislative liaisons, or "LLs."

The role of congressional liaisons cannot be overstated. The Navy must maintain a unified voice and synchronized message on Capitol Hill. Utilizing OLA and FMBE as the clearinghouse for all congressional interaction ensures consistent messaging of Navy equities. The rule of thumb is simple: no direct communication between the Navy Staff and Congress should occur that is not coordinated in some way through OLA or FMBE.

CONGRESSIONAL CALENDAR AND BUDGET PROCESS

As an action officer on the Pentagon staff, it is important to understand the congressional calendar and budget process, and how annual recurring events influence the defense budget process inside the Pentagon. Like the defense budget process (discussed in depth in chapter 7), the congressional budget process is fluid—certain milestones are mandated by law whereas others require deliberation and consensus before proceeding. Lack of consensus can lead to partisan gridlock and budget uncertainty, which affects the service's ability to support the force and plan for the future. The following section highlights the key elements of the federal budget and appropriations process and lists notional dates that are subject to change given political dynamics and other emergent events.

PRESIDENT'S BUDGET SUBMISSION

The process begins with the President's budget (PB) submission to Congress, which is required by statute to be delivered by the first Monday in February.

POSTURE HEARINGS

Following budget submission, the four defense committees (HASC, SASC, HAC-D, and SAC-D) hold "posture" or budget hearings with department civilian and military leadership. The Secretary of Defense typically testifies alongside the Chairman of the Joint Chiefs of Staff on the defense budget as a whole; the service secretaries and service chiefs subsequently testify on their specific service budgets. Combatant commanders also testify on budgetary impacts to their AOR.

MARKUP

After testimony is complete, the defense committees edit the NDAA and the Defense Appropriations Bill, a process that begins in the respective

Annual posture hearings are important opportunities for Congress to exercise oversight over military policies and budgets. *U.S. Navy photo by MC1 Nathan Laird/ Released*

subcommittees and is then moved to the full committee. "Markup," as this is called, is simply the editing of the draft legislation, often by adding amendments, for eventual consideration by the full House and Senate. For the authorizing committees (HASC and SASC), markup includes the addition of new policy provisions or the revision of previous provisions in the NDAA. It also includes a funding table that authorizes funding levels for programs.

For the appropriations committees, markup primarily consists of a line-by-line review of the defense budget with additions or subtractions to programmatic funding levels based on justifications provided by DOD. In Pentagon vernacular, if your program was "marked" it means it was targeted for a reduction by either HAC-D or SAC-D. These decisions are not final, however, until the NDAA or Defense Appropriations Bills are passed and signed into law by the President. This leaves time for an appeal process in which DOD highlights key program reductions or undesirable policy provisions and generates written appeals that urge the committees to reconsider their positions.

FLOOR ACTION
When markup is complete, the legislation is voted out of committee and debated on the floor of the House and the Senate before a vote is held in each respective chamber to reconsider their positions, called a "reclama."

CONFERENCE
Once the House and the Senate have passed their respective versions of a bill, a conferencing committee is formed consisting of elected members from both chambers who are charged to develop a compromise version of the bill. Staffers will informally conference items before members proceed to formal conferencing to gauge reaction in the other chamber. The outcome of conference is typically a compromise bill and a conference report that summarizes conference activity, which is then returned to each chamber for consideration. Additionally, for the NDAA, a "joint explanatory statement" is often published. This document is an executive summary and explains the individual provisions in more concise language, which can be helpful when trying to comprehend a lengthy bill.

FINAL VOTE
Once conference is complete, a final vote is held on the compromise legislation in both the House and the Senate. After the bill passes both chambers

Table 14-1. Budget and Appropriations Timeline

January	★ State of the Union address
February	★ President's budget request sent to Congress (first Monday in February)
March	★ Budget/posture testimony to Armed Services and Appropriations Committees
April	★ 15 April: Statutory deadline for budget resolution completion*
May	★ Appropriations Committees issue 302(b) allocations to subcommittees** ★ NDAA subcommittee/full committee markup ★ Appropriations Bill subcommittee/full committee markup
June	★ House/Senate Floor Debate
July	★ House/Senate Staff begin conference negotiations
August	★ Recess
September	★ Formal House/Senate NDAA and appropriations bill conference ★ Target completion for appropriations activity. If there is no compromise imminent on funding, Congress will typically pass a Continuing Resolution to serve as a stopgap***
October	★ Start of the new Fiscal Year
November	★ Continued negotiation of NDAA or appropriations bills if compromise has not previously been reached
December	★ End of the legislative session

Note: This notional timeline reflects a traditional appropriations timeline but exact dates may vary.

* Budget Resolution: A resolution passed by the House and Senate that serves a "budget blueprint." Although not enforceable by law, it provides guidance on spending levels to the appropriations committee so the appropriations process can move forward.

** 302(b) Allocations: Individual spending allocations provided by the full appropriations committee to the 12 appropriations subcommittees.

*** Continuing Resolution: A stopgap spending resolution that provides appropriations at the prior-year spending rate. Utilized when new appropriations legislation cannot be passed prior to the start of the new fiscal year.

it becomes law when signed by the President. If the President vetoes the bill, it is sent back to Congress. Per Article I Section 7 of the Constitution, Congress can override a presidential veto with a two-thirds majority in both chambers.

INTERACTING WITH CONGRESS

Military officers interact with Congress throughout the year for a variety of reasons. As alluded to earlier, some of these interactions are driven by the calendar as the budget process runs its legislative course; others occur on an "as needed" basis. Any interaction with Congress can be a challenge in terms of preparation required but it is also an opportunity to gain exposure to a different part of the federal government. Officers stationed at the Pentagon should anticipate these interactions and know what to expect from them.

ANNUAL POSTURE TESTIMONY AND OTHER APPEARANCES

Appearances on Capitol Hill by the SECNAV and CNO constitute one of the most significant events for the Navy Staff. During hearings with the four defense oversight committees, the SECNAV and CNO must be prepared to answer questions about the entire Navy portfolio—from programmatic details to strategic plans and policy. Both the sheer volume of material and the importance of appearing before four congressional committees necessitate significant preparation for the principals. Action officers may be called on to draft information papers on individual programs, write responses to sample questions, or review written testimony submitted to the committees to ensure accuracy.

In addition to annual posture testimony, the CNO and SECNAV can be invited to testify at any time by any of the four defense oversight committees. Other flag and general officers can also be invited to testify on any topic within their area of expertise, often in smaller subcommittee hearings. Some may occasionally travel to the Hill for office calls with members or staff to discuss important issues.

REPORTS TO CONGRESS

Both the NDAA and the Defense Appropriations Bill direct the services to prepare a number of written reports to Congress on a variety of topics, usually detailing the status of and projections for Navy programs. These reports are typically drafted by action officers and routed through the chain of command for SECNAV or CNO signature.

PROGRAM AND ISSUE BRIEFS

Following the submission of the President's budget to Congress, professional staffers on the four defense oversight committees are briefed on the entire Navy program portfolio. These briefings include the latest budget data from the recent budget submission, including historic performance, milestones, future goals, and schedules. Additionally, personal and professional staff may periodically request briefings throughout the course of the year—these are often time sensitive and require in-person congressional engagement. Some of these briefings are to junior staff and can be spearheaded by uniformed briefers in the grades of O-6 and below. The majority of briefings are to professional staffers and usually involve one- or two-star briefers—often a resource sponsor (such as OPNAV N96) who may be accompanied by a member of a program office (typically the O-6 program manager but potentially the PEO flag officer, depending on the importance or sensitivity of the topic).

WRITTEN REQUESTS FOR INFORMATION

If questions arise that do not require an in-person briefing, staffers will often submit written questions to the Navy through an RFI. These are typically received by OLA or FMBE, formally tracked by the Director, Navy Staff (the current system in use is the Congressional Information Management System, or CIMS), and assigned to the appropriate office for action. Timely and accurate responses to RFI are important to build trust and maintain a positive working relationship with Congress.

CONGRESSIONAL TRAVEL

Congressional delegations (CODEL) and staff delegations (STAFFDEL) are official travel events that enable members and staff to conduct congressional oversight outside Washington, DC. For defense-related matters, CODELs and STAFFDELs are important because they allow Congress to observe the military firsthand and compare their experiences with information they receive in congressional hearings. The Navy supports dozens of CODELs and STAFFDELs each year, ranging from day trips for staffers to the Norfolk waterfront to weeklong trips with multiple members of Congress across several continents. In short, CODELs and STAFFDELs provide an opportunity for the Navy to showcase the force that is resourced by Congress.

Travel support is one of the primary responsibilities of OLA's House and Senate liaison offices, especially for larger Navy-led CODELs and STAFFDELs. Other branches within OLA, such as LA-5, organize trips centered on specific Navy programs while FMBE handles most appropriator travel. OLA is not the only element of the Navy Staff that provides support to CODELs and STAFFDELs. The Navy Staff will often provide briefings prior to travel or follow-up briefings to answer any member or staff questions resulting from the trip. These questions may also be submitted in an RFI, requiring a timely and accurate response from the Navy.

BEST PRACTICES

When working or briefing on Capitol Hill, below are a few best practices to keep in mind:

- *Avoid partisan politics.* Congress is a political organization. Discussion of partisan politics is a normal part of everyday conversation on Capitol Hill and is an underlying factor in daily business. Despite your personal beliefs, it is important for military officers to remain unbiased and apolitical, even in conversations that appear to be informal. Doing so will maintain your personal credibility and the credibility of the military as a whole.
- *Limit use of acronyms.* Acronyms are unavoidable in the military's vernacular. Although many staffers deal with defense issues on a daily basis, it is best to assume that your congressional counterparts do not have a robust knowledge of acronyms. Speak in clear and unambiguous terms and avoid colloquialisms and acronyms in written correspondence and briefings.
- *Treat everyone as a VIP.* Aside from the standard professional decorum you already practice, treating everyone on Capitol Hill as VIPs will reflect well on you and on the service as a whole. Remember: you may be the only uniformed person from your service with whom your civilian counterparts have interacted so their impressions of you will shape their broader opinions.
- *Address members and staff appropriately.* Despite the relative seniority granted to congressional staff, it is acceptable to address them using their first name. For members of Congress, representatives should be addressed as "Congressman" or "Congresswoman" and senators should be addressed as "Senator." It is also acceptable to simply refer to members as "sir" or "ma'am."

- *Dress appropriately.* For officers who are authorized to wear civilian clothes on Capitol Hill (OLA, FMBE, and Legislative Fellows), take the time to invest in a professional wardrobe. For officers going to Capitol Hill to provide formal testimony, service dress blues are the appropriate uniform. For informal briefings on the Hill, summer whites are often worn in the summer but service dress blues are a common sight in Washington, DC, year round and may be more appropriate when briefing members and staff wearing business attire.

- *Use congressional liaisons as they were intended.* This was emphasized earlier in this chapter but it is worth repeating. All congressional communication between the Navy and Congress must flow through OLA or FMBE to choreograph efforts and maintain a complete picture of Navy equities on the Hill.

- *Understand how congressional tasking is generated and best answered.* Action officers should familiarize themselves with the process for receiving, assigning, and tracking congressional RFIs. As a rule, ensure responses are accurate and timely. Additionally, it is generally advised that one should craft responses that answer the question in clear and concise language and not offer information beyond what was outside the scope of the original question asked.

- *Build relationships.* Establishing relationships based on trust and mutual respect are critical to accomplishing business on Capitol Hill. Solid relationships with members and staff provide the foundation for candid feedback and frank discussion, which are essential for effective two-way communication between the Navy and Congress.

- *Defend the President's budget.* Despite potentially divergent views expressed internally by commands or offices within the Pentagon, the only position that should be carried to Congress is the information contained in the President's budget. Once submitted to Congress, it is the job of every member of the executive branch to defend the President's budget.

- *Do not get ahead of the President.* The President's budget is typically submitted to Congress in February. Keep in mind, however, that prior to submission the Pentagon has been working on that budget for over a year. In your communication with Congress, take care to ensure you do not reveal any pre-decisional budget details until formal submission of the President's budget. You are not at liberty to discuss internal DOD budget deliberations or preparation info with anyone in industry or on Capitol Hill until the President's budget is delivered to Congress.

WORKING IN LEGISLATIVE AFFAIRS

There are many opportunities for naval officers to work in legislative affairs at almost all career levels. For junior officers (O-3), the OLA liaison offices of the House and the Senate provide the opportunity to travel with members and staff and directly represent the Navy on Capitol Hill. For those slightly more senior (O-4/O-5), OLA and FMBE have several congressional liaison billets that manage critical relationships with professional staff on the Armed Services and Appropriations Committees. In addition, Joint Staff LA and COCOM LA offices have congressional liaison billets, which allow for concurrent completion of a legislative affairs tour and a joint duty assignment. There are also a number of post-command and post–major command legislative affairs jobs, demonstrating that legislative experience is a highly valued skillset in the Navy at all career points.

LEGISLATIVE FELLOWS PROGRAM

In addition to billets in legislative affairs organizations, the Navy has a program that places active-duty officers into fellowships in select member offices (typically with members who serve on the Armed Services Subcommittee on Defense or the Appropriations Subcommittee on Defense). Unlike the officers in OLA—who do not work for a specific member— legislative fellows are embedded in the office of a member of the House of Representatives or the Senate as fully integrated personal staffers for one year and are often charged with handling a portion of the member's national security portfolio. According to the announcement message, the Legislative Fellows Program also "enhances the ability of the Navy to fulfill its role in the national policy development process." Candidates typically apply in the spring, interview with OLA in the summer, and commence their yearlong fellowship in November. After completing a year on Capitol Hill, the Navy will seek to place these officers into key legislative affairs billets so their newfound skills can be put to effective use. Like most high-visibility and demanding jobs, the surest way to be competitive for a legislative affairs position is to demonstrate sustained superior performance at sea.

RESOURCES

Various resources and entities exist to aid those serving in legislative affairs positions. One such organization is the Government Affairs Institute (GAI)—originally created as part of the U.S. Office of Personnel Management but has since been privatized—which facilitates courses and seminars designed to familiarize participants with congressional culture, organization, procedures, and policy matters. GAI operates a tailored, weeklong program called the Navy Capitol Hill Workshop, in which participants interact with members of Congress and their staff, news media professionals, executive branch officials, and Navy OLA on legislative processes and issues of particular interest to the Navy. Those who enroll in additional classes have the opportunity to earn a certificate in legislative studies from Georgetown University, which currently administers the program. Attendance is subject to approval based on schedule availability, funding, etc. More information is available online (https://gai.georgetown.edu).

CONCLUSION

The Constitution grants Congress the sole authority to provide and maintain a Navy. Because Congress has a unique role in resourcing national defense and providing oversight to the executive branch, it is vital that the Navy maintains a healthy relationship with the legislative branch. By understanding the way Congress functions, supporting its various methods of oversight, and effectively messaging Navy priorities, the Navy can work with Congress to ensure the Navy is properly manned, trained, and equipped for its Title 10 mission of prompt and sustained combat operations at sea.

LCDR James Hagerty is a native of Baldwin, New York; he is a surface warfare officer and a 2003 graduate of the U.S. Naval Academy. At sea, he served as first lieutenant in USS *Shiloh* (CG 67), training officer in USS *Chancellorsville* (CG 62), flag lieutenant to commander, *Theodore Roosevelt* Carrier Strike Group, operations officer in USS *Higgins* (DDG 76), and N3 in Destroyer Squadron SEVEN. Ashore, he served as flag aide to the Director of Surface Warfare (OPNAV N86), surface warfare congressional liaison (OPNAV N96), and most recently as deputy legislative assistant to the Chairman of the Joint Chiefs of Staff.

15

INTERAGENCY COORDINATION

CDR MICHAEL WISECUP, USN

W here does policy creation begin? The answer may surprise you: it starts with people like you. The challenges posed by the modern security environment demand expertise beyond proficiency in one's warfare area, trade, or craft. A modern leader in the profession of arms—from tactician to strategist—must now be able to work with other branches, departments, and agencies throughout the U.S. government (USG) in order to accomplish missions both large and small. Modern military officers are also de facto uniformed diplomats who must work side by side and hand in hand with traditional and nontraditional allies around the world to ensure the Department of Defense (DOD) is contributing to national objectives.

The roster of USG agencies with which you may work during your tour—a veritable "acronym soup"—may be unfamiliar to many who have spent their careers away from Washington on the waterfront or flight line; however, these groups are instrumental in developing national policy and strategy and you may be called to work with them during your assignment. This chapter will introduce you to those organizations—known collectively as "the interagency"—the interagency collaborative process, and how to work with it (and within it) during your tour in Washington, DC. Although this could encompass the full breadth of all USG activities, we will focus on the interagency as it relates to national security.

WHAT IS THE INTERAGENCY?

Placing aside for a moment the tactical knowledge you have gained through numerous deployments and a career of professional development milestones, duty in Washington will broaden your horizons beyond simply your warfare specialty in which you have likely spent the majority of your time to date. Your warfare community makes up one small part of the

Defense Department and the collection of military and civilian agencies, departments, organizations, and entities within the executive branch—an area known in policy circles as the interagency.

The interagency is not a place or organization with a fixed structure; rather, it describes a coordination process that encompasses multiple USG agencies. This framework is guided by presidential direction and informs the national policy and strategic guidance that is created across the executive branch to drive DOD and Navy decision-making. Interagency coordination is influenced by actors within their respective organizations and can be complicated by overlapping authorities among agencies—an amorphous jurisdictional structure that defies simple explanation. There is no interagency professional development program and there is no exact interagency process that is easily replicated for all situations. Much of this has to be learned through on-the-job personal experience. Nevertheless, your effort and that of your peers in other agencies is critical to ensure that military, diplomatic, economic, and other capabilities are aligned and leveraged to address increasingly complex national security challenges.

The interagency process is noteworthy because it is collaborative rather than competitive, although it would be naive to think that every actor or agency sees an issue the same way. Each agency brings its own authorities, budgets, core missions, jurisdictions, and expertise. This diversity of thought and experience provides an opportunity to view problems from multiple perspectives, generate innovative solutions, and bring together an array of capabilities to accomplish national security objectives.

Despite the wide array of agencies, departments, and stakeholders, achieving unity of effort through unified action is essential to meeting strategic goals—something made possible by effective and efficient interagency cooperation. This point is underscored in the "3D Planning Guide: Diplomacy, Development, and Defense," a collaborative document produced by the State Department, U.S. Agency for International Development (USAID), and Defense Department that was unveiled in 2012: "To achieve unity of effort, it is not necessary for all organizations to be controlled under the same structure, but it is necessary for each agency's efforts to be in harmony with the short and long-term goals of the mission." Moreover, according to Joint Publication 3-0, the Department of Defense understands that interagency "coordination occurs between elements of the Department of Defense and engaged U.S. government agencies for the purpose of achieving an objective."

As alluded to earlier in this chapter, participants can be forgiven for viewing issues solely through the lens of their own experience and perspective (a common practice in "multi-stakeholder" enterprises); however, parochial approaches to problem-solving rarely result in furthering the broader team's goals. Something to keep in mind as you deal with actors from different organizations is that compared to other executive branch agencies and departments, the Defense Department enjoys an embarrassment of riches in money, manpower, and resources. For those who lack introspection, these resources may mask alternative solutions—policy, authority, doctrine, organization, training, etc.—that may reside in other agencies and can be leveraged for the nation's benefit. It is therefore especially important for uniformed and civilian DOD employees to approach interagency collaboration with an open mind.

In Washington, you will sometimes hear an old policy hand mention that an issue is being "addressed across the DIMEFIL"—that is to say using all instruments of power to include diplomatic, information, military, economic, financial, intelligence, and legal. Given that the military is *one but not the only* instrument of power, it is not surprising that DOD is

The interagency process is collaborative, bringing together uniformed leaders and civilian officials from across the executive branch. In this iconic photo taken on May 1, 2011, members of the Obama administration national security team monitor Operation Neptune Spear, the raid that captured and killed Osama bin Laden, in real time. *Official White House photo by Pete Souza*

often not the lead agency in interagency coordination. More often than not, in fact, the Department of State drives the collaborative process with DOD acting as a supporting agency. As Prussian military theorist Carl von Clausewitz observed, "War is not an independent phenomenon, but the continuation of politics by different means."

Within the DOD realm, the Office of the Secretary of Defense and Joint Staff lead the formal interagency coordination process. By instruction—specifically, Chairman of the Joint Chiefs of Staff Instruction (CJCSI 5715.01C signed January 2012)—the NSC systems "provide the institutional channels through which the Chairman discharges a substantial part of the statutory responsibilities as the principal military advisor to the President and the Secretary of Defense." This instruction further stipulates that the "Joint Staff maintain active liaison and full coordination with the Office of the Secretary of Defense, NSC Staff, and in dealing with intradepartmental issues. . . . The Services implement national security policy, but they do not participate directly in the policy-making activities of the interagency process; rather, they are represented primarily by the Chairman."

BRIEF HISTORY OF THE INTERAGENCY PROCESS

IMPORTANCE OF COOPERATION

"One of the principal obstacles with which naval forces are confronted in small war situations has to do with the absence of a clean-cut line of demarcation between the State Department authority and military authority."
—*Small Wars Manual* (USMC, 1940)

Since the dawn of formalized systems of government, inter- and intra-organizational coordination has been vital—and difficult. The nation's modern-day interagency process was formed in the National Security Act of 1947, which created the NSC as the coordinating hub for national security power. This resulted in the major restructure of military and intelligence agencies following the conclusion of World War II. The legislation was a deliberate response to the emerging security challenges—a rising Soviet Union, nascent stages of a nuclear arms race, etc.—that would require a more coordinated whole-of-government approach to tackle.

ACHIEVING INTERAGENCY AND CIVIL INTEROPERABILITY

"[There is an] imperative that our Joint Forces also enhance their ability to operate in consonance with other U.S. Government agencies, and with non-governmental organizations [and] international organizations . . . in a variety of settings. The specialized access and knowledge these organizations possess can facilitate prompt, efficient action to prevent conflict, resolve a crisis, mitigate suffering, and restore civil government upon conflict termination. Achieving interagency and civil interoperability through the continuing development of our doctrine and interagency participation in our training exercises is important to unity of effort upon which success in many missions depends."
—National Military Strategy of 1997

While the National Security Act established the position of Secretary of Defense and Chairman of the Joint Chiefs of Staff, the services still maintained disjointed, stovepiped access to the President and continued to develop doctrine and strategy within parochial service lines. The Goldwater-Nichols Department of Defense Reorganization Act of 1986 made notable changes to the national security apparatus that are still visible today, including elevating the role of the Chairman of the Joint Chiefs of Staff and Secretary of Defense. The cumulative effect of these changes consolidated the flow of national security policy making within DOD under the purview of these two senior leaders while relegating the services to an advisory role in the creation of military strategy.

The need for more efficient and effective coordination became apparent in an instant on September 11, 2001. The response to those terrorist attacks spotlighted the need for interagency coordination not just in Washington but on the battlefield, as well. Significant shortcomings were uncovered in these early days in the organization and operation of the executive branch—most notably, within the intelligence community (IC). The *9/11 Commission Report* underscores the criticality of government coordination to meet twenty-first-century security challenges: "Long-term success demands the use of all the elements of national power: diplomacy, intelligence, covert action, law enforcement, economic policy, foreign aid, public diplomacy, and homeland defense. . . . Defeating insurgents and terrorists is not based on traditional war tactics; it encompasses a national strategic effort that employs all elements of national power."

Structurally, the results of the *9/11 Commission Report* recommended the establishment of the Director of National Intelligence, a singular head to oversee the seventeen separate agencies that collectively compose the U.S. intelligence community, and to act as the senior intelligence advisor to the NSC (though this arrangement was later modified such that both the DNI and CIA director advise the NSC equally). Additionally, though it was once commonplace to encounter peers from other government agencies only during tours of duty in Washington, DC, or in select positions abroad, the Global War on Terrorism and Iraq War galvanized pioneering interagency collaboration at the tactical level. Not only does this effectively expose a larger cadre of junior officers to the interagency process, it also creates an understanding and appreciation for the results that are achieved through cooperation.

Each administration takes a different approach to organizing and delineating roles and responsibilities by means of policy, executive order, national security directives, and memoranda. For example, *Presidential Policy Directive—1 (PPD-1)* formed President Barack Obama's NSC organization, while his successor, President Donald Trump, reshaped the NSC in a document called *National Security Presidential Memorandum—2 (NSPM-2)*, which was subsequently modified by *NSPM-4*. Irrespective of the naming convention, every President since Harry Truman—who signed the National Security Act of 1947, which shaped our modern defense establishment—used some type of national security directive to organize his administration.

YOUR ROLE IN THE INTERAGENCY PROCESS

Cabinet members or flag officers rarely write draft policy documents; instead, they are researched, composed, and staffed by action officers within the services, the Joint Staff, or OSD. Those stationed with OSD or the Joint Staff will take a leading role in coordination with other agencies while those on the Navy Staff or in combatant command Washington offices will engage with the interagency by working through JS or OSD channels. The Secretary of Defense and Chairman of the Joint Chiefs of Staff regularly attend NSC meetings and their staffs liaise regularly.

Similarly, services and global combatant commander staffs work with (and through) their OSD and Joint Staff counterparts to facilitate interagency coordination, and to establish and maintain dialogue on objectives specific to their interests. Synchronized interagency coordination at each of these levels—OSD, Joint Staff, GCCs, and services—ensures the Secretary and Chairman are fully informed and best prepared to represent DOD in meetings and key deliberations. Decisions made by senior leaders are only as good as the information on which they are based—a serious responsibility that begins with you.

Coordination starts by establishing a common view of the operational environment on which future discussions and decision-making are based. Forge a collective definition of the problem in clear and unambiguous terms. Define the objectives, priorities, and desired conditions for success for each organization involved. Understand the differences between national objectives; military end state and transition criteria; and the goals of other governments, international organizations, NGOs, private sector entities, and other interested parties.

The NSC's formal committee structure is composed of principals and deputies committees. Like an iceberg, these formal committees represent "above the waterline" interagency coordination at the senior-most levels. The more informal process, which occurs out of sight below the waterline, is paradoxically more comprehensive but less defined. These engagements take place continuously by lower-level staff and account for the majority of initial interagency collaboration—in short, the place where "first draft" products are formulated. It is in this sphere that you may find yourself in the interagency process.

During the informal interagency process—those engagements that occur below the NSC, principals, and deputies committee levels—initial efforts should identify and define the legislative and financial authorities and boundaries resident in each agency involved. Doing so will increase the chances of a thorough coordination process and result in a stronger recommendation to senior leadership so they can best represent DOD equities at the highest level of government. Officers who may find themselves in a position to work with other agencies should understand the common vernacular that indicates the level of positional approval and authority it represents:

- A *DOD position* is one that has been approved by the SECDEF or designated representative following full coordination among all appropriate DOD elements.
- A *Chairman, Joint Chiefs of Staff (JCS) position* is one that has been approved verbally or in writing by the Chairman following full coordination among appropriate elements.
- A *JCS position* is one that has been approved during a JCS tank meeting and includes consideration of any dissenting views.
- A *proposed position* is one presented by, or on behalf of, one of the Joint Staff directors that does not fall into one of the above categories. Such a position should never claim to represent the holistic or approved views of the DOD, the chairman, or be confused with an official Joint Staff position.

Many of your colleagues in joint billets and those positioned across the executive branch will welcome your assistance as they manage their own portfolios and may have limited knowledge in your area of expertise. Such coordination can be both personally and professionally rewarding: as you work across the interagency your counterparts will learn about the Navy and you, in turn, will gain an understanding of topics that will better position you to support your chain of command. You will meet like-minded people whose interests at and outside of work likely converge with yours, creating opportunities for career networking and lifelong friendships. These relationships are the metaphorical foundation on which interagency coordination rests and they are best established prior to a crisis. Personal credibility—developed through subject matter expertise and integrity in your interactions—is essential. Early and repeated interactions with your counterparts can lay the groundwork for trust, which creates open communication lines and makes you more effective in your duties.

Building this wide network can seem daunting. To overcome institutional barriers and facilitate interagency coordination, there are a number of military liaison officers permanently assigned throughout the government. Whether from combatant commands, services, Joint Staff, OSD, or even the National Guard Bureau, a uniformed officer can likely provide an introduction to the appropriate office or point you in the right direction. These liaisons ensure coordination is synchronized across DOD so seek them out and use them extensively. Doing so will enhance the speed and quality of your work and ensure your efforts support your organization.

KEY AGENCIES WITHIN THE NATIONAL SECURITY SYSTEM

The executive branch is organized by function with each agency performing certain core tasks that are codified in, and funded by, legislation. The ability of an agency to execute specific missions is therefore constrained by both its legal authority and the availability of funding to perform those activities—an important nuance that underscores the notion that an agency's ability to do something does not inherently mean it is allowable (per legislation) or that the agency has the means (money). As a result, collaborating across agencies may be the only manner in which some organizations can accomplish the mission—a veritable force multiplier.

Though interagency coordination can—depending on the subject or mission—theoretically span the entire executive branch, there are naturally a few departments with which DOD employees are more likely to deal on a regular basis. The list below, while not exhaustive, should give naval officers stationed at the Pentagon some insight into a few of those key agencies represented on the NSC.

DEPARTMENT OF STATE
The Department of State is responsible for planning and implementing foreign policy. The Secretary of State is the ranking member of the cabinet and fourth in the line of presidential succession; the President's top advisor on foreign policy; and the official person principally responsible for U.S. representation abroad. The Defense Department partners with the Department of State to ensure defense-related activities support national foreign policy objectives and facilitate defense activities aboard.

DEPARTMENT OF ENERGY
The Department of Energy establishes policies regarding energy and safety in handling nuclear material. Its defense-related responsibilities include executive oversight of the nation's nuclear weapons program, nuclear reactor production for the U.S. Navy, energy conservation, energy-related research, radioactive waste disposal, and domestic energy production.

DEPARTMENT OF THE TREASURY
This department overseas administration of the American economy and promotes conditions that enable economic growth, job opportunities, and stability at home and abroad. Additionally, the Treasury Department combats economic security threats, protects the integrity of the financial system, and proposes and enforces economic sanctions.

DEPARTMENT OF HOMELAND SECURITY

DHS is charged with homeland security to prevent terrorism and enhance security, secure and manage the nation's borders, enforce and administer U.S. immigration laws, protect cyberspace and critical infrastructure, and strengthen national preparedness and resilience to disasters. Moreover, the Secretary coordinates the domestic all hazards preparedness efforts of all governmental departments and agencies in consultation with state, local, tribal, and territorial governments; NGOs; the private sector; and the general public. The components within DHS that DOD most frequently interfaces with are the U.S. Coast Guard and the air and marine operations of the U.S. Customs and Border Protection.

OFFICE OF THE DIRECTOR OF NATIONAL INTELLIGENCE

This agency singularly heads intelligence integration across the intelligence community that delivers the most complete, thorough, accurate, and timely intelligence possible. DNI assimilates foreign, military, and domestic intelligence capabilities to inform policymakers, warfighters, homeland security officials, and law enforcement personnel.

CENTRAL INTELLIGENCE AGENCY

The CIA provides impartial intelligence relevant to strategic policy and national security interests of senior U.S. policymakers. The CIA's primary mission is to collect, analyze, and produce timely analysis of foreign intelligence to assist the President and senior government policymakers to facilitate accurate and informed decisions in support of national interests and goals. The CIA does not make policy; it is a single, independent source of intelligence information for those who do. The CIA may also conduct covert action at the direction of the President to preempt threats or achieve national policy objectives.

DEPARTMENT OF JUSTICE

The DOJ enforces federal laws, safeguards the public against foreign and domestic threats, oversees anti-crime efforts, and ensures fair and impartial administration of justice for all Americans. The offices within DOJ with which DOD most frequently interfaces includes the Criminal Division; National Security Division; Drug Enforcement Agency; Federal Bureau of Investigations; Bureau of Alcohol, Tobacco, Firearms, and Explosives; International Criminal Police Organization; U.S. National Central Bureau (Interpol Washington); and U.S. Marshals Service.

CLEAR WATERS, SHOALS, AND DANGERS: BEST PRACTICES AND LESSONS LEARNED

Like any new endeavor, it is wise to be mindful of best practices to employ and pitfalls to avoid for your tour during which you may find yourself part of the interagency collaborative process. Here are some tips:

- Strive to understand partner agency organization, culture, and command/coordination structure.
- Develop trust through "early and often" coordination.
- Communicate broadly to ensure all equities are known and addressed.
- Never get ahead of your boss or senior leaders; understand your role in the process.
- Treat civilian counterparts as equal professionals, regardless of age.
- Strive to be collaborative, rather than competitive.
- Assume positive intent—others don't wake up in the morning with the purposeful intention of making your life miserable.
- Listen intently and use that information and context to inform your position and recommendations.
- Use common and clear language; avoid institutional jargon or doctrine.
- Recall that personal relationships strengthen collaboration efforts.
- Approach problems with introspection and thoughtfulness; most problems or issues are not confined to a single agency.
- Bear in mind that your interagency peers have (potentially conflicting) guidance from their superiors just as you do.
- Identify your peers and coordinate at your level, not your boss's level.
- View problems from your counterpart's perspective to uncover unforeseen solutions.
- Be mindful that how you frame a problem often defines how you try to solve it.
- Handle inquiries from your interagency colleagues with courtesy and respect—many may know little about the Navy, your background, or your portfolio.
- Match your attire to your counterparts whether in uniform or civilian clothes. Service dress blues are a common sight in DC year round and may be more appropriate than the short-sleeves and open collar of summer whites (especially when others are in business suits).
- No one said this process would be easy; "strategic patience" will be required to work issues that cross interagency seams and boundaries.

- Avoid falling prey to a "winner takes all" approach—inevitably, the people with whom you negotiate and coordinate on one issue will work beside you on other policy challenges.
- Remember: You represent the service! One day you will return to the fleet, so never forget those for whom you are crafting policy.

CDR Michael Wisecup is a 1998 U.S. Naval Academy graduate and 2007 Olmsted Scholar to Mumbai, India. He has spent his career as a naval special warfare officer and has extensive experience working with the interagency on the battlefield, in embassies and consulates throughout the world, and within the National Capital Region. He was also the aide-de-camp to the Chairman of the Joint Chiefs of Staff, GEN Martin Dempsey, USA (Ret.), which gave him unprecedented insight into the highest levels of national decision making and policy formulation.

16

THINK TANKS AND FELLOWSHIPS

CDR MICAH MURPHY, USN

I t comes as no surprise that the nation's capital is home to nearly all major federal administrative, legal, and policy decisions. As a military officer, what may be less obvious is how these decisions are made, who influences them, and what organizations outside the DOD may be involved. Indeed, the CNO and SECNAV do not draft or enforce policy on their own—most major policy decisions are the result of a combination of forces and organizations both inside and outside DOD. For example, Congress—as part of their funding and oversight mandate—is often involved and crafts policy through annual National Defense Authorization Act (NDAA) legislation.

In addition to Congress, there are myriad other stakeholders who influence how and why senior military leaders craft policy, including industry, academia, and the general public. One important such source of research, analysis, and recommendations are "think tanks." This chapter explores the three main sources of policymakers and influencers in Washington, explains what a think tank is and does, highlights opportunities unique to DC, and offer some tips on how to earn selection for and succeed in fellowships at some of our nation's premier think tanks.

WHAT IS A THINK TANK?

"Think tank" is a relatively modern term (dating to the mid-twentieth century) that can mean different things to different people. Merriam-Webster defines it as "an institute, corporation, or group organized to study a particular subject (such as a policy issue or a scientific problem) and provide information, ideas, and advice." Because the term is broadly defined, it is easily misapplied or misunderstood. Nevertheless, institutions or organizations that categorize themselves as think tanks have proliferated over the last fifty years and today there are nearly seven thousand in existence worldwide. Most that are U.S.-based entities are nominally

LAW VS. REGULATION VS. POLICY

There are hierarchical differences between a law, regulation, and policy. For starters, only Congress can make a *law*. Federal executive branch agencies and departments write *regulations* to implement and execute laws; while subordinate to laws, these regulations are still enforceable. *Policy* is generally a written directive that aims to communicate a standard or stance across a department or agency to achieve a desired end but does not carry the weight of law. These are important distinctions to understand when examining particular issues so you understand how, what, and who may influence any desired change.

considered by the Internal Revenue Service to be so-called 501(c)(3) organizations—nonprofits characterized as "charitable" in nature. Some of the more prominent U.S. think tanks are well known, including the Brookings Institution, the Center for Strategic and International Studies (CSIS, cofounded by ADM Arleigh Burke), the Heritage Foundation, and the Council on Foreign Relations.

This small sample of organizations comprises a wide variety of specializations, political leanings, organizational models, funding sources, and fundraising methodologies; indeed, they share as many differences as they do similarities. This chapter will not delve too deeply into the nuanced permutations of these unique organizations—for example, how a particular think tank is funded can offer insights into its potential biases or advocacy efforts. Rather, the aim is to familiarize officers stationed in Washington with the basic roles and functions of think tanks.

PURPOSE AND FUNCTIONS

Enrique Mendizabal, who founded a nonprofit organization called On Think Tanks, offers a succinct yet thorough overview of the purpose and function of these organizations:
- Educating policymakers on an diverse range of issues
- Creating spaces for debate and facilitating open discussions
- Offering insights into the policymaking process

- Channeling intellectual resources and ideas to political parties, interest groups, academics, and military and civilian leaders
- Legitimizing ideas, policies, and practices—and individuals or groups
- Monitoring and auditing public policy and behavior

Think tanks can provide experts, venues, channels, methods, and products for clients. One of the largest consumers of think tank services and products is the U.S. government (particularly DOD), which seeks outside perspectives and diverse viewpoints to inform policy decisions. As a result, it is not uncommon for senior DOD officials to meet with think tanks in off-the-record conversations, participate in a public-facing panel discussion, offer remarks at a book or report launch, or leverage specific venues to announce a major policy decision (while complying with legal and ethical guidance). Further, many of these events are open to the public and provide exceptional opportunities for junior officers to hear from a senior leader or policy expert as you learn more about a specific policy area (many organizations will also post these events on their websites providing another resource for officers interested in a specific speaker or policy area). Below are some examples of how DC-based think tanks achieve some of these functions:

Report Launch. Most commissioned projects culminate in some sort of launch event—usually a keynote speech by the author or panel discussion. For large projects with broad potential interest, some organizations will host these events at popular venues in Washington and broadcast the proceedings on their website in order to maximize attendance and exposure.

Panel Series. Panel discussions are one way for think tanks to attract leaders and experts in particular fields or subject areas. These may be thematic series, such as the U.S. Naval Institute (USNI) and Center for Strategic and International Studies Maritime Security Dialogue series, which invites naval leaders to discuss current issues and challenges.

White Papers. Think tanks often generate short, focused papers to educate and/or influence decision-makers on specific policy matters.

Policy Reviews. These opportunities to examine a particular topic or issue area bring together experts from across the public and private sectors. Think tanks can initiate them on their own, or they can be requested or commissioned by congressional or executive branch leadership.

Off-the-Record Meetings. Senior civilian and military leaders use off-the-record sessions to have candid two-way conversations with a variety

Think tanks provide venues for leaders to discuss important policy issues. *Official DOD photo from defense.gov*

of audiences to receive unvarnished feedback from subject matter experts on their ideas or concepts.

Conferences. Think tanks typically hold a signature annual event that attracts a diverse range of of keynote speakers and includes panels and more intimate breakout sessions. These conferences usually culminate in a reception or banquet that afford attendees an opportunity to socialize, share ideas, and build personal and professional relationships.

FEDERAL EXECUTIVE FELLOWSHIP

The Navy's Federal Executive Fellowship (FEF) program offers an opportunity for a select group of officers to serve in think tanks for a one-year rotation.

WHAT IS A FEDERAL EXECUTIVE FELLOW?
The FEF program places twelve to fifteen mid-to-senior-grade officers in national security–related think tanks around the world each year every year. A summertime naval message outlines eligibility (usually all O-4 to O-6 unrestricted line and some restricted line officers), the application process, and any obligated service time incurred for this opportunity (generally three months for every month of the fellowship). Upon completion of the FEF tour, officers are awarded a naval strategist subspecialty code

and are subsequently assigned to strategist-coded billets on the Navy Staff, Joint Staff, combatant command, or OSD staff. Though the participating institutions can vary slightly over the years, the following list reflects the think tanks that participate regularly in the FEF program:

- Atlantic Council, Washington, DC
- Brookings Institution, Washington, DC
- Center for a New American Security (CNAS), Washington, DC
- Center for Strategic and Budgetary Assessments (CSBA), Washington, DC
- Center for Strategic and International Studies, Washington, DC
- Chicago Council on Global Affairs, Chicago, Illinois
- Harvard University, John F. Kennedy School of Government, Cambridge, Massachusetts
- Hudson Fellowship, Oxford University, Oxford, UK
- Johns Hopkins University Applied Physics Laboratory (JHU APL), Laurel, Maryland
- Massachusetts Institute of Technology (MIT), Security Studies Program, Cambridge, Massachusetts
- RAND Corporation, Arlington, Virginia
- Stanford University, Hoover Institution on War, Revolution, and Peace, Stanford, California
- Stimson Center, Washington, DC
- Tufts University, the Fletcher School of Law and Diplomacy, Medford, Massachusetts
- U.S. Naval Institute, Annapolis, Maryland

WHY PARTICIPATE?

There are few times in your naval career that will afford you the opportunity to exchange a uniform for a coat and tie or dress and integrate fully with a civilian staff. Participants spend a year away from the typical grind of staff work or frenetic pace of operational tours, which serves multiple purposes: it affords the space and time to reflect, think, study, and write about strategic issues that matter to you, the Navy, or broader defense department; it provides exposure to some of the sharpest minds in the national security field; it empowers you to serve as a de facto in-house consultant and source of operational experience that may be lacking (or outdated) on the staff; it highlights how folks outside your service may approach issues differently than you (or the Navy); it sharpens your writing skills; and it broadens your network by introducing you to accomplished people—some of whom may become lifelong friends. This once-in-a-lifetime experience represents an investment in you by the Navy to help develop a cadre of future naval strategists.

WHAT DO FELLOWS DO?

There is no such thing as a standard "day in the life" at a think tank. It is an open opportunity to explore a portfolio or research a topic that you find particularly interesting. Former FEF participants would generally agree that a typical week at a think tank likely includes some of the following activities:

- Attending two or three events at other local think tanks
- Participating in panel discussions
- Consulting or providing insights on ongoing projects
- Working on research topics
- Reading, reading—and then more reading
- Authoring short form articles or blogs for security studies or Navy-centric journals, periodicals, or websites
- Meeting with junior staff members about potentially joining the military service
- Joining senior fellows or executives for coffee or meet-and-greets

Like most commands and military staffs, these organizations each have their own unique culture, though there are pronounced differences between the two: think tanks employ a "flat" organizational structure that differs from a hierarchical military chain of command. Additionally, executives and staff are customarily on a first-name basis and fellows are given latitude to pursue research topics or contribute to an array of projects (with one caveat: FEFs are not allowed to participate in any work related to a bid proposal or fundraising).

VISITING THINK TANKS

Although many think tanks are nonpartisan 501(c)(3) organizations, that does not necessarily mean they are neutral or apolitical. Before attending a think tank event, it is important to research the organization or speaker to understand their background, goals, and political leanings—in short, anything that may influence their products. Doing so will allow you to read, think, and listen critically during your visits and interactions.

THINK TANKS IN DC

Regardless of whether you want to concentrate on a certain region or area of interest, explore a broader view of world affairs, work outside your day job to create actionable policy or tactics recommendations, or just get to know other folks interested in national security matters, Washington, DC, is home to numerous think tanks and organizations that cover a wide array of issues seeking to influence governmental outcomes. These include many that focus primarily on defense, foreign policy, and homeland security issues that will be of particular interest to military officers serving in the Pentagon:

- American Enterprise Institute (http://www.aei.org)
- American Foreign Policy Council (http://www.afpc.org)
- Aspen Institute (https://www.aspeninstitute.org)
- Atlantic Council (http://www.atlanticcouncil.org)
- Brookings Institution (https://www.brookings.edu)
- Business Executives for National Security (http://bens.org)
- Carnegie Endowment for International Peace (http://carnegieendowment.org)
- Cato Institute (https://www.cato.org)
- Center for Naval Analyses (https://www.cna.org/centers/cna/)
- Center for a New American Security (https://www.cnas.org)
- Center for Strategic and Budgetary Assessments (http://csbaonline.org)
- Center for Strategic and International Studies (https://www.csis.org)
- Council on Foreign Relations (www.cfr.org)
- The Heritage Foundation (http://www.heritage.org)
- International Institute for Strategic Studies (https://www.iiss.org/en)
- Lexington Institute (http://www.lexingtoninstitute.org)
- RAND Corporation (https://www.rand.org)
- Stimson Center (https://www.stimson.org)
- United States Institute of Peace (https://www.usip.org)
- Washington Institute for Near East Policy (http://www.washingtoninstitute.org)
- Woodrow Wilson International Center for Scholars (https://www.wilsoncenter.org)

UNIQUE OPPORTUNITIES

While a job in the Pentagon can be professionally rewarding and eye-opening in and of itself, there are more learning opportunities outside of work in Washington than in any other city or duty station. In fact, seizing these opportunities will likely help you in your job by exposing you to the dynamics, personalities, and landscape involved with strategy and policy decision-making.

Overcoming the centrifugal pull of your desk in the Pentagon can be difficult; however—not unlike a trip to the gym—exercising your brain by exploring new ideas, listening to different opinions, and interacting with professionals outside the military or government can be equally as important and rewarding. Importantly, in a town that prizes relationships, meeting like-minded professionals may help you cut through bureaucratic red tape when you or your boss need something on short notice—people are more likely to take a call, answer an email, or do a favor for someone whom they have already met. Although naval officers are not politicians, they still deal in "political capital"; either developing or diminishing trust, goodwill, or influence with each encounter. Below is a representative sample of the kinds of opportunities open to officers seeking to broaden their personal interests and professional horizons.

Center for a New American Security Next Generation National Security Leaders Program. Every year, the Center for a New American Security selects a diverse group of twenty to twenty-five emerging national security leaders between the ages twenty-seven to thirty-five to participate in a year-long, part-time professional development fellowship. The Next Generation National Security Leaders Program brings together young professionals from across the national security field for a year of learning best practices and lessons in leadership and management through roundtable discussions with former and current national security leaders, leadership development retreats, staff rides, mentorship, writing opportunities, and an international study tour. (https://www.cnas.org/next-generation-programs/nextgeneration)

Council on Foreign Relations (CFR) Term Membership. The Stephen M. Kellen Term Member Program offers promising young leaders in government, media, NGOs, law, business, finance, and academia the opportunity to participate in an ongoing conversation on international affairs and U.S. foreign policy. The program allows these younger members to interact with seasoned foreign policy experts and participate in a wide variety of events designed especially for them. Each year a new class of term members, between the ages of thirty and thirty-six, is elected to a five-year membership term. (https://www.cfr.org/membership/term-member-program)

Defense Entrepreneurs Forum (DEF). The Defense Entrepreneurs Forum is a not-for-profit network of emerging defense leaders, civilian innovators, and social entrepreneurs who promote a culture of innovation and act upon transformational ideas that address national security challenges. (http://defenseentrepreneurs.org/)

Foundation for the Defense of Democracies (FDD) National Security Fellows Program. FDD sponsors a competitive National Security Fellows Program (NSFP) for rising leaders in U.S. national security leaders. The program includes thought-provoking national security discussions, as well as opportunities for professional development, networking, mentorship, and the opportunity to participate in the subsidized weeklong military trip to Israel. (http://www.defenddemocracy.org/project/national-security-alumni-network/)

Securing America's Future Energy (SAFE) Fellows Program. The SAFE Fellows Program seeks to connect emerging professionals in energy and national security fields to engage in conversations on the future of American foreign policy and energy security. (http://secureenergy.org/apply-now-safes-energy-security-fellows-program/)

Young Professionals in Foreign Policy Fellow. This intensive eight-month fellowship is designed to develop expertise by encouraging writing and assisting with writing on security studies issues, which are published regularly in major print and online media outlets. (http://www.ypfp.org/fellowship)

Because these extracurricular opportunities fall outside the scope of your day job, it is always wise to ensure your chain of command is aware of and supports your participation and that doing so adheres to all departmental ethical guidance. If there are any doubts about whether a given event is appropriate for you to attend in a professional or private capacity (including attending events in uniform or in civilian clothes), your command staff judge advocate is also an essential resource to consult. Doing so will not only keep you on solid legal footing but will also make your experience more rewarding.

CDR Micah Murphy is a surface warfare officer with four DC and two command tours. At the time of this writing, he was the post-collision commanding officer of the USS *John S. McCain* (DDG 56). Postings in Washington, DC, included fellowships at CSIS, USNI, and in the office of Senator John McCain. He also served as Special Assistant to the Chief of Naval Operations and Executive Assistant to the Chief of Legislative Affairs. He encourages you to make the most of your time in DC by getting out of your cubicle as often as possible, reading beyond the headlines, and engaging with those you wouldn't normally have interacted in other Navy jobs.

17

RESEARCH AND DEVELOPMENT ORGANIZATIONS

CDR KYLE GANTT, USN

Now that you are getting your hands around the relationships required to succeed inside the Pentagon, you need to understand the role that organizations outside the Pentagon—both within other parts of the federal government and in civilian sectors—play in shaping and delivering capabilities for the future naval force. Across the nation, numerous organizations specialize in addressing DOD research and development (R&D)—and almost all have representation in or around Washington, DC. No matter where you are assigned—in a manpower management role, on a strategic concept development team, or as a requirements officer—you may be required to conduct, lead, or interpret outside analysis during your Pentagon tour.

INTERACTING WITH OUTSIDE RESEARCH ORGANIZATIONS

A newly reporting staff officer in the Pentagon could be assigned to lead analytic research in support of an important decision. Several factors dictate how you should proceed. First you must ask, "Is the research beyond my expertise or level of knowledge?" If not, get to work! However, if the answer lies beyond your ability, you must frame the timeline, the funding available, the decision to be supported, and the ultimate audience for the analysis (e.g., DOD decision-makers, Congress). Each of these factors can lead you to a different outcome.

If the timeline calls for an immediate answer, then your options are limited to those organizations that can respond rapidly to your analytic questions. This generally means you will need to use a for-profit analysis firm (such as Systems Planning and Analysis [SPA] or METRON), or Federally Funded Research and Development Centers (FFRDCs) and University Affiliated Research Centers (UARCs). To execute such analysis, you will need to have an existing contract vehicle to deliver funding to the study team—check with your DCNO (e.g., N3/N5 or N9) or the program you are resourcing (either via the program manager or the PEO).

If your timeline is more flexible, more options exist. For example, the Navy sponsors an Integrated Analytic Agenda (IAA) each year, historically led by OPNAV N81 or potentially through the newly established Navy Analytic Office (NAO). The IAA sets aside funding each year and solicits input for projects to be supported. Seek out the point of contact for the IAA and understand the nuances of submitting a successful proposal because if your proposal is selected, the IAA will solicit performers to conduct the work, put the work on contract, and fund the effort (usually a very competitive process).

THE ROLE OF NAVY ACADEMIC INSTITUTIONS

Beyond the IAA, there are other options to pursue programmatic research. The Naval War College and the Naval Postgraduate School offer analytic resources and faculty-led research. This analysis can be some of the best in the world on topics specific to the Navy and is appropriate to deliver to all audiences.

There are also programs that align student research to problems relevant to decisions being made at higher headquarters. While student-led efforts are generally low or no cost to the sponsor, you must weigh how the research is to be used. A student thesis is appropriate to support internal Navy deliberations; however, if you are responding to official inquiries from Congress, you would likely want to underpin that response with more recognized analysis.

NAVAL WAR COLLEGE (NWC)

The U.S. Naval War College is home to world-class faculty and research staff. Not only does the college serve as a high quality advanced educational opportunity for mid-grade and senior officers, it also directly supports the analytic requirements of the Navy and Marine Corps. If you are assigned a task to analyze a future concept, determine the impact of a future capability, are presented with a theater-specific analytic challenge, or are looking to understand a problem across the tactical, operational, and/or strategic level of war, the Naval War College can be a useful resource.

Specifically, the Center for Naval Warfare Studies (CNWS) serves as NWC's research, analysis, publication, and war-gaming arm. Within CNWS, the Strategic and Operational Research Department (SORD) consists of several research entities that play a critical role in validating future concepts and defining how technological advances should be incorporated into militarily useful capabilities. The Naval War College describes each research center as follows:

Cyber and Innovation Policy Institute (CIPI). Advances and promotes research, education, and analysis in cyber conflict at the international, national, and operational levels.

China Maritime Studies Institute (CMSI). Leverages relationships with government research centers, civilian academic institutions, and other relevant organizations to produce mostly unclassified and primary source research on China's evolution as a maritime power.

Russia Maritime Studies Institute (RMSI). Examines regional maritime issues on behalf of the U.S. Navy and NATO partners and then disseminates finished research to Navy leadership and the fleet.

Institute for Future Warfare Studies (IFWS). Established in 2017 to serve as a focal point for research and analysis on future warfare trends and challenges, the future operating environment, warfare innovation, and future strategy and force structures. The IFWS research program focuses on the options, assumptions, costs, and risks of near-term decisions that will affect the Navy and the nation in the years 2050 and beyond.

The CNWS also operates advanced research programs (ARPs) for exceptional resident students. The ARPs include:

Gravely Group. Conducts research centered on the development of emerging technologies to support fleet capability development, inform program office projects, and advise systems commands and joint force leadership.

Halsey Alfa. Examines high-intensity conventional warfare at the tactical and operational levels of war through collaborative student-faculty research, military operations research, and wargaming.

Halsey Bravo. Complements Halsey Alfa's analysis on high-end competition by focusing on competition scenarios involving slightly less technologically advanced adversaries.

Mahan Scholars. Focused on deterrence and related strategic concepts, including nuclear, space, cyberspace, and special operations issues.

Holloway Advanced Research Program. Conducts research, free-play wargaming, and open-source Russian-language research to conduct detailed studies of high-intensity conventional warfare.

NAVAL POSTGRADUATE SCHOOL (NPS)

The Naval Postgraduate School offers several opportunities for higher headquarters staffs to align ongoing or planned NPS research to current challenges. Moreover, several warfare communities have assigned senior officers to NPS to coordinate student- and faculty-led research to address pressing warfighting questions.

One program that is particularly noteworthy is NPS' Naval Research Program (NRP), which supports research projects for higher echelon staffs of the Navy and Marine Corps. The NRP is a competitive program that selects limited projects from multiple candidates. If selected, a NPS faculty member will lead a team of faculty and/or students in the research. Since all the research under NRP is funded by SECNAV (and not the topic sponsor), the process is quite competitive. Topics are selected for funding each year through a Navy and Marine Corps review board.

GOVERNMENT R&D-FOCUSED ORGANIZATIONS

Within the government, DOD maintains a robust research capability through government-funded research institutions. In addition to the academic institutions described above these include technical research organizations. Each provides a dedicated corps of researchers, scientists, engineers, and strategists who focus solely on issues impacting the Department of the Navy.

DEFENSE ADVANCED RESEARCH PROJECTS AGENCY (DARPA)

The Defense Advanced Research Projects Agency (DARPA) is focused across the DOD on delivering transformational change in military capability. DARPA does not take on routine problems; rather, it focuses on problems whose solution will fundamentally change the way we fight and win wars. DARPA selects program managers from academia, industry, and government agencies for three- to five-year rotational tours to deliver technological advancement in support of national security objectives. As a result, you will likely interact with DARPA if you are involved in a program whose timeline looks far to the future or is involved in "leap ahead" technology. To facilitate this engagement, the Navy has senior uniformed liaison officers stationed at DARPA headquarters who report to the agency director. Once you understand the scope of your job, seek out the Navy's DARPA liaison to ensure you are aware of all the ongoing research related to your program—much of which will likely be highly classified.

OFFICE OF NAVAL RESEARCH

The Office of Naval Research (ONR) is the Department of the Navy's principle R&D organization with work ranging from basic research to prototype system development. According to the Naval Research and Development Framework, ONR—in concert with the Naval Research Laboratory and the Marine Corps Warfighting Laboratory—aligns early research, development, and demonstration to prioritized technology requirements; allocates investments for systems integration and interoperability; and accelerates capability adoption to match the pace of technology innovation.

ONR's principal areas of research are defined by their six codes:

- *Code 30:* expeditionary maneuver warfare and combating terrorism
- *Code 31:* command, control, communications, intelligence, surveillance, and reconnaissance (C4ISR)
- *Code 32:* ocean battlespace sensing
- *Code 33:* surface warfare and weapons
- *Code 34:* warfighter performance
- *Code 35:* naval air warfare and weapons

WARFARE CENTERS

Warfare centers reside within the Navy's SYSCOMs. Principally, these organizations exist to manage system research, development, test, and evaluation (RDT&E) to deliver new technologies and capabilities to the fleet. Pentagon action officers primarily deal with those warfare centers that are aligned to the community or program they support. For example, the Naval Surface Warfare Center (NSWC) oversees eight divisions specializing in various aspects of surface warfare; the Naval Undersea Warfare Center (NUWC) maintains two divisions supporting undersea warfare; and the Naval Aviation Warfare Center (NAWC) comprises three divisions supporting the development of aircraft, weapons, and training systems.

In contrast to these warfare centers that work predominantly for a specific warfare community, the Space and Naval Warfare Systems Command (SPAWAR) supports the development, delivery, and maintenance of C4ISR systems employed across the warfighting domains. These warfare centers must prioritize the projects they accept against their limited capacity so action officers should engage the analytic teams at the warfare centers directly and communicate with them frequently to leverage their background, expertise, and research capability.

FEDERALLY FUNDED RESEARCH AND DEVELOPMENT CENTERS (FFRDC)

FFRDCs are nonprofit organizations sponsored by government departments or agencies to address R&D, engineering, and analytic needs that cannot be met as effectively by existing government resources. FFRDCs (and UARCs, which are described in the next section) exist under a special provision in U.S. code, which gives them exclusive, "sole source" ability to build and maintain a cadre of highly specialized researchers, engineers, scientists, and strategists. Because of this statutory relationship, FFRDCs and UARCs are required to act in the public interest, rather than in the interest of shareholders; in short, they are considered nonprofit firms and are barred from competing against for-profit firms for many of the more lucrative production contracts. They are, however, granted privileged access to government information in order to provide DOD with an unbiased R&D option.

The first FFRDC, the RAND Corporation (whose name was adopted from a contraction of the phrase "research and development"), was established in 1948 and several others soon followed. As of March 2017, there were forty-three FFRDCs across the U.S. government. The Department of the Navy sponsors one FFRDC: the Center for Naval Analyses (CNA), which is administered by the CNA Corporation. CNA evolved from the U.S. Navy's Operations Research Group, which was formed during World War II to defeat the challenge posed by German U-boats. Today, CNA's core competencies include analysis of defense and national security issues, as well as maritime operations, programs, resources and strategy.

The DOD sponsors the FFRDCs listed in table 17-1. Many of the technologies used by the Navy have come from research initiated and/or developed by an FFRDC sponsored by another service or agency.

UNIVERSITY AFFILIATED RESEARCH CENTERS (UARC)

Similar to FFRDCs, University Affiliated Research Centers grew out of the relationships between academic institutions and the military during the Second World War and are now formally established in U.S. Code Title 10. UARCs are university-operated research organizations established by an executive department or branch to provide long-term research and development capabilities. The Navy sponsors five UARCs, each with specific core competencies. Much like FFRDCs, it is highly likely you will work with researchers beyond those sponsored by the Navy. Navy sponsored UARCs and their core competencies are listed following table 17-1; however, given their specialties and relative proximity to Washington, officers stationed in the Pentagon may find themselves working predominantly with the applied laboratories at the first two institutions listed.

Table 17-1. Federally Funded Research and Development Centers (FFRDC)

Sponsor	FFRDC	Website
Department of the Air Force	Aerospace Federally Funded Research and Development Center	http://www.aerospace.org/
	Project Air Force	https://www.rand.org/paf.html
Department of the Army	Arroyo Center	https://www.rand.org/ard.html
Department of the Navy	Center for Naval Analyses	https://www.cna.org/
National Security Agency / Central Security Service	Center for Communications and Computing	https://www.ida.org/ en/IDAFFRDCs/ CenterforCommunications .aspx
Office of the Under Secretary of Defense for AT&L	Lincoln Laboratory	https://www.ll.mit.edu//
	National Defense Research Institute	https://www.rand.org/nsrd /ndri. html
	National Security Engineering Center	https://www.mitre.org /centers/national-security -and-engineering-center /who-we-are
	Software Engineering Institute	https://www.sei.cmu.edu/
	Systems and Analyses Center	https://www.ida.org/en /SAC.aspx

THE JOHNS HOPKINS UNIVERSITY APPLIED PHYSICS LABORATORY (JHU/APL)

- Strategic systems test and evaluation
- Submarine security and survivability
- Space science and engineering
- Combat systems and guided missiles
- Theater air defense and power projection
- Information technology
- Simulation, modeling, and operations analysis

THE APPLIED RESEARCH LABORATORY OF THE PENNSYLVANIA STATE UNIVERSITY (ARL/PSU)

- Guidance, navigation and control of undersea systems
- Advanced thermal propulsion concepts and systems for undersea vehicles
- Advanced propulsors and other fluid machinery for marine systems and submarine/surface platforms
- Naval materials and manufacturing technology
- Atmosphere and defense communications systems research

THE APPLIED RESEARCH LABORATORIES OF THE UNIVERSITY OF TEXAS AT AUSTIN (ARL/UT)

- Ocean acoustic environment, electromagnetic propagation, and high frequency sonar
- Navigation in space, air, water, and on land
- Command, control, communications, computers, and intelligence (C4I) as applied to information warfare and capability modeling and simulation

THE APPLIED PHYSICS LABORATORY OF THE UNIVERSITY OF WASHINGTON (APL/UW)

- Ocean environment and acoustic propagation as it relates to the operation performance of Navy systems
- Development of specialized underwater instrumentation and equipment for undersea warfare, mine countermeasures, and general data acquisition
- Corrosion studies

THE APPLIED RESEARCH LABORATORY OF THE UNIVERSITY OF HAWAII (ARL/UH)

- Ocean environmental effects on littoral antisubmarine warfare, marine life, mammals, and other naval experiments

- Astronomical research
- Advanced electro-optical systems, detection systems, arrays, and instrumentation

All DOD-sponsored UARCs are listed in table 17-2.

PARTNERING WITH INDUSTRY

Outside the government and beyond the special contractual relationships the government maintains with FFRDCs and UARCs reside for-profit firms that play a vital role in technological and capability development. These private sector groups range from large corporations that produce systems such as communication networks, weapons systems, or platforms to smaller analytic firms.

To develop capabilities that may be of interest to the government, the larger defense contractors generally allocate a significant amount of their annual budget to independent or internal research and development (IRAD), which drives their investment decisions. While this analysis is usually thorough, it is not always objective—the intent of IRAD investment by for-profit firms is to deliver return to shareholders. In addition to research conducted under IRAD, for-profit organizations can also use IRAD to develop prototype systems, which can be used to demonstrate a system's performance but also validates production cost and schedule.

For-profit firms generally employ business development (BD) teams—knowledgeable professionals who often hold security clearances—whose job is to liaise with staff officers in the Pentagon to generate new or increased business for their firm (this is especially true for requirements officers who define the "warfighting need" for systems). Though government officials should not share pre-decisional or competition sensitive information with corporate counterparts, maintaining a formal relationship with business development teams is generally advantageous for both sides.

Communicating warfighting or programmatic challenges to industry affords opportunities to align official requirements with corporate interests. Firms may then target IRAD to tackle these pressing issues, which can potentially expedite capability delivery and drive down costs. Though you should be judicious in your interaction with BD teams to avoid the appearance of a conflict of interest, it is prudent to establish these relationships so you know whom to call when you have questions.

Table 17-2. University Affiliated Research Centers (UARCs)

Sponsor	UARC	Website
Navy	Johns Hopkins University: Applied Physics Laboratory	http://www.jhuapl.edu/
	Pennsylvania State University: Applied Research Laboratory	http://www.arl.psu.edu/
	University of Texas at Austin: Applied Research Laboratories	https://www.arlut.utexas.edu/
	University of Washington: Applied Physics Laboratory	http://www.apl.uw.edu/
	University of Hawaii at Manoa: Applied Research Laboratory	http://www.hawaii.edu/arl/
Army	University of California at Santa Barbara: Institute for Collaborative Biotechnologies	https://www.icb.ucsb.edu/
	University of Southern California: Institute for Creative Technologies	http://ict.usc.edu/
	Georgia Institute of Technology: Georgia Tech Research Institute	https://www.gtri.gatech.edu/
	Massachusetts Institute of Technology: Institute for Soldier Nanotechnologies	http://isnweb.mit.edu/
Missile Defense Agency	Utah State University: Space Dynamics Laboratory	http://www.spacedynamics.org/
Office of the Secretary of Defense	Stevens Institute of Technology: Systems Engineering Research Center	http://www.sercuarc.org/
U.S. Strategic Command	University of Nebraska: National Strategic Research Institute	https://nsri.nebraska.edu/

CONCLUSION

At some point during your Pentagon tour you could be called on to conduct, lead, or interpret analysis conducted by organizations outside the Pentagon. This chapter provides a glimpse into the expansive research and development universe that represents the infrastructure in place to support the senior leaders and decision-makers within the DOD. As you begin your new assignment, invest the time early in your tour to understand the resources at your disposal. Use this chapter as a launching point to begin your own personal discovery into how research and development organizations outside the Pentagon can help you to become a better staff officer and, ultimately, a better decision-maker.

CDR Kyle Gantt was commissioned via the U.S. Naval Academy in 1997, earning a BS in history. He served division officer and department head tours in a frigate, a cruiser, and a destroyer; he was executive officer in a destroyer. He commanded USS *Hurricane* (PC 3), USS *Sirocco* (PC 6), and USS *Gonzalez* (DDG 66). Ashore, Commander Gantt earned an MBA (financial management) from the Naval Postgraduate School, where he was selected a Conrad Scholar for outstanding achievement. Additional shore tours include flag aide to Commander, Naval Surface Forces Atlantic; aide-de-camp to the Commander, U.S. Joint Forces Command; and branch head for Destroyers and Future Ship Requirements, OPNAV N96.

PART V

LIFE IN WASHINGTON, DC

18

FINDING THE RIGHT PLACE TO LIVE

LCDR DOUG ROBB, USN

Deciding where to live is arguably the most important personal decision one can make and preparation can only carry you so far. Moving is always stressful, and moving to a new duty station in a new city as you prepare to begin a demanding assignment can take stress to a new level. Choosing a place to live—especially if you have a family—requires planning, compromise, and communication before the moving truck rolls up to your house.

While some issues are easily resolved, others that relate to lifestyle choices are often frustratingly convoluted. For example, does your family prefer a more pastoral setting or the bustling anonymity of an urban neighborhood, including the easy access it can offer to shops, restaurants, entertainment, and other amenities? Do you choose to own a car, or is public transportation more your style? How does the prospect of a long commute sit with you—especially one that eats up time and takes you away from home?

These are but a few of the simpler choices that can quickly add up to affect your perceptions of your new assignment. Though one might think that living and working in Washington should not be all that dissimilar to life in other metropolitan areas, it is in many ways quite the opposite: carefully selecting where to live in the DC area is an anecdotal yet surprisingly accurate indicator of one's overall satisfaction of working there. This chapter offers a brief overview of some of things to consider during your search, as well as areas that have been well regarded by service members who have in the past found themselves in a position similar to yours.

CONSIDERATIONS FOR YOUR HOUSING SEARCH

BALANCE COST AND SPACE

For starters, do not be deceived: the Greater Washington Area—the District of Columbia and surrounding areas in Maryland and Northern

Virginia—are among the nation's costliest when it comes to real estate (whether rented or purchased). As a general rule, real estate "cost per square foot" increases as you inch closer to downtown Washington (just as it does in other desirable cities). Not surprisingly, the city and surrounding neighborhoods have a higher cost of living than outlying suburban areas in Virginia and Maryland. Consequently, an honest assessment of your personal financial means, housing allowance, family situation, and projected tour length should be balanced to find the home that is right for you, your family, and your budget.

Consider parking, for example: inside the city itself, parking is typically limited to the street, though residents (including active duty military with proof of residence) are eligible to apply for parking permits in order to avoid hourly charges. Apartment or condo buildings typically offer onsite parking (either in an adjacent outdoor lot or in an underground garage) for an added monthly fee, and this amount can climb into triple digits for some locations in the city center. Additionally, many single-family homes have dedicated driveway and/or garage space for storing cars or other household items.

PLAN YOUR COMMUTE

As one might expect, when asked of their perception of work at the Pentagon—and of their general satisfaction with their tour(s) in Washington—there is often an understandable correlation between time spent in traffic and job satisfaction. In other words, many people find that less time commuting (and, conversely, more time to accomplish work in the office and return home to their families) creates a more satisfying overall experience.

We explored various commuting choices available to people working in Washington in chapter 2: driving personal vehicles or carpooling, metro or commuter rail, city or coach busses, and biking. If you have time or are in a position to take house hunting leave prior to relocating, consider making a "test run" commute in actual weekday conditions before finalizing your neighborhood or housing decision to ensure it accurately reflects what you may experience. As the 1970s Holiday Inn hotel chain advertising slogan famously observed, "The best surprise is no surprise."

CHOOSE AMENITIES RIGHT FOR YOU

Newer apartment buildings, condominium complexes, and townhome communities typically have onsite amenities, including common spaces, gyms, pools, or playgrounds that are included in homeowners association

(HOA) fees. Exterior work and yard care are often included, as well, which can reduce your family's list of chores that cut into leisure activities. Perhaps not surprisingly, HOA fees tend to be higher for buildings in the city or communities offering more options. Something else to consider is the annual climate in the DC area can be extreme—cold with snowfall in the winter and seemingly relentless heat and humidity in the summer. As a result, it would be wise to consider both heating and cooling needs in any housing search both for your family's comfort and for the potential impact to your utility expenses, which could be substantial.

CONSIDER WHETHER TO RENT OR BUY
For officers who have received longer twenty-four- or thirty-six-month orders, expect to be on shore duty in the area for an extended period of time, or for those who have an opportunity to serve multiple or successive tours in Washington, investing in real estate may be a positive financial investment for you and your family—depending on your finances, the location, potential re-sale value, and other considerations like the local school district. Conversely, for those expecting to serve shorter tours in DC, or who are in between sea duty assignments that will necessitate multiple moves in a short period of time, rental housing that provides greater flexibility may prove the wiser decision.

Additionally, taxes—real estate, state and local, property, and sales taxes—vary between Maryland, DC, and Virginia. If you plan to register your car in Virginia, be aware that automobiles are subject to annual state personal property taxes—an added annual expense (that in fairness, might be counterbalanced with higher relative tax burdens in Washington, DC, and Maryland). Popular housing search websites like Zillow, Trulia, Renter .com, and Military by Owner (just to name a few) list property inventories, price guides, and local neighborhood research that can aid your search.

TIME YOUR SEARCH
As a general rule, more military families tend to move in the spring and summer months as a way to take advantage of more moderate weather and to optimally align with school calendars. The trend is particularly pronounced for people moving to Washington, as summer interns and seasonal workers flood the capital and university students arrive to begin the school year. Though dependent on the timing of your orders, your expected report date, and family considerations, the ability to research the market, schedule visits, or finalize leases or purchases during the

off-peak months may provide a broader selection and more reasonable pricing and the opportunity to acquaint yourself more fully with your new surroundings and its charm.

DECIDE TO WORK WITH A REALTOR OR SEARCH ON YOUR OWN

If you are unfamiliar with the area, you may find it useful to work with a licensed realtor during your housing search. Given the number of federal government and seasonal employees who live and work in Washington, realtors are accustomed to dealing with the needs of "transient" residents. In addition to their familiarity with local neighborhoods and commuting options, realtors often have access to housing databases not available to the general public, which may be of considerable value as your search progresses and can hopefully reduce your level of stress.

SELECT A SCHOOL DISTRICT OR CHILD-CARE OPTION

For service members with children, perhaps no variable is more important than finding a school district that meets your child's needs. The quality or ratings of public schools varies markedly by neighborhood. In some (though not all) instances, public schools in the outlying suburban areas outperform those closer to downtown, which can create trade-offs with respect to cost and commuting. Researching the local school district in the area you are considering can affect future resale considerations and should be carefully appraised. And while you are examining school options, be sure to check the number and type of private schools and day care options—to include military child development centers (CDCs)—nearby.

DECIDE IF MILITARY BASE HOUSING IS RIGHT FOR YOU

Several bases in the Washington Metropolitan Area offer on-base housing for active duty service members stationed in the area. If buying or renting out in town seems like an unattractive option, base housing may be a better alternative for you and your family. Table 18-1 lists the military bases in the area and some of the services they offer (including housing).

UNDERSTAND YOUR RIGHTS AND OPTIONS

As a service member, there are several contractual caveats to keep in mind should you choose to rent in the Washington area. First, though the Servicemembers' Civil Relief Act (SCRA) entitles military members to a wide range of legal benefits and protections, it is still wise to ensure your lease includes the standard "military clause" that enables you to terminate the lease early in the event you receive new orders before the end of your contract. If your landlord has previously rented to military (or State Department) tenants, this should not be an issue. However, if you rent from a party who is on active duty, clarify that your lease provides for adequate notification should your landlord receive orders to return before you expect to move. Finally, if purchasing a house or condo from a service-member or veteran, there may be additional financing options available to you; for instance, if the previous owner used a Veterans Affairs (VA) loan, you may be eligible to assume their loan, which could provide long-term cost savings.

CHOOSING YOUR NEIGHBORHOOD

For a variety of reasons—expansion of the Metrorail system, construction of the Washington Nationals ballpark at the Navy Yard, and ongoing neighborhood revitalization efforts—parts of the city and other suburban neighborhoods are enjoying a renaissance. This revival brings new shops, restaurants, museums, entertainment, and cultural activities. It also illustrates how rapidly neighborhoods can evolve. If you have been stationed in Washington before, the neighborhood in which you lived previously may no longer be recognizable and costs may not be as you remember them.

There are also personal issues or preferences to consider when choosing a neighborhood: do you have children or pets and want access to expansive outdoor areas, or do you prefer an urban environment? Do you have family or friends in the area you would like to be near? Are you a member of a church, community center, or fitness center from a previous tour that you plan to rejoin? Will you be commuting to an institution of higher learning? Are there stores or shops that appeal to you? Is the neighborhood safe?

Numerous online resources exist to help you research neighborhood attractions, school districts, commuting options, crime rates, and available housing. Some local universities and offices also publish "Moving to DC" guides for incoming students and seasonal interns that can help guide you, as well. Though the following list is not intended to be definitive, it may provide useful insights to guide your search.

WASHINGTON, DC, METRO AREA

Metro Area—North (Dupont Circle, Woodley Park, Cleveland Park, U Street, Columbia Heights). Home to a number of young professionals, these trendy neighborhoods in DC offer easy access to new and diverse surroundings, though housing prices can often be shocking. Head farther west for quieter, more residential streets between the National Zoo and Washington National Cathedral.

Metro Area—East (Capitol Hill, Eastern Market, H Street Corridor). This DC Metro area has undergone a major revival in recent years, thanks in large part to a large weekend farmers market and a number of new local restaurants. Young parents pushing strollers are frequently spotted in the area, which is particularly convenient for those working on Capitol Hill. Most of the housing in this area tends to be older and smaller than areas of DC with more recent construction.

Metro Area—Central (Chinatown/Gallery Place, Logan Circle). In the heart of the city, residents have easy access to the basketball/hockey/concert arena and a number of top museums, including the Smithsonian American Art Museum/National Portrait Gallery. Take a short walk south to the National Mall with easy access to the Washington Monument, the United States Capitol, and many other Smithsonian museums.

Metro Area—South/Southwest (Navy Yard, Southwest Waterfront). Long-suffering and diehard sports fans will appreciate the close proximity to Nationals Park (baseball) and Audi Field (soccer) in this area, which is rapidly expanding with new (but pricey) high-rise apartment buildings and lively restaurants. Located just south of I-395, this area offers easy highway access to travel east into Maryland or west into Virginia.

Metro Area—West (Foggy Bottom, Georgetown). Brimming with George Washington University students during the academic year, Foggy Bottom offers quick eateries and food trucks amid academic buildings and apartments. Journey a few blocks west into Georgetown for colonial-era brick-lined streets filled with boutiques, upscale eateries, and the amenities of Georgetown University. Escape the city by heading into Rock Creek Park or Theodore Roosevelt Island, or visit the John F. Kennedy Center for the Performing Arts for a show.

VIRGINIA

Virginia Suburbs—North (Arlington/Alexandria). Pentagon City and Crystal City in Arlington offer convenient commutes (a short Metro or bike ride, or even walking distance) to the Pentagon from a number of apartment buildings, as well as easy access to retail chains and chain restaurants. More diverse housing options are available in Arlington south of Crystal City. Alexandria offers a waterfront community with local restaurants and

Table 18-1. MILITARY BASES AND SERVICES IN THE GREATER WASHINGTON AREA	ABERDEEN PROVING GROUNDS	FORT A.P. HILL	FORT BELVOIR	FORT MCNAIR	FORT MEADE	JOINT BASE ANACOSTIA-BOLLING (JBAB)	JOINT BASE ANDREWS - NAVAL AIR FACILITY WASHINGTON
Auto Shop	◆	-	◆	-	◆	◆	◆
Bowling	◆	-	◆	-	◆	◆	-
Chapel / Chaplain Services	◆	-	◆	◆	◆	◆	◆
Child Development Center	◆	-	◆	-	◆	◆	◆
Commissary	◆	-	◆	-	◆	◆	◆
Exchange / Package Store	◆	◆	◆	-	◆	◆	◆
Family Support Center	◆	-	◆	-	◆	◆	◆
Gas	◆	-	◆	◆	◆	◆	◆
Golf Course	◆	-	◆	◆	-	-	◆
Gym / Fitness Center	◆	◆	◆	◆	◆	◆	◆
Housing / Referral Office	-	-	◆	-	◆	◆	◆
ID / CAC Card Office	◆	◆	◆	◆	◆	◆	◆
Legal Services	◆	-	◆	◆	◆	◆	◆
Library	◆	-	◆	◆	◆	◆	◆
Lodging (temporary)	◆	◆	◆	◆	◆	◆	◆
Medical Treatment Facility	◆	◆	◆	◆	◆	◆	◆
Morale, Welfare & Recreation / Tickets	◆	◆	◆	-	◆	◆	◆
Pers. Property / Household Goods / Transp.	◆	-	◆	-	◆	◆	◆
Thrift Shop	◆	-	◆	-	◆	◆	◆
Veterinary Services	◆	-	◆	-	◆	-	◆

Table 18-1. Military Bases and Services in the Greater Washington Area

MILITARY BASES AND SERVICES IN THE GREATER WASHINGTON AREA	JOINT BASE MYER-HENDERSON HALL (JBMHH)	MARINE CORPS BASE QUANTICO	NAVAL AIR STATION PATUXENT (PAX) RIVER	PENTAGON	U.S. NAVAL ACADEMY / NAVAL SUPPORT ACTIVITY ANNAPOLIS	WALTER REED NATIONAL MILITARY MEDICAL CENTER (WRNMMC)	WASHINGTON NAVY YARD (WNY)
Auto Shop	◆	◆	◆	-	◆	-	-
Bowling	◆	◆	◆	-	-	◆	-
Chapel / Chaplain Services	◆	◆	◆	◆	◆	◆	-
Child Development Center	◆	◆	◆	-	◆	◆	-
Commissary	◆	◆	◆	-	◆	-	-
Exchange / Package Store	◆	◆	◆	-	◆	◆	◆
Family Support Center	◆	◆	◆	◆	◆	◆	◆
Gas	◆	◆	◆	-	◆	◆	-
Golf Course	-	◆	◆	-	◆	-	-
Gym / Fitness Center	◆	◆	◆	◆	◆	◆	◆
Housing / Referral Office	◆	◆	◆	-	◆	◆	◆
ID / CAC Card Office	◆	◆	◆	◆	◆	◆	◆
Legal Services	◆	◆	◆	◆	◆	◆	◆
Library	◆	◆	-	-	-	-	-
Lodging (temporary)	◆	◆	◆	-	◆	◆	-
Medical Treatment Facility	◆	◆	◆	◆	◆	◆	◆
Morale, Welfare & Recreation / Tickets	◆	◆	◆	◆	◆	◆	◆
Pers. Property / Household Goods / Transp.	▲	▲	▲		▲	▲	▲
Thrift Shop	◆	◆	-	-	◆	-	◆
Veterinary Services	◆	◆	◆	-	-	-	-

LIFE IN WASHINGTON, DC

boutiques, and housing options include apartment buildings, townhomes, and single-family homes. Affectionately known as "NOVA" (pronounced "NO-vah"), Northern Virginia is also laden with playgrounds, dog and splash parks, bike trails, libraries, and weekly farmers markets that will keep you and your family busy.

Virginia Suburbs—South/Southwest (Mount Vernon, Springfield, Wood-bridge, Burke). Extending farther out from the DC area involves trade-offs between more spacious homes and commutes. Metro and commuter rail services are available in some areas, but consider those options when looking at homes. For those who enjoy spending time outdoors, notable sights in these areas include George Washington's homestead, Huntley Meadows Park, Lake Accotink Park, and Burke Lake Park.

Virginia Suburbs—West/Northwest (Annandale, Fairfax, Vienna, McLean, Herndon, Oakton). Many suburbs of DC offer excellent public education, and the west/northwest suburbs are no exception. Great for families, these areas offer welcoming communities, comfortable homes, and recreational facilities. The Patriot Center at George Mason University often hosts events, and the City of Fairfax Historic District offers some old-time charm and local restaurants.

MARYLAND

Maryland Suburbs—North (Montgomery County: Bethesda, Gaithersburg, Rockville, Silver Spring). Maryland is home to a number of military bases and federally funded research centers just across the border from DC, so this might be an ideal location for service members who know their job will require frequent travel to these locations. Additionally, these regions offer more spacious and affordable housing accommodations then you may find in city center and may be a good option for families with children.

Maryland Suburbs—East (Annapolis, Bowie, Laurel, Prince George's County). Head farther east into Maryland for more housing options and closer access to the U.S. Naval Academy, downtown Annapolis, and water-front property options. Bowie is a convenient intermediate location to split the commute between Washington and Annapolis, and also affords easy driving access to Baltimore.

LCDR Doug Robb is a surface warfare officer who lived in the Georgetown neighborhood of Washington, DC, while attending graduate school and who, while on shore duty, rented an apartment in Arlington and bought a home in Alexandria. His wife attended George Washington University in Foggy Bottom and has worked at the Washington Navy Yard for more than ten years.

19

PURSUING GRADUATE EDUCATION IN DC

LT KAITLIN SMITH, USN

M any jobs in the Pentagon offer sufficient flexibility to pursue part-time study in graduate education. Your ability to enroll in advanced education during your tour in DC will depend on numerous factors, including your daily workload, the targeted program's focus of study, campus location, cost, and your own professional goals inside or outside the Navy. The purpose of this chapter is to provide an overview of options and considerations for pursuing graduate education while stationed at the Pentagon. This chapter is not exhaustive but may assist prospective officer students searching for a graduate program during their time in Washington.

SCHOOLS TO CONSIDER

There are numerous avenues and opportunities to complete advanced education in the DC area, which is home to some of the nation's premier brick-and-mortar institutions. Online distance learning programs, or a combination of on-site and online programs, could provide added flexibility. Being mindful that where you intend to live, whether you are eligible for reduced tuition rates for in-state residents, what you aim to study, and how you prefer to learn—whether by interacting with a professor or classroom in person, or by working at your own pace on your own time—will likely influence your school or program choice. The following universities are located in the Washington metropolitan area, each with an array of graduate education program options well suited for military officers:

DISTRICT OF COLUMBIA
- American University
- Catholic University of America

- George Washington University
- Georgetown University
- Howard University
- The Institute of World Politics
- University of the District of Columbia

VIRGINIA

- George Mason University (campuses in Arlington and Fairfax)
- George Washington University Virginia Science & Technology Campus (Ashburn)
- Marymount University (Arlington)
- University of Mary Washington (campuses in Stafford and Fredericksburg)
- University of Virginia (Falls Church—certificate programs only; main campus in Charlottesville)

MARYLAND

- Johns Hopkins University (Baltimore)
- Loyola University Maryland (Baltimore)
- University of Maryland, College Park
- University of Maryland, University College (multiple campuses)

DISTANCE LEARNING AND OTHER OPTIONS

A number of universities across the country offer online graduate education. Many universities local to the DC area also offer a combination of in-person classes and online classes. In addition, there are a number of local public and private community colleges, as well as proprietary (for-profit) institutions, which offer classes and professional certificates through online study.

JOINT PROFESSIONAL MILITARY EDUCATION

Title 10 established requirements for joint professional military education for all military officers. Joint Staff instruction (CJCSI 1800.01) outlines policies and procedures for the five complementary levels of JPME: pre-commissioning, primary, JPME Phase-I, JPME Phase-II, and general officer/flag officer courses. Pre-commissioning and primary training are accomplished through commissioning programs and initial tours of duty.

By Navy policy, JPME Phase-I must be completed by unrestricted line officers prior to assuming O-5 command status (per NAVADMIN 136/10).

Duty in Washington may afford you an opportunity to pursue a civilian graduate degree or complete your professional military education. *U.S. Navy photo by MC Jess Rodrguez/Released*

JPME Phase-I can be completed on site at the Naval War College or via distance learning programs. Though some may seek assignment to a service war college following duty at the Pentagon, completing JPME Phase-I in advance or via alternate means could open up more options for detailing in later tours.

Officers seeking to complete JPME Phase-I while stationed at the Pentagon can choose to enroll in the Naval War College Fleet Seminar Program, which offers on-site classes at multiple locations in the DC area: the Pentagon, Washington Navy Yard, Joint Base Myer-Henderson Hall, the Center for Naval Analysis, Capitol Hill, and the GAO. Additionally, classes are offered in Maryland (Annapolis and Patuxent River) and Virginia (Dahlgren). Alternatively, the Naval War College offers a web-enabled program designed to be completed within eighteen to twenty-four months.

More information regarding JPME programs (on site and distance) is available on the BUPERS website (http://www.public.navy.mil/bupers-npc/

officer/detailing/jointofficer/pages/jpme.aspx) and on the Naval War College website (https://www.usnwc.edu/). For post-command commanders and captains, all JPME Phase-II courses in DC are conducted on site and are offered through the National Defense Universities syndicate and at all service war colleges.

PART-TIME PROGRAMS OF INTEREST

Academic programs vary with respect to credit requirements and time commitment; however, the following schools and programs have been historically popular with military officers stationed in DC. Further information about graduate programs is available on the universities' websites, including admissions deadlines and semester timelines.

SECURITY STUDIES/INTERNATIONAL SECURITY (MA)
- George Mason Schar School of Policy and Government (thirty-nine credits)
- George Washington University Elliott School of International Affairs (forty credits)
- Georgetown University Center for Security Studies (twelve courses/ thirty-six credits)
- Johns Hopkins School of Advanced International Studies (twelve courses—onsite and online)

STRATEGIC STUDIES (MA)
- Johns Hopkins School of Advanced International Studies (sixteen courses/sixty-four credits, plus demonstrated proficiency in a second language)

FOREIGN POLICY/FOREIGN AFFAIRS/INTERNATIONAL RELATIONS (MA)
- George Washington University Elliott School of International Affairs (various programs)
- Georgetown University Walsh School of Foreign Service (various programs; some are full-time only)
- The Institute of World Politics (thirteen courses/fifty-two credits)

STRATEGIC INTELLIGENCE
- National Intelligence University (forty-three credits full and part time)
- The Institute of World Politics (thirteen courses/fifty-two credits and OPNAV N2/N6 will grant a 2400 Subspecialty in Strategic Intelligence to Information Warfare Corps graduates)

BUSINESS (MBA)

- Georgetown University McDonough School of Business (sixty credits/ three years part time)
- George Washington University School of Business (fifty-five-and-a-half credits, two to five years, online option)
- George Mason University School of Business (forty-eight credits, flexible completion, online option, in-state tuition rates for Virginia, Maryland, and DC residents)
- University of Maryland Robert H. Smith School of Business (fifty-four credits; two to five years; online option; multiple locations—Rockville, Baltimore, or Washington, DC)
- University of Maryland, University College MBA (thirty-six credits; online only; eighteen months)

PUBLIC POLICY AND PUBLIC ADMINISTRATION (MPP/MPA)

- George Mason University Schar School of Policy and Government (thirty-six to thirty-nine credits)
- George Washington University Trachtenberg School of Public Policy & Public Administration (three years part time, two years full time; forty credits)
- Georgetown University McCourt School of Public Policy (three years part time, two years full time; forty-eight credits)

ACCREDITATION

Choosing an accredited program is generally recommended, and is a requirement for receipt of federal financial aid or veterans' education benefits. Regional accreditation tends to be more prestigious than national accreditation. The Middle States Commission on Higher Education (MSCHE) handles accreditation for institutions of higher learning in Maryland and DC, and the Southern Association of Colleges and Schools (SACS) handles accreditation for Virginia. Online degree programs should be accredited by one of the seven regional members of the Council for Higher Education Accreditation (which includes MSCHE and SACS), or by an agency recognized by the Department of Education.

PhD PROGRAMS

Doctoral programs tend to be more time-intensive and require more self-study than master's degree programs, but it may be possible to complete a PhD during your Pentagon tour. Programs vary widely based on program and field of study.

PICKING A PROGRAM

UNIVERSITY SERVICES

If deciding between different programs, you may want to consider the quality of the university's services for veterans—particularly if you intend to fund your study using veterans' benefits—and the quality of the university's career center, if you are considering separation from active duty. Additionally, some programs allow broad latitude in taking courses in other schools of the university, or at other universities in the area (called a "consortium"), whereas other programs may have a more restrictive curriculum. Many professional organizations offer free assistance to veterans regarding education benefits and career counseling, including the Military Officers Association of America (MOAA), Veterans of Foreign Wars of the United States (VFW), and Service to Service (S2S).

COMMUTING TO CLASS

To balance full-time employment with part-time education, it is important to consider the commute when choosing a program, both from the Pentagon to class, and from class to your home. Parking is not guaranteed for all Pentagon employees, though parking is available for a daily fee at the nearby Pentagon City Mall or a monthly fee in the Post Pentagon Row building. Similarly, parking in the District is both sparse and expensive. Universities in DC are accessible via public transit—Metrorail and bus—though transfers between Metro stops or busses can lengthen travel times. Parking may be more affordable and more readily accessible at universities outside the Washington city center.

FUNDING OPTIONS

General information about Navy graduate education, including Navy-funded and non-funded programs, is available in OPNAVINST 1520.23.

GRADUATE EDUCATION VOUCHER

Graduate Education Voucher (GEV) funds up to twenty-four months of off-duty graduate education in a Navy-relevant program. GEV covers education costs up to $20,000 per year ($24,000 total). GEV requires a minimum service obligation of either two years, or of three times the number of months of education (with a maximum of three years), whichever is greater. More information on eligibility and policies is available in OPNAVINST 1520.37.

FLEET SCHOLAR EDUCATION PROGRAM

Fleet Scholar Education Program (FSEP) funds up to twenty-four months of full-time in-person graduate education. Because FSEP is full-time, selectees would not be able to fill a billet at the Pentagon, but may have opportunities to intern at the Pentagon during breaks in classes. All selectees are obligated for an additional three years of service following completion of the program. Refer to http://www.nps.edu/academics/CIVINS/index.html for additional information.

TUITION ASSISTANCE

Tuition assistance (TA) funds up to sixteen semester hours per fiscal year, with a cap of $250 per semester hour. These funds can be used for graduate or certificate programs. TA only covers tuition and cannot be used to pay for books or other educational expenses. Using TA can incur a two-year obligation that can be served concurrently with other obligated service. More information is available at http://www.navycollege.navy.mil/tuition-assistance/.

COMMUNITY BONUSES FOR OBLIGATED SERVICE

If your unrestricted line, restricted line, or staff corps community offers a bonus for signing on for additional obligated service, you may consider using these funds to pay for graduate education. Reinvesting your bonus in education may be an appealing option for those who wish to transfer veterans' education benefits to other family members, or for those who either are not interested in or not accepted to other obligated service graduate education programs (e.g., GEV or FSEP).

MONTGOMERY GI BILL (CHAPTER 30)

The Montgomery GI Bill offers monthly stipends to cover up to thirty-six months of education benefits. Service-member eligibility is defined by four categories based on date of entrance to service. The rate of payment depends on the type of training, length of service, and past contributions to the program. For more information, refer to https://www.benefits.va.gov/gibill/mgib_ad.asp.

POST-9/11 GI BILL (CHAPTER 33)

The Post-9/11 GI Bill funds full tuition and fees for in-state public schools, and up to a capped national maximum for private schools and out-of-state public schools, for up to thirty-six months. The Post-9/11 GI Bill also

Table 19-1. Post–9/11 GI Bill (Chapter 33)

Member Serves	Maximum Benefit Payable
At least 36 months	100%
At least 30 continuous days on active duty and must be discharged due to service-connected disability	100%
At least 30 months, but less than 36 months	90%
At least 24 months, but less than 30 months	80%
At least 18 months, but less than 24 months	70%
At least 12 months, but less than 18 months	60%
At least 06 months, but less than 12 months	50%
At least 90 days, but less than 06 months	40%

provides a stipend for books and other expenses. Veterans no longer serving on active duty are eligible for a monthly housing allowance, pro-rated for dates when classes are in session (note that rates are different if you take all online classes versus taking at least one course on campus). The percentage of the maximum benefit payable is based on length of active duty service (table 19-1).

For service members whose undergraduate education was funded via scholarship, length of service for Post-9/11 GI Bill eligibility begins at completion of the minimum active duty service requirement. One unique feature of the Post-9/11 GI Bill is the ability to transfer benefits to dependents; however, doing so incurs additional service time. Additional information, including the annual maximum rate for tuition, is available at https://www.benefits.va.gov/gibill/post911_gibill.asp.

YELLOW RIBBON PROGRAM

Active duty service members are not eligible for the Yellow Ribbon Program but it is an option for veterans and members separating from active duty (and hence does not entail an additional service commitment). Through the Yellow Ribbon Program, universities enter into agreement with the VA to offer additional funding that covers the difference between the Post-9/11 GI Bill cap and the actual costs charged by the university. Some schools will fund the total difference while other schools may offer more modest subsidies. Only service members qualified at the 100 percent rate for the Post-9/11 GI Bill are eligible for the Yellow Ribbon Program. Additional information is available at https://www.benefits.va.gov/gibill/yellow_ribbon.asp.

FREE APPLICATION FOR FEDERAL STUDENT AID

The federal government offers grants and loans for advanced education through application to the office of Federal Student Aid (FAFSA). Unlike student loans that must be repaid, grants do not require repayment. While active duty military officers may not qualify for grants, they may be eligible for loans or scholarship opportunities. States and universities use data submitted through FAFSA to consider students for additional funds or scholarships, so even applicants who do not expect to receive grants or intend to take out loans may find it beneficial to submit FAFSA. Applying for aid through FAFSA incurs no additional service obligation. Additional information is available at https://studentaid.ed.gov/sa/.

VOCATIONAL REHABILITATION & EMPLOYMENT AND VETSUCCESS ON CAMPUS (VSOC)

Service members with a service-connected disability rating of 20 percent of more may be eligible for additional benefits and services to assist in pursuing advanced education. Many schools in the DC area have a VetSuccess on Campus (VSOC) office and assigned counselor to assist veterans in taking advantage of benefits and career services. For more information, refer to https://www.benefits.va.gov/vocrehab/index.asp.

FELLOWSHIPS/SCHOLARSHIPS

Many public and private foundations offer academic fellowships and scholarships. Graduate scholarships are less prevalent and tend to offer lower awards than undergraduate scholarship opportunities. Graduate scholarships often have eligibility criteria to cater to students working in a particular field (e.g., the Thomas R. Pickering Foreign Affairs Fellowship), or associated with professional organizations (e.g., Surface Navy Association). Additionally, some grants and scholarships are designated for specific groups on the basis of race/ethnicity, gender, religion, or other factors.

ADMISSIONS CONSIDERATIONS

Graduate programs often require applicants to submit scores from standardized tests for admission. Requirements vary among programs, so it is important to identify programs of interest and their requirements early on in the application process. This section will provide a brief overview of commonly required exams.

TESTING

Graduate Record Examination (GRE). The GRE is the most commonly accepted standardized test for graduate programs, and is increasingly accepted by business schools, as well as select law schools in the area (including Georgetown Law). The GRE has three timed sections: verbal reasoning, quantitative reasoning, and analytical writing. The test is administered at scheduled times at locations worldwide and GRE scores are valid for five years from completion of the test. The cost of the exam is around $200. Find more information or register for a test online at https://www.ets.org/gre.

Graduate Management Admission Test (GMAT). While many business schools and MBA programs do not require the GRE, some programs may still require applicants to submit GMAT scores for admission. The GMAT has four timed sections: analytical writing assessment, integrated reasoning, quantitative, and verbal. Like the GRE, the GMAT is offered at test centers worldwide at scheduled times and scores are valid for five years. The cost of the exam is $250. Find more information or register for a test online at https://www.mba.com.

Law School Admission Test (LSAT). Nearly all law school applications require submission of LSAT scores. The LSAT has five timed sections: reading comprehension, analytical reasoning, two logical reasoning sections, and an unscored section used to test new or unique questions. The LSAT schedule is more restrictive than the GRE and GMAT schedules because the LSAT is only offered four times per year: February, June, September, and December. The LSAT must typically be completed by December if the prospective applicant seeks to matriculate the following fall semester. Tests are offered worldwide at a cost of $180 and scores are valid for five years. The Defense Activity for Non-Traditional Education Support (DANTES) does not reimburse fees for the LSAT. Find more information or register for a test online at https://www.lsac.org/.

BEING MINDFUL OF ADMISSIONS TIMELINE

Some graduate programs offer rolling admissions throughout the year while other programs have fixed annual deadlines for admissions. Depending on projected rotation date, officers pursuing graduate education may consider applying to schools prior to their arrival at the Pentagon. Alternatively, if reporting to the Pentagon in the middle of or "off-cycle" from the academic year, there may be opportunities to enroll in classes in a desired academic program through a school's continuing studies office; that is, enrolling in the very same classes à la carte, rather than as a matriculated member of the degree-granting program. Subject to the school's academic regulations, these classes will familiarize prospective students with the program and professors and can, in some instances, be counted as credits toward the degree program—an added benefit. Continuing studies programs may also be an appealing option for students who need more time to decide on a degree program, complete required standardized tests, and/or submit applications.

COMPLETING APPLICATIONS

Begin working on applications early to ensure adequate time to gather recommendations and transcripts. Most programs require transcripts from all previous undergraduate and graduate education, as well as two or three letters of recommendations. As a professional courtesy, allow the authors of your recommendations—many of whom are busy with jobs of their own—adequate time to prepare the recommendations prior to the admissions deadline. While many schools offer online submission for recommendations and transcripts, some schools still require hard-copy mailed submissions.

TIP

Service members are eligible to have one graduate-level exam reimbursed via DANTES. Refer to http://www.dantes.doded.mil/examinations/funding-and-reimbursement-eligibility/reimbursement-eligibility.html for more information. Additionally, veterans and active-duty service members are entitled to a 50 percent discount if they sign up at service2school.org for a test prep discount.

CONDUCTING INTERVIEWS

Some programs—particularly MBA programs—require interviews as part of the admissions process. Engage early with admissions offices to determine whether an interview is required and to determine whether you have operational commitments that could preclude completion of the interview.

CONCLUSION

Should your work schedule and family commitments permit, service members stationed at the Pentagon are uniquely positioned to take advantage of a diverse array of graduate education opportunities. Many DC-area graduate programs are tailored to students who work full time in Washington's military, government, or private sectors and are accustomed to accommodating hectic personal schedules. Though it can be challenging to balance competing priorities, pursuing graduate education in the nation's capital can be a rewarding opportunity to enhance your assignment and overall DC experience.

LT Kaitlin Smith is a reservist assigned to Naval Reserve Operations & Plans on the Navy Staff. Prior to joining the Reserves, Lieutenant Smith worked for the Director, Surface Warfare (N96) in the Office of the Chief of Naval Operations. During this tour, she began pursuing her master's degree in public policy part time at George Washington University. Previously, Lieutenant Smith served in USS *Donald Cook* (DDG 75) in Rota, Spain, and USS *Stockdale* (DDG 106) in San Diego, California. She lives in Washington, DC, and holds a BS from Duke University.

20

ENRICHMENT OPPORTUNITIES

LCDR DOUG ROBB, USN

M any people find serving at the Pentagon to be demanding yet rewarding—in part because the work can be both challenging and meaningful. But there are myriad other stimulating cultural and educational opportunities offered in the National Capital Region that contribute to this satisfaction, as well. Not surprisingly, Washington attracts world-class scholars, political luminaries, and military strategists from across a diverse spectrum; indeed, there is no shortage of interesting people doing interesting and important work. As a result, outside the office you will find a wide array of opportunities to expand your mind—and your horizons.

The District is also a magnet for trade shows, expos, conventions, and conferences—to say nothing of commemorative or celebratory naval and military events that provide numerous occasions for networking and socializing with people who can support and challenge you. The area, which includes nearby cities like Baltimore and Annapolis, is home to world-class institutions—universities, museums, libraries, theaters, galleries, and attractions both historical and contemporary. This somewhat eclectic chapter, which is neither exhaustive nor definitive, seeks to reveal those professional and personal activities that may be of interest to naval officers—and their families—embarking on this new adventure in Washington.

PROFESSIONAL ENGAGEMENTS

A SHORT LIST OF DEFENSE-RELATED CONFERENCES
AND TRADE SHOWS IN WASHINGTON
- U.S. Navy League Sea-Air-Space (SAS) Exposition
  (http://www.seaairspace.org)
- Surface Navy Association (SNA) National Symposium
  (http://navysna.org)

- American Society of Naval Engineers (ASNE) Convention (http://www.navalengineers.org)
- Armed Forces Communications and Electronics Association (AFCEA) Summits and Symposia (https://www.afcea.org/site/)
- Office of Naval Research (ONR) Naval Future Force Science and Technology (S&T) Expo (https://www.onr.navy.mil/Conference-Event-ONR/)
- Air Force Association Air, Space & Cyber Conference (https://www.afa.org/airspacecyber/home)
- Association of the U.S. Army's Annual Meeting and Exposition (https://www.ausa.org/)
- National Defense Industrial Association's Annual SO/LIC Symposium & Exhibition (http://www.ndia.org/)
- The Naval Submarine League's Annual Symposium and Industry Update (https://www.navalsubleague.org/events/annual-symposium/)

These events provide opportunities for military officers to interact with professionals from the defense industry and government. Typically organized around a "theme" that can vary from year to year, these conferences attract expert speakers for panels, sponsor collaborative exercises, host social hours, and offer a wealth of worthwhile interactive sessions. Washington and its immediate suburbs in Virginia and Maryland have numerous venues—hotels, conference or convention centers, and other event spaces—that are popular conference locations and are often easily accessible by car, public transit, or shuttle bus from the Pentagon.

SPEAKER SYMPOSIA AND SEMINARS

- USNI Maritime Security Dialogue. Co-hosted by two distinguished nonpartisan institutions—USNI and the Center for Strategic and International Studies (CSIS)—this monthly series focuses on topical maritime, security, organizational, or budgetary challenges facing the Navy, Marine Corps, and Coast Guard. (https://www.usni.org/events/maritime-security-dialogue-1)
- USNI Defense Forum Washington. This annual forum brings together senior military and political leaders to discuss timely security topics. (https://www.usni.org/events/defense-forum-washington)
- Service Academies Global Summit (SAGS). This annual gathering attracts service academy graduates to discuss issues related to military, civilian,

and government service. (https://serviceacademiesglobalsummit
.com)

- Officer Women Leadership Symposium (OWLS). An annual conference
that hosts panel discussions, practical workshops, and networking
events for military women seeking to continue their service in the
military, or in the public or private sector. (http://academywomen.org
/events/home.php/)

- U.S. Naval Academy Greater Washington Chapter/Collegiate Alumni
Association events. Many universities have local alumni chapters in
Washington that host breakfasts, luncheons, happy hours, open houses,
and speaker series. (http://www.usnaaagwc.org)

- SNA Greater Washington Chapter. This local chapter hosts luncheons
and happy hours for active and retired Navy Surface Warfare and Coast
Guard personnel, as well as industry professionals. (http://www.chapter
.navysna.org/washington/GWCIndex.htm)

- Think Tank Events. As you learned in chapter 16, think tanks play
an important role in working with the defense community to shape
security strategy. Often times these organizations host speaker series
that are either open to the public or selectively invite active and reserve
servicemembers. Think tanks and local universities often attract and
employ notable civilian or retired military leaders who offer important
perspectives from their experiences in the highest rung of government,
and nearly every institution's website has an "Events" section detailing
upcoming programs.

SPORTING EVENTS AND OTHER OPPORTUNITIES

Many Navy program offices, professional associations, and private defense-
related organizations host annual or semiannual golf tournaments at
private or military golf courses in Virginia or Maryland that attract active
and retired servicemembers and industry representatives for camaraderie
and friendly competition. Most tournaments that seek to attract active-
duty members enjoy recurrent approval from military ethics advisors
for participation; however, if in doubt, be sure to consult one (see inset
on following page). Additionally, opportunities abound to participate
in leagues and clubs for various sporting events, such as softball, tennis,
squash, running, cycling, triathlons, and general fitness. Not only are
these pursuits enrichment activities, they also offer opportunities to build
relationships with like-minded professionals.

FORMAL CELEBRATORY DINNERS AND BALLS
- Navy Birthday Ball
- Submarine Birthday Ball
- Navy Supply Corps Birthday Ball
- U.S. Marine Corps Birthday Ball
- Battle of Midway Dinner

ETHICS DETERMINATION FOR ATTENDANCE

It is not uncommon for active-duty military personnel in Washington to be offered complimentary admission to one of the many dinners, conferences, or other events hosted by industry, academia, or other private foundations or organizations that are offered to civilian attendees for a fee. It is important to consult a judge advocate general, civilian government counsel, or designated ethics advisor to ensure your attendance is appropriate, TAD/TDY travel (if required) is permitted, and your acceptance of the admission gift does not violate department policy.

For certain events sponsored by private professional organizations (for example, the U.S. Navy Memorial Foundation, Surface Navy Association), a JAG may issue a "widely attended gathering" (WAG) finding memo or message justifying your attendance in according to federal statute and department instruction. These findings determine if there is an "agency" interest in your attendance at the event; evaluate whether your attendance outweighs any concern that you may, or may appear to be, improperly influenced in the performance of your official duties by attending; appraise the appropriateness of gifts (e.g., the cost of dinner, parking, mementos) based on their estimated monetary value; gauge the department's relationship with the host organization and other attendees; and balance whether the informal contacts you make during the course of your attendance could benefit the department. If in doubt as to whether your attendance would be appropriate, err on the side of caution and consult a legal or trained ethics advisor.

RECREATIONAL AND EDUCATIONAL OPPORTUNITIES

LOCAL MUSEUMS AND ATTRACTIONS

Museums listed with an asterisk (*) offer admission free of charge, and those marked (S) are part of the Smithsonian Institution complex of museums and research and education centers.

- American Art Museum*
- Bureau of Engraving and Printing*
- Clara Barton Missing Soldiers Office Museum
- Daughters of the American Revolution Museum*
- Drug Enforcement Administration Museum & Visitors Center*
- FBI Headquarters*
- Ford's Theatre
- Hirshhorn Museum and Sculpture Garden (S)*
- International Spy Museum
- The John F. Kennedy Center for the Performing Arts*
- Museum of the Bible
- National Air & Space Museum (S)*
- National Air & Space Museum Udvar-Hazy Center (annex near Washington Dulles International Airport) (S)*
- National Archives*
- National Building Museum
- National Gallery of Art*
- National Geographic Museum
- National Law Enforcement Museum
- National Museum of African American History and Culture (S)*
- National Museum of African Art (S)*
- National Museum of American History (S)*
- National Museum of the American Indian (S)*
- National Museum of Civil War Medicine
- National Museum of Health and Medicine*
- National Museum of the Marine Corps*
- National Museum of Natural History (S)*
- National Museum of the United States Navy*
- National Museum of the U.S. Army* (opening in 2020)
- National Portrait Gallery (S)*
- National Postal Museum (S)*
- National Zoo (S)*
- Red Cross National Headquarters Museum*

- Smithsonian American Art Museum (S)*
- Smithsonian Institution Building ("The Castle") (S)*
- United States Botanic Garden*
- United States Capitol Visitor Center*
- United States Holocaust Memorial Museum*
- U.S. Navy Memorial Naval Heritage Center*
- U.S. State Department's Diplomatic Reception Rooms
- Voice of America Studio Tour*
- Washington National Cathedral
- The White House*

CIVIL WAR BATTLEFIELDS WITHIN 90 MILES OF WASHINGTON, DC

- Antietam (Sharpsburg, Md.)
- Bristoe Station (Bristow, Va.)
- Chancellorsville (Spotsylvania, Va.)
- Fredericksburg (Va.)
- Gettysburg (Pa.)
- Manassas (Va.)
- Monocacy (Frederick, Md.)
- Harper's Ferry (W.Va.)

Civil War battlefields—like this one at Chancellorsville—are among the many personal and professional enrichment opportunities available to those stationed in the DC area. *National Park Service photo by Buddy Secor/Released*

NATIONAL PARK SERVICE HISTORIC PRESIDENTIAL
HOMES WITHIN 140 MILES OF WASHINGTON, DC

- George Washington's Mount Vernon (Mount Vernon, Va.)
- Thomas Jefferson's Monticello (Charlottesville, Va.)
- James Madison's Montpelier (Orange, Va.)
- James Monroe's Oak Hill (Loudon County, Va.)
- John Tyler's Sherwood Forest (Charles City, Va.)
- James Buchanan's Wheatland (Lancaster, Pa.)
- Woodrow Wilson House (Washington, DC)
- Dwight Eisenhower's Home (Gettysburg, Pa.)

LCDR Doug Robb is a surface warfare officer who has served two tours in the Pentagon on the Navy Staff and one on Capitol Hill.

INDEX

action officers (AO), 79, 134, 173; attributes of, 134–35; best practices, 145; developing expertise, 135–36; education and collaboration, 132, 140–42; Joint Staff, 95; JSAP and, 93–94; NJOIC and, 86; NMCC and, 88; PBAD and, 91; portfolio decisions, 139–40; portfolio driving action, 136–39; tools of the trade, 142–45

Adaptive Planning and Execution (APEX), 81

administrative command (ADCON), 47, 81

Administrative Instruction (AI) 88, 25–26

aide position, 45, 149, 150–51, 154, 169, 199–200

All-Volunteer Force (AVF), 67

appropriators, 52, 206. See also House Appropriations Subcommittee on Defense (HAC-D); Senate Appropriations Subcommittee on Defense (SAC-D)

Arnold, Henry "Hap," 77

Assistant Chairman Joint Chiefs of Staff (ACJCS), 84

assistant for administration (DON/AA), 70

Assistant Secretary of Defense for Acquisition, 106

Assistant Secretary of Defense for Legislative Affairs (ASD[LA]), 111

Assistant Secretary of Defense for Nuclear, Chemical, and Biological Defense Programs, 106

Assistant Secretary of Defense for Special Operations and Low-Intensity Conflict (SO/LIC), 108

Assistant Secretary of Defense for Sustainment, 106

Assistant Secretary of the Navy, 60, 61

Assistant Secretary of the Navy (Aeronautics) (ASN[Air]), 64

Assistant Secretary of the Navy (Energy, Installations, and Environments) (ASN[EI&E]), 66, 69, 72

Assistant Secretary of the Navy (Financial Management and Comptroller) (ASN[FM&C]), 52, 66, 70, 72, 74, 128, 130–31, 210; front office, 147

Assistant Secretary of the Navy (Manpower and Reserve Affairs) (ASN[M&RA]), 47, 66, 72

Assistant Secretary of the Navy (Research and Development), 64–65

Assistant Secretary of the Navy (Research, Development, and Acquisition) (ASN[RD&A]), 66, 68, 72–73, 130

Assistant to the Chairman of the Joint Chiefs of Staff (ACJCS), 84

Assistant to the President for National Security Affairs (APNSA). See National Security Advisor (APNSA)

Assistant to the Secretary of Defense (Public Affairs) (ATSD[PA]), 30, 111

authorizers, 206. See also House Armed Services Committee (HASC); Senate Armed Services Committee (SASC)

Bancroft, George, 61

Base Realignment and Closure Commissions (BRAC), 50, 69

Bergstrom, George Edwin, 9, 12, 13

Board of Inspection and Survey (INSURV), 60

Board of Navy Commissioners, 39

Bradley, Omar, 78

briefs, 144–45, 179, 215

budget process, 118, 132; ASN(FM&C) and, 66; budget and appropriations timeline, 213; CNO guidance (CNOG), 49; defense committee hearings, 211; DON/AA and, 74; Future Years Defense Program (FYDP), 41, 51, 65, 119; key POM stakeholders, 126–32; OPA and, 65–66; OPNAV 8 and, 51–54; PPBE process and timeline, 118–25; PPBS, 39; President's budget (PB) submission, 211, 213–14; Program Objective Memorandum (POM), 41; supporting processes to PPBE, 125–26. See also OPNAV N82/FMB

Budget Submitting Offices (BSOs), 121, 130

Bureau of Medicine and Surgery (BUMED), 54, 60

Bureau of Naval Personnel (BUPERS), 60, 156, 266

Burke, Arleigh, 233

Bush, George H. W., 197

calendars, 142–43

Capabilities Gap Assessment (CGA), 80, 91

CAPSTONE program, 90

Carter, Jimmy, 67
Casey, Patrick "Pat," 8
Center for a New American Security Next Generation National Security Leaders Program, 181, 239
Center for Naval Warfare Studies (CNWS), 243–44
Center for Strategic and International Studies (CSIS), 181, 233, 277
Central Command, 67
Central Intelligence Agency (CIA), 98, 190, 192, 225, 229
Chafee, John, 67
Chairman of the Joint Chiefs of Staff (CJCS), 41, 77, 78, 79–80, 82, 84, 85, 87, 88, 91, 100, 125, 149, 189, 192, 211, 223, 224, 225, 227
Chairman of the National Security Resources Board, 189
Chairman's Action Group, 85
Chairman's Program Assessment (CPA), 80
Chairman's Program Recommendation (CPR), 80
Chairman's Readiness System (CRS), 80
Chairman's Risk Assessment (CRA), 80, 89
Chandler, Williams E., 61
Chief Management Officer (CMO), 109–10
Chief of Chaplains (N097), 55
Chief of Information (CHINFO) (N09C), 55, 62
Chief of Legislative Affairs (CLA) (N09L), 55, 208–9
Chief of Naval Information (CHINFO), 74
Chief of Naval Operations (CNO), 79; budget process and, 119–20, 127, 214; creation of, 39, 58, 61; delegation of authority by, 45; front office, 149; as key POM stakeholder, 127; Maritime Strategy, 68; officers reporting to, 42, 52, 55; OPNAV reorganizations by, 44; personal flag of, 40; POM and, 118; responsibilities of, 38–39. See McNamara, Robert; Zumwalt, Elmo
Chief of Naval Personnel (CNP). See Deputy CNO for Manpower, Personnel, Training, and Education (MPTE) (OPNAV N1)
Chief of Naval Research (CNR), 53, 74
Chief of Navy Reserve (N095), 54
Civil Engineer Corps (CEC), 50
civilian employees, 56–57, 92–93, 102, 111, 155, 171, 179–80
Clare, Thane, 97–115
Clarke, Gilmore, 10, 11, 12

Clausewitz, Carl von, 223
Clinton, William J., 197
CNO guidance (CNOG), 49, 128
Cold War, 15, 16, 39, 63–64, 67–68, 69, 98, 100, 114, 190–91, 223
Combat Command Staff, 39, 114
combat logistics force (CLF), 50
combatant command (CCMD) staffs, 81, 86–88
combatant command (COCOM), 81, 102
combatant commanders (CCDRs), 80, 81, 82, 88, 89, 91, 119
Commandant of the U.S. Coast Guard, 79
Commandant of the U.S. Marine Corps, 79
Commander, Naval Installations Command (CNIC), 50
Commander, Navy Safety Center (NAVSAFCEN), 55
Commander in Chief, U.S. Fleet (COMINCH), 39
commuting/commuters: additional commuting options, 24; commuter and coach bus, 22; Commuter Connections, 24; commuter rail, 23; commuting stipends, 21; costs of, 21; graduate education and, 269; Guaranteed Ride Home (GRH), 24; GWRide Connect, 24; High Occupancy Vehicle (HOV) lanes, 22; mass transit, 20–22; parking, 24–26; pedestrian tunnel, 30; personally owed vehicles (POVs), 24; plans, 255; ridesharing, 23–24; SmarTrip payment cards, 21; vehicle registration, 25. See also parking
computer software, 142
conferences, 212, 235, 276–77
Congress, 181, 204–5, 219; best practices, 216–18; BRAC and, 69; branches of government, 205–6; budgeting and, 121, 122, 123–24, 141; CJCS and, 78; congressional calendar and budget process, 210–14; congressional delegations (CODEL), 215–16; congressional interaction, 214–15; congressional liaisons, 208–10; congressional staff, 207–8; congressional travel, 215–16; DOD and, 188–89; DON CIO and, 69; Goldwater-Nichols Act of 1986, 68, 100; interacting with, 214–15; JSC and, 79, 82; national defense and, 98; offices mandated by, 66; OPNAV N8 and, 51; OSD and, 102–3, 106; oversight committees, 206;

recommendations to, 52; SECDEF and, 99–100; working in legislative affairs, 218–19

congressional liaisons: appropriate use of, 217; FMBE, 210; Navy OLA, 208–9; other legislative liaisons, 210

consumer services, 260–61

continuing resolutions (CRs), 124

continuity of government (COG), 88

continuity of operations (COOP), 87–88

contractor support employees, 56–57

Cooperative Strategy for 21st Century Seapower, A (2007), 70

Council on Foreign Relations (CFR) Term Membership, 239

Cox, Samuel, 40

Crowder, Doug, 175–83

Cutler, Thomas J., 57

Daniels, Josephus, 61

Davidson, Janine, 70

Defense Acquisition Board, 84

Defense Acquisition System (DAS), 125, 126

Defense Acquisition University (DAU), 125, 132

Defense Advanced Research Projects Agency (DARPA), 245

defense agencies, 101, 102, 106–7, 110, 113

Defense Appropriations Bill, 206, 211, 212, 214

Defense Contract Audit Agency, 109

Defense Entrepreneurs Forum (DEF), 240

defense field activities, 101, 102, 106–7, 110, 113

Defense Finance and Accounting Service, 109

Defense Information Systems Agency, 111

Defense Intelligence Agency (DIA), 86, 109

Defense Legal Services Agency, 110

Defense Planning Guidance (DPG), 119

Defense POW/MIA Accounting Agency, 108

defense reforms, 64–68

Defense Security Cooperation Agency, 108

Defense Strategic Guidance (DSG), 119

Defense Technology Security Administration, 108

Delano, Frederic A., 10

Department of Defense (DOD), 15; budget process and, 141, 212; building passes, 30; Chief Information Officer (CIO), 110, 111, 113; components of, 102; Defense Acquisition University (DAU), 125; EOP and, 188; establishment of, 99, 188; General Counsel, 71–72, 110, 113; Inspector General (IG), 102, 110, 113; interagency

coordination, 220–21, 225–26; J-7 and, 90; J-32 and, 87; J-35 and, 88; J-39 and, 88; NSC and, 190, 201; positions in, 227; Reorganization Act of 1958, 39; SECDEF and, 100; Tank meetings, 181

Department of Energy, 45, 228

Department of Homeland Security, 79, 229

Department of Justice (DOJ), 110, 229

Department of State, 228

Department of the Navy offices: Assistant for Administration (DON/AA), 74; Assistant Secretary of the Navy, Energy, Installations, and Environment (ASN[EI&E]), 72; Assistant Secretary of the Navy, Financial Management and Comptroller (ASN[FM&C]), 72; Assistant Secretary of the Navy, Manpower and Reserve Affairs (ASN[M&RA]), 72; Assistant Secretary of the Navy, Research, Development, and Acquisition (ASN[RD&A]), 72; Chief Information Officer, 69; Chief of Naval Information (CHINFO), 69, 74; Deputy Undersecretary of the Navy for Policy (DUSN), 74; Naval Audit Service, 74; Navy Inspector General (NAV IG), 74; Navy Judge Advocate General (JAG), 74; Office of Legislative Affairs (OLA), 75; Office of the Chief Management Officer (OCMO), 75; Office of the General Counsel of the Navy (OGC), 75; Office of the Secretary of the Navy (SECNAV), 75; Office of the Undersecretary of the Navy (UNSECNAV), 75; Sexual Assault Prevention Office (SAPRO), 75; Special Access Program Coordinator (DON SAPCO), 54

Department of Treasury, 228

deployment orders (DEPORDS), 88

Deputies Committee (DC), 195–96, 197

deputy assistant secretaries of defense (DASDs), 105

Deputy Assistant Secretary of the Navy (Budget), 52

Deputy Assistant to the President for National Security Affairs (DAPNSA). *See* Deputy National Security Advisor (DAPNSA)

Deputy CNO for Fleet Readiness and Logistics (OPNAV N4), 50, 129

Deputy CNO for Information Dominance (OPNAV N2/N6), 48–49, 129

Deputy CNO for Integration of Capabilities and Resources (OPNAV N8), 51–52, 127–28, 147

Deputy CNO for Manpower, Personnel, Training, and Education (MPTE) (OPNAV N1), 46–47, 128–29

Deputy CNO for Operations, Plans, and Strategy (OPNAV N3/N5), 49, 119, 129

Deputy CNO for Warfare Systems (OPNAV N9), 53–54, 129–31

Deputy CNO for Warfighting Development (N7), 50

Deputy Commandant for Plans, Policies, and Operations (PP&O), 182

Deputy Commandant for Programs and Resources, 130

Deputy Director for Force Protection, 91–92

Deputy Director for Global Policy and Partnerships, 89

Deputy Director for Operations: National Military Command Center (NMCC), 87–88

Deputy Director for Politico-Military Affairs, 89

Deputy Director for Requirements, 91

Deputy Director for Resources and Acquisition, 91

Deputy Director for Simulations and Analysis, 91

Deputy Director for Strategic Planning, 89–90

Deputy Director of Naval Intelligence (N2/N6I), 48–49

deputy executive assistant (DEA) position, 45, 149–50, 152, 155

Deputy National Security Advisor (DAPNSA), 191, 195–96

Deputy Operations Deputies (DEPOPSDEPs), 84–85

Deputy Secretary of Defense (DEPSECDEF), 103, 106, 113, 131, 195

deputy undersecretaries of defense (DUSDs), 105, 106

Deputy Undersecretary of the Navy, 70

Deputy Undersecretary of the Navy for Policy (DUSN), 74

Deputy's Management Action Group (DMAG), 121

Design for Maintaining Maritime Superiority, A (Richardson), 50

Dewey, Thomas, 61

Digital Warfare Office (DWO), 53

Director, Air Warfare Division (N98), 54

Director, Assessments Division (N81), 51–52

Director, Energy and Environmental Readiness Division (N45), 50

Director, Expeditionary Warfare Division (N95), 53–54

Director, Financial Management Division (N10), 47

Director, Fiscal Management Division (N82), 52

Director, Flag Officer Management and Development (PERS-00F), 47

Director, Fleet Readiness Division (N83), 52

Director, Global Integration and Engagement Division (N5I), 49

Director, Innovation, Technology Requirements, and Test and Evaluation Division (N94), 53

Director, J-8 (DJ-8), 91

Director, Logistics Programs Division (N41), 50

Director, Military Personnel Plans and Policy Division (N13), 47

Director, Naval Criminal Investigative Service (NCIS) (N09N), 55

Director, Naval History and Heritage Command, 40

Director, Naval Nuclear Propulsion Program (N00N), 42, 45, 149

Director, Navy Cyber Security Division (N2/N6G), 48

Director, Navy Staff (DNS), 42, 46

Director, Oceanography and Navigation Division (N2/N6E), 48

Director, Operations and Plans Division (N31), 49

Director, Programming Division (N80), 51

Director, Shore Readiness Division (N46), 50

Director, Special Programs Division (N9SP), 54

Director, Strategic Mobility and Combat Logistics Division (N42), 50

Director, Strategy Division (N50), 49

Director, Surface Warfare Division (N96), 54

Director, Total Force Manpower, Training, and Education Requirements Division (N12), 47

Director, Twenty-First Century Sailor Officer (N17), 47

Director, Undersea Warfare Division (N97), 54

Director, Warfare Integration Division (N2/N6F), 48

Director, Warfare Integration Division (N9I), 53

Director of Cost Assessment and Program Evaluation (CAPE), 110–11, 113, 121
Director of Management (DOM), 84
Director of National Intelligence (DNI), 109, 225; NSC and, 192
Director of Net Assessment (DNA), 112, 113
Director of Operational Test and Evaluation (DOT&E), 111
Director of the Joint Staff (DJS), 84
Directorate of Management (DOM), 85–86
directorates, 42, 45–56
divisions, 42, 45–56, 91
Dobbin, James C., 60
Douds, Doug, 77–96
dress code, 217
Duffy, Matthew, 146–58

education, 264, 275; admissions, 273–75; distance learning, 265; funding for, 269–73; graduate schools, 264–65, 267–68; Joint Professional Military Education, 265–67; JPME, 90; Naval Postgraduate School (NPS), 40, 51, 243, 245; navy academic institutions, 243–45; part-time programs of interest, 267–68; PhD programs, 268; picking a program, 269; PME, 49; senior leader education, 90; testing, 273; tuition assistance, 270
Eisenhower, Dwight D., 14, 99, 190
email, 143
employee access, 26–27
England, Gordon, 57, 70, 172
enrichment opportunities in DC, 276; professional engagements, 276–79; recreational and educational opportunities, 280–82
ethics: ethics advisors, 153; ethics determination for attendance, 279
execution orders (EXORDS), 81, 88
executive assistant (EA) position, 45, 149, 150, 151–52, 155, 169
Executive Office of the President (EOP), 188

Federal Executive Fellowship (FEF): activities of, 237; FEF fellows, 235–36, 237; OPNAV N3/N5 and, 49; participation in, 236–37
Federally Funded Research and Development Centers (FFRDC), 51, 242, 247, 248
fellowships/scholarships, 218, 240, 272–73
final votes, 212, 214
flag secretary position, 45, 149, 150, 153, 155
flag writer position, 149, 150, 151, 155

food and beverage options, 31–34
foreign area officer (FAO) community, 49
foreign policy advisor position, 149
Forrestal, James V., 15, 62–63, 98
Fox, Gustavus V., 60
Front End Assessment (FEA), 128
front office, 85, 146; compositions of, 148–50; four-star front office, 149; one-star front office, 150; roles and responsibilities, 147–48; securing an assignment, 156–57; three-star front office, 149–50; two-star front office, 150. See also Chairman of the Joint Chiefs of Staff
Functional Capabilities Board (FCB), 91
Future Years Defense Program (FYDP), 41, 51, 65, 119, 120

Gagliano, Joseph A., 186–203
Gainey, William J. "Joe," 85
Gantt, Kyle, 242–52
gift exchanges, 151
Global Employment of the Force (GEF), 89
global force management (GFM), 49, 87, 88
Global Positioning System (GPS), 63
Goldberg, Alfred, 98
Goldwater-Nichols Act of 1986, 40, 68, 78, 84, 100, 224
Gosnell, Rachael, 7–18
Government Accountability Office (GAO), 110, 219
government branches, 205–6
government civilian employees, 56–57, 92–93, 149
Groves, Leslie R., 12, 13

Hagerty, James, 204–19
Haynes, Peter, 40
hearing impaired visitors, 30
Hidalgo, Edward, 67
Homeland Security Council (HSC), 79
House Appropriations Committee, 10
House Appropriations Subcommittee on Defense (HAC-D), 206, 208, 211, 212
House Armed Services Committee (HASC), 181, 206, 208, 211, 212
housing, 254; amenities, 255–56; commute, 255; cost and space considerations, 254–55; military base housing, 257; neighborhoods, 258–62; realtor use, 257; rent or buy, 256; rights and options, 257–58; school districts/child-care options, 257; search considerations, 254–58; time for search, 256–57

Ickes, Harold L., 11
identification requirements, 30, 94
individual augmentee (IA) sailors, 70
information operations (IO), 88
Integrated Analytic Agenda (IAA), 243
integrated priority list (IPL), 119
interagency coordination, 220; best practices/
    lessons learned, 230–31; brief history of
    interagency process, 223–25; interagency
    defined, 220–23; key agencies within
    national security system, 228–30; role in
    interagency process, 225–27
interviews, 156–57, 275

J-1 Manpower and Personnel Directorate, 86
J-2 Intelligence Directorate, 86
J-3 Operations Directorate, 49, 87–88
J-4 Logistics Directorate, 88–89
J-5 Strategic Plans and Policy Directorate, 49,
    88, 89–90
J-6 Command, Control, Communications,
    and Computers/Cyber Directorate, 90
J-7 Joint Force Development Directorate, 90
J-8 Force Structure, Resources, and
    Assessment Directorate, 91–92, 131–32, 147
J-32 Deputy Director for Intelligence,
    Surveillance, Reconnaissance Operations,
    87
J-33 Deputy Director for Nuclear, Homeland
    Defense, and Current Operations, 87
J-35 Deputy Director for Regional Operations
    and Force Management, 88
J-37 Deputy Director for Special Operations
    and Counter Terrorism, 88
J-39 Deputy Director for Global Operations,
    88
J-codes, 42, 82
Johnson, Louis A., 99
Joint Capabilities Board (JCB), 91
Joint Capabilities Integration and
    Development System (JCIDS), 91, 125–26
Joint Chiefs of Staff (JCS), 77, 79, 102, 227
joint duty assignment list, 82, 94
Joint Forces Command, 88, 90
Joint Integrated Air and Missile Defense
    Organization (JIAMDO), 92
Joint Logistics Enterprise (JLEnt), 88
Joint Logistics Operations Center (JLOC), 88
Joint Professional Military Education (JPME),
    90, 265–67
Joint Qualification System (JQS), 94
Joint Requirement Oversight Council (JROC),
    80, 84, 91, 125–26

Joint Staff: brief history of, 77–79; CCDRs and,
    81, 119; CCMD and, 81, 86–88; Chairman
    of the Joint Chiefs of Staff (CJCS), 80–82;
    COCOM and, 81; DOD and, 102; Force
    Structure, Resources, and Assessment
    directorate, 131–32; front office, 147, 148;
    functions of, 79–82; identification badges,
    94; interagency coordination, 225–26;
    Joint Qualification System (JQS), 94; Joint
    Staff Action Process (JSAP), 93–94; Joint
    Staff Inspector General, 84; Joint Staff
    Planning System (JSPS), 80; OPNAV N095
    and, 54; OPNAV N81 and, 52; organization
    and titles of, 82–83; organizations and
    directorates, 85–92; OSD and, 92, 114;
    principal officers, 84–85; workforce
    composition, 92–93
Joint Strategic Capabilities Plan (JSCP), 80
Judge Advocate General of the Navy (JAG)
    (N09J), 55, 74, 153, 171, 279

Kacher, Fred, 169–74
Kelso, Frank, 42, 53
Kennedy, John F., 63, 190–91
KEYSTONE program, 90
Kimball, Dan A., 63
King, Ernest J., 3, 39, 77
Kissinger, Henry, 195
Knox, Frank, 62
Korean War, 15, 63
Korth, Fred, 65

Laird, Melvin, 67
Law School Admission Test (LSAT), 273
Leahy, William, 77
legal advisor position, 45, 153
Lehman, John, 68–69
L'Enfant, Pierre, 10
limited duty officers (LDOs), 153
Livingstone, Susan M., 70
local museums and attractions, 280–81
Long, John D., 61
Lushenko, Jonathan "Shank," 19–36
Lynn, William J., 106

Mabus, Ray, 70
Mahan Scholars, 244
Manpower Personnel Training and
    Education, 130
Marine Air-Ground Task Force (MAGTF), 63
Marine Corps Warfighting Laboratory, 246
Marine Expeditionary Force (MEF), 70

Maritime Strategy, 49, 68
markup, 211–12
Marshall, George C., 8
Mason, John Y., 60
mass communications specialists (MCs), 153
Master Chief Petty Officer of the Navy
    (MCPON) (NooD), 55
masters-at-arms (MA) specialists, 155–56
material solution analysis (MSA), 126
McNamara, Robert, 15, 39, 64, 65, 111, 118
McShain, John, 12
Mediterranean Squadron, 60
Mendizabal, Enrique, 233
Mexican-American War, 60
Meyer, George von Lengerke, 61
military and civilian pay grades, 56–57
military assistant (MA) position, 152
military construction (MILCON), 50
Military Construction/Veterans Affairs
    (MILCON/VA) Appropriations Bill, 206
military information support operations
    (MISO), 88
Military Legislative Assistant (MLA), 207
Military Sealift Command (MSC), 50, 128
Modly, Thomas, 70, 71
Montgomery GI Bill (Chapter 30), 270
morale, welfare, and recreation (MWR)
    programs, 50, 108, 260
Mullen, Michael, 86
Murphy, Micah, 232–41
Musser, Grady, 134–45
Myers, Richard, 85

National Command Authority (NCA), 81
National Defense Authorization Act (NDAAs),
    97, 106, 110, 211, 212, 214, 232
National Defense Strategy (NDS), 89, 119
National Geospatial-Intelligence Agency
    (NGA), 109
National Guard, 79, 108, 227
National Intelligence University, 267
National Joint Operations and Intelligence
    Center (NJOIC), 86
National Military Command Center (NMCC),
    15, 81, 86, 87–88
National Military Establishment, 15, 98, 99. See
    Department of Defense (DOD)
National Military Strategy (NME), 80, 89, 119
National Nuclear Security Administration, 45
National Security Act Amendment of 1949, 189
National Security Act of 1947, 15, 77, 98, 189, 191,
    223–24, 225

National Security Advisor (APNSA), 190, 191,
    194–95, 196, 198, 201
National Security Agency, 109
National Security Council (NSC): background
    and history, 77, 78, 98, 187, 188–89; CJCS
    and, 79–80; committees, 195–97; DNI
    and, 225; evolution and makeup, 189–91;
    interagency integration, 197–99, 226;
    J-5 and, 89; leadership, 191, 194–95; OSD
    and, 102; purpose and functions, 191–92;
    structure and composition, 192–94; USD(P)
    and, 108. See also White House
National Security Fellows Program (NSFP), 240
National Security Strategy (NSS), 89, 100, 119
National Security System, 79, 228–29
Naval Academy, 61, 262, 278
Naval Air Systems Command (NAVAIR), 130,
    136
Naval Audit Service, 74
Naval Aviation Warfare Center (NAWC), 246
Naval Education and Service Training
    Commands (NETC/NSTC), 47
Naval Facilities Engineering Command
    (NAVFAC), 50, 130
Naval History and Heritage Command, 40
Naval Installations Command, 130
Naval Nuclear Propulsion Program (NooN),
    45, 149
Naval Personnel Command (NPC), 47
Naval Postgraduate School (NPS), 40, 61, 243,
    245
Naval Reactors (NR), 45, 149
Naval Research Laboratory (NRL), 63, 246
Naval Research Program (NRP), 245
Naval Reserve Officer Training Corps
    (NROTC), 46
Naval Sea Systems Command (NAVSEA), 130,
    136
Naval Supply Systems Command, 130
Naval Surface Warfare Center (NSWC), 246
Naval Undersea Warfare Center (NUWC), 246
Naval War College (NWC), 61, 243–44, 266,
    267
NavCivGuide: A Handbook for Civilians in the
    United State Navy (Cutler), 57
navigating the Pentagon, 19–20, 36; entering
    the building, 26–27; fitness facilities, 34–35;
    food and beverage options, 31–34; getting
    to, 20–24; navigating within the building,
    27–29; parking, 24–26; personal consumer
    services, 35–36; taking a tour, 29–31
NAVSEC 08. See Naval Nuclear Propulsion
    Program (NooN)

Navy Analytic Office (NAO), 243
Navy Appropriations Matters Office, 208
Navy Capabilities Board (NCB), 51
Navy Capitol Hill Workshop, 219
Navy Criminal Investigative Service (NCIS), 149, 155
Navy Department, 38–39
Navy Information Section, 62
Navy Inspector General (NAV IG) (N09G), 55, 74
Navy Munitions Requirements Program (NMRP), 52
Navy Office of Legislative Affairs (OLA), 209
Navy Operations Center (NOC), 49
Navy Reserve Force, 42, 54, 61
Navy Safety Center (NAVSAFCEN) (N09F), 55
Navy Secretariat, 54, 59–76; Cold War, 63–64; current Department of Navy offices, 72–75; defense reforms, 64–68; early twentieth century, 61–62; front office, 147; further reading, 75–76; late twentieth century, 69; nineteenth century, 59–61; organizational chart, 73; Reagan and Lehman era, 68–69; twenty-first century, 70–72; World War II, 62–63
Navy Staff. See OPNAV (Office of the Chief of Naval Operations) Staff
N-codes, 42, 45, 149
NCS Deputies Committee, 84
Niemeyer, Rob, 118–33
9/11 attacks, 16–17, 31, 70, 182, 224–25
Nitze, Paul H., 64
Nixon, Richard, 67
"no hat, no salute" zones, 13
noncommissioned officers (NCOs), 85
North Atlantic Treaty Organization (NATO), 31, 64

Obama, Barack, 225
office coded directorates, 39, 42
Office of Appropriations Matters (FMBE), 52, 210
Office of Assistant Secretary of the Navy, 210
Office of Civilian Human Resources, 72
Office of Director of National Intelligence, 229
Office of Legislative Affairs (OLA), 74, 208–10, 218–19
Office of Management and Budget (OMB), 52, 109, 121, 123, 131
Office of Naval Research (ONR), 53, 63, 130, 246

Office of Personnel Management (OPM), 56, 219
Office of Program Appraisal (OPA), 65–66
Office of Strategy and Innovation, 70–71
Office of Systems Analysis, 111
Office of the Chairman Joint Chiefs of Staff. See Chairman of the Joint Chiefs of Staff (CJCS)
Office of the Chief Management Officer (OCMO), 71, 74
Office of the Chief of Naval Operations (OPNAV). See OPNAV (Office of the Chief of Naval Operations) Staff
Office of the Chief of Naval Operations Principal Officers (OPOs). See OPNAV Principal Officers (OPOs)
Office of the Chief of Naval Operations Staff. See OPNAV (Office of the Chief of Naval Operations) Staff
Office of the Department of Defense Inspector General, 102, 110, 113
Office of the General Counsel of the Navy (OGC), 63, 74
Office of the Joint Chiefs of Staff (OJCS). See Joint Staff
Office of the Secretary of Defense (Comptroller) (OSD[Comptroller]), 121, 123, 131, 148
Office of the Secretary of Defense (OSD), 65, 89, 97, 103, 114; brief history of, 97–100; budget process, 52, 119, 121; coordination with Service, Joint, and Combatant Command staffs, 114; defense agencies, 101; defense field activities, 101; front office, 148; importance of, 66; interagency coordination, 225–26; J-7 and, 90; Joint Staff and, 92; OPA and, 66; OPNAV N81 and, 52; other principal staff assistants, 109–12; principal staff assistants, 105; purpose of, 100–102; SECDEF and, 92; structure of, 102–5; undersecretaries of defense, 105–9; workforce composition, 112–13
Office of the Secretary of Defense Cost Assessment and Program Evaluation (OSD[CAPE]), 110–11, 121, 123, 131, 132
Officer Women Leadership Symposium (OWLS), 278
off-the-records meetings, 234–35
O'Keefe, Sean, 68, 69
operating tempo (OPTEMPO), 108
operational control (OPCON), 81

Operations Deputies of the Joint Chiefs of Staff (OPSDEPs), 84
OPNAV (Office of the Chief of Naval Operations) Staff, 38, 58; brief history of, 38–40; front office, 148; interagency coordination, 225; organizational functions and titles, 41–42; principal officers (OPOs), 42–55; purpose of, 40–41; workforce composition, 56–57. *See also* OPNAV Principal Officers (OPOs)
OPNAV N093, 54
OPNAV N095, 54
OPNAV N097, 55
OPNAV N1, 46–47, 128–29
OPNAV N2/N6, 129
OPNAV N3/N5, 49, 119, 129, 182
OPNAV N4, 50, 128, 129
OPNAV N5I, 49
OPNAV N7, 50, 53
OPNAV N8, 53, 127, 130, 147
OPNAV N9, 52–53, 129–31
OPNAV N9I, 53
OPNAV N9SP, 54
OPNAV N31, 49
OPNAV N41, 50
OPNAV N42, 50
OPNAV N45, 50
OPNAV N46, 50
OPNAV N50, 49
OPNAV N80, 51, 119–21, 126, 127, 132
OPNAV N81, 120, 127–28, 243
OPNAV N82/FMB, 52, 121, 122, 126, 128
OPNAV N83, 52, 128
OPNAV N94, 53
OPNAV N95, 53
OPNAV N96, 54
OPNAV N97, 54
OPNAV N98, 54
OPNAV Operations and Organization Manual (OOOM), 42, 45
OPNAV Principal Officers (OPOs), 42–56
OPNAV Protocol Handbook, 56
OSD Cost Assessment and Program Evaluation, 131
OSD principal staff assistants, 103, 105–12. *See also specific assistants*
oversight committees, 206

Pace, Peter, 85
Pacific Fleet, 39, 60, 130
Papadopoulos, Sarandis, 59–76
papers, 143–44

parking, 21, 24–26, 30, 36
pay scale, 56–57
Pentagon (building): brief history of, 7–18; during Cold War, 15–16; construction, 12–13, 20; construction cost, 13; controversy, 10–12; design, 9–10; facility statistics, 13–15, 20; location, 8–9, 19; map of, 28; naming of, 13; navigating, 19–36; need for, 7–8; 9/11 attack, 16–17, 31; Pentagon Athletic Center (PAC), 26, 34; Pentagon Concourse Food Court, 32, 34; Pentagon Library, 26; post–World War II, 15; Project Phoenix, 17; renovation projects, 17, 19; as symbol, 15–16, 18; today, 17–18
Pentagon Access Control Branch (PACB), 26
Pentagon Force Protection Agency (PFPA), 26, 27, 110
Pentagon Reservation, 13, 19, 25, 26
Pentagon service, 175–76; briefings, 179; civilians, 179–80; complaining, 177; discussion groups, 180–81; Joint Chiefs meetings, 181–82; language issues, 180; learning curve, 177–78; personal relationships, 178–79; power of ideas, 182; starting strong, 176–77; understanding Congress, 181
Perry, Matthew C., 60
personal staff: overview, 146; positions, 150–56; securing an assignment, 156–57; summary of tips, 157, 170
personnel tempo (PERSTEMPO), 108
PINNACLE program, 90
plan of action and milestones (POAM) approach, 137
Planning, Programming, and Budgeting System (PPBS), 39, 51, 65
Planning, Programming, Budgeting, and Execution (PPBE) system, 118–19; budgeting, 121; CAPE and, 110–11; execution phase, 123; overlapping timelines, 124; planning/strategy phase, 119; POM and, 118, 138; PPBS and, 65; program/budget review phase, 121–23; programming, requirements assessment, resource integration phase, 119–20; supporting processes to, 125–26. *See also* budget process: PPBE process and timeline
planning orders (PLANORDS), 81
political advisor (POLAD) position, 149, 155
political-military (pol-mil) strategist, 49

portfolios, 136–37; major decisions, 139–40; results-focused routine, 137–38; reviews, 138–39; updating of, 140–42

Post-9/11 GI Bill (Chapter 33), 270–71

President (POTUS): APNSA and, 194–95; budgeting and, 123, 124, 141, 211, 213–14, 217–18; CJCS and, 79, 80, 81; EOP and, 188; J-3 and, 86; J-35 and, 88; NSC and, 189–92, 198–99, 200–201; NSC committees and, 195; OSD and, 92, 102; presidency and, 186–87; SECDEF and, 97–98, 100; VCJCS and, 84; WHMO and, 199; working for, 200–201. See also National Security Council; White House

President, Board of Inspection and Survey (INSURV) (N09P), 55

President's budget (PB) submission, 211, 217–18

Preston, William B., 60

Principals Committee (PC), 195–96, 197, 201

Procurement Legal Division, 63

professional engagements, 276–79

professional military education (PME), 49, 61, 90

professional staff members (PSMs), 208

Program and Budget Analysis Division (PBAD), 91

Program Budget Coordinating Group (PBCG), 121

Program Budget Information System (PBIS), 120, 132

program executive offices (PEOs), 66, 74

Program Objective Memorandum (POM), 41, 51, 52, 118, 119–20, 122, 124, 127, 138

Program Objective Memorandum (POM) stakeholders, 126–32

program requirements reviews (PRR), 129

programs of record (POR), 122

protective service detail (PSD), 155–56

protocol officer position, 154

public affairs officer (PAO) position, 153–54, 171

Rapid Deployment Force, 67

read-ahead (RAH) materials, 147, 151

Reagan, Ronald, 68–69, 198

recreational and educational opportunities, 280–81, 281, 282

relationship building, 151, 152, 172, 178–79, 217

renovation projects, 16–17, 19

reorganizations, 40, 42, 44, 45, 49, 68, 78, 84, 107

research and development organizations, 242, 252; Federally Funded Research and

Development Centers (FFRDC), 247; government R&D-focused organizations, 245–46; interacting with outside research organizations, 242–43; ONR principal areas of research, 246; partnering with industry, 250; role of navy academic institutions, 243–45; University Affiliated Research Centers (UARC), 247–50, 251

reserve force, 42, 54, 108

Resource Management Division (RMD), 123

resources: constraints on, 67; energy programs, 50; Future Years Defense Program (FYDP), 41, 51; legislative affairs and, 219; MILCON and, 50; Navy Staff and, 39; OPNAV N8 and, 51; OPNAV N94 and, 53; OPNAV N96 and, 54; OPNAV N97 and, 54

Revenue Cutter Service, 60

Richardson, John, 50

Rickover, Hyman, 45

Robb, Doug, 38–58, 254–63, 276–82

Roosevelt, Franklin D., 7, 8, 10–11, 12, 14, 77, 97, 188, 191

Roosevelt, Theodore, 61, 199

Roper, William B., Jr., 107

safety tips, 169–73

scheduler position, 45, 149, 151, 154, 155

Schlesinger, James, 97

scope of work (SOW), 93

Scowcroft, Brent, 198

Secretary of Defense (SECDEF): authority of, 99; budget process and, 91, 131, 211; CJCS and, 78, 79, 80, 81; CNO and, 41; comparisons, 113; CPRs and, 91; DOD budget and, 131; DOT&E and, 111; establishment of, 224; interagency coordination, 225; J-2 and, 86; J-3 and, 86–87; J-35 and, 88; JCS and, 77; JS and, 82; Navy Secretariat and, 67; NSC and, 189; POMs and, 120; POTUS and, 40; PPBS amd, 39; PSAs and, 105; responsibilities of, 97, 98, 100; SEAC and, 85; Truman and, 15; USD(I) and, 109; USD(P) and, 108

Secretary of State, 189

Secretary of the Air Force, 189

Secretary of the Army, 189

Secretary of the Navy (SECNAV), 74; Afghan and Iraqi wars, 70; approval of, 45; BRAC and, 69; budget process and, 126–27, 214; fiscal challenges and, 65; as key POM stakeholder, 126–27; NRP and, 245; NSC and, 189; officers reporting to, 42, 52, 55

Securing America's Future Energy (SAFE) Fellows Program, 240
security detail lead position, 155–56
security guidelines, 30
Selective Service system, 67
Senate Appropriations Subcommittee on Defense (SAC-D), 206, 208, 211, 212
Senate Armed Services Committee (SASC), 106, 107, 181, 206, 208, 211, 212
Senior Enlisted Advisor to the Chairman of the JCS (SEAC), 85
senior executive service (SES), 56, 69, 92–93
Senior Readiness Oversight Council (SROC), 84
Service Academies Global Summit (SAGS), 277–78
Servicemembers' Civil Relief Act (SCRA), 257
Sexual Assault Prevention Office (SAPRO), 74
Smith, Harold D., 10–11
Smith, Kaitlin, 264–75
Snodgrass, Guy, 159–68
social media, 154
Somervell, Brehon Burke, 8, 9, 10, 11, 12, 13, 17
Space and Naval Warfare Systems Command (SPAWAR), 130, 136, 246
Special Assistant for Inspection Support, 55
Special Assistant for Legal Services, 55
Special Assistant for Legislative Support, 55
Special Assistant for Material Inspection and Surveys, 55
Special Assistant for Naval Investigative Matters and Security, 55
Special Assistant for Public Affairs Support, 55
Special Assistant for Safety Matters, 55
special technical operations (STO), 88
speechwriters, 45, 149, 153, 154, 159; gather information, 162–63; keys to success, 167–68; knowing the audience, 163–65; knowing your message, 165–66; speechwriting, 159–60; trust, flexibility, and priorities, 165–67; understanding the boss, 160–61
Spencer, Richard V., 71–72
staff delegations (STAFFDEL), 215–16
standard joint duty assignment list (S-JDAL), 82, 94
Stephen M. Kellen Term Member Program, 239
Stevenson, Charles A., 97
Stimson, Henry L., 8, 10
Stoddert, Benjamin, 59

Strategic and Operational Research Department (SORD), 243–44
Strategic Capabilities Office (SCO), 107
Strategy Discussion Group (SDG), 180–81
subject matter experts (SMEs), 56, 85, 92–93, 135–36, 208, 227, 235
Surgeon General of the Navy (N093), 54

tactical control (TACON), 81
tasker system, 46, 152
terrorism, 49, 69, 70, 88, 89, 114, 224–25
think tanks and fellowships, 232; events, 181, 278; Federal Executive Fellowship, 235–37; OPNAV N81 and, 51; purpose and functions, 233–35; think tank defined, 232–33; visiting, 237–40
Thomas, Charles S., 63
Thompson, Smith, 60
tools of the trade, 142–45
Total Naval Force concept, 57
Total Obligation Authority (TOA), 119, 123, 128
tours: formal Pentagon tours programs, 30; self-guided, 31; taking a tour, 29–30; tour guides, 30
transportation: bicycles, 24; bus terminal, 19; commuter and coach bus, 22; commuter rail, 23; Guaranteed Ride Home (GRH), 24; GWRide Connect, 24; mass transit, 20–22; ridesharing, 23–24; slugging, 24; Zip Cars, 24. See also commuting/commuters
Trask, Roger, 98
Truman, Harry S., 15, 79, 97–98, 190
Trump, Donald, 225

Undersecretary of Defense (Comptroller) (USD[C]), 109
Undersecretary of Defense for Acquisition and Sustainment (USD[A&S]), 105–7
Undersecretary of Defense for Acquisition, Technology, and Logistics (USD[AT&L]), 106, 107
Undersecretary of Defense for Intelligence (USD[I]), 109
Undersecretary of Defense for Personnel and Health (USD[P&H]), 108–9
Undersecretary of Defense for Personnel and Readiness (USD[P&R]), 108–9
Undersecretary of Defense for Policy (USD[P]), 108
Undersecretary of Defense for Research and Engineering (USD[R&E]), 107

Undersecretary of the Navy (UNSECNAV), 62, 63, 70, 74
United State Naval Institute (USNI), 277
University Affiliated Research Centers (UARCs), 242, 247–48, 250, 251, 255
Upshur, Abel P., 60
U.S. Air Force, 31, 39, 66, 79, 95, 98, 148
U.S. Army, 39, 79, 98, 148
U.S. Coast Guard, 31, 49, 55, 60, 79, 95, 148, 277, 278
U.S. Fleet Forces Command, 53, 119, 130
U.S. House of Representatives, 205
U.S. Marine Corps (USMC), 49, 52, 53–54, 59, 60, 61–63, 65, 67–72, 73, 79, 95, 130, 148, 182, 243, 245, 277
U.S. National Guard Bureau, 79, 148, 227; front office, 148
U.S. Naval Academy, 61, 262, 278
U.S. Senate, 205–6

VetSuccess on Campus (VSOC), 272
Vice Chairman of the Defense Acquisition Board (DAB), 84
Vice Chairman of the Joint Chiefs of Staff (VCJCS), 79, 84, 85, 126, 149, 195
Vice Chief of Naval Operations (OPNAV N09) (VCNO), 42, 45, 121, 149
Vice Director Joint Staff (VDJS), 84
Vietnam War, 16, 39, 64, 65, 67
visually impaired visitors, 30
vocational rehabilitation & employment, 272

War Department, 7–8, 11
Warfare Integration Division (N9I), 130
Warfighting and Support Capability Assessment (WSCA), 128
Warner, John, 67
Washington, DC, life: enrichment opportunities, 276–82; finding the right place to live, 254–63; Metro Area

neighborhoods, 258–59; pursuing graduate education in DC, 264–75
Washington Headquarters Service Employee and Customer Resources, 36
Washington Headquarters Services (WHS), 110
Washington Headquarters Services (WHS) Parking Management Branch (PMB), 25
Washington Metropolitan Area Transit Authority "Metro" (WMATA), 20–21, 24
Webb, James, 68
Welles, Gideon, 60
White House, 186–87, 203; duties at, 200–203; Easter Egg Roll, 202; grounds, 187–88; Halloween trick-or-treating, 202; holiday decorations, 202; Lobby, 202; Mess, 202; NSC and, 188–99; Oval Office, 202; presidential staff, 188; Press Briefing Room, 202; Rose Garden, 202; special events, 202; tours, 202; WHMO, 199–200; WHSR, 191
white papers, 234
widely attended gathering (WAG) memos, 279
Wilson, Woodrow, 11, 39
Winter, Donald, 70
Wisecup, Michael, 220–31
Work, Robert, 70
workforce composition: Joint Staff, 92–93; Navy (OPNAV) staff, 56–57; OSD, 112–13
World War II, 62–63, 77, 97–98, 188, 223

Y2K challenge, 69
Yellow Ribbon Program, 271–72

Zumwalt, Elmo, 67

ABOUT THE AUTHORS

RDML Fred W. Kacher has deployed multiple times at sea and commanded USS *Stockdale* (DDG 106) and Destroyer Squadron SEVEN. An author of numerous articles on naval affairs and recipient of the Elmo Zumwalt Award for Visionary Leadership and the U.S. Navy League's John Paul Jones Award for Inspirational Leadership, he has also served ashore at the White House and the Pentagon. A graduate of the U.S. Naval Academy and Harvard's Kennedy School, he is also the author of the *Newly Commissioned Naval Officer's Guide*, 2nd edition (Naval Institute Press, 2018).

LCDR Douglas A. Robb is a surface warfare officer who has served at sea on board USS *Halsey* (DDG 97) and USS *Kidd* (DDG 100), and on the staff of Commander, Destroyer Squadron SEVEN, where he received the Navy League's Stephen Decatur Award for Operational Competence. Ashore, he served as a liaison to the House of Representatives, in the Pentagon on the Navy Staff, and as speechwriter for the Chief of Naval Operations. He is a graduate of the U. S. Naval Academy, Georgetown University's Walsh School of Foreign Service, and the U.S. Naval War College.